A GALLERY
OF SOUTHERNERS

A GALLERY
OF SOUTHERNERS

Louis D. Rubin, Jr.

Louisiana State University Press
Baton Rouge and London

Designer: Albert Crochet
Typeface: Linotron Trump Medieval
Typesetter: Graphic Composition, Inc.
Printer: Thomson-Shore, Inc.
Binder: John H. Dekker and Sons, Inc.

LIBRARY OF CONGRESS CATALOGING IN PUBLICATION DATA

Rubin, Louis Decimus, 1923–
    A gallery of Southerners.

    Includes bibliographical references and index.
    1. American literature—Southern States—History and criticism—Addresses, essays, lectures. 2. American literature—20th century—History and criticism—Addresses, essays, lectures. I. Title.
PS261.R64   810'.9'975   82–64
ISBN 0–8071–0997–5   AACR2

For my friend, counselor, and collaborator
of a quarter-century

C. Hugh Holman
1914–1981

In that extremity I bore me well.
A true gentleman, valorous in arms.
Disinterested and honorable.

Contents

Polemical Preface to Another Gallery of Southerners

Said the Duke of Gloucester, upon being presented with yet another volume of the *Decline and Fall of the Roman Empire*, "Another damn'd, thick, square book! Always scribble scribble scribble! Eh? Mr. Gibbon?" Without his prose style or his subject, nevertheless I understand the distinguished historian's feelings upon such an occasion. For here is one more volume of my writings on southern literature. This time I am led to preface it with some speculation on what it has all been about.

When I was twelve years old or so, in Charleston, South Carolina, back in the mid-1930s, my aunt telephoned me one day to say that in the office of the legal firm for which she worked there was a large quantity of books of poetry, which were about to be discarded, and if I liked I might come and select some for myself. So I rode downtown on the streetcar to Broad Street, and soon confronted a room in the law offices of Huger, Wilbur, Miller, and Mouzon, bereft of furniture and with many hundreds of volumes of poetry stacked along the floor. Now understand that I was not notably precocious, and that my idea of a good poem was something like Longfellow's "Building of the Ship" or the *Barrack-Room Ballads*. Going entirely by the colors of the dust jackets and the bindings, the look of the print, the wording of the titles, I selected some twenty or so books, which I loaded into a large carton and took back home.

Today, almost a half-century later, I am awed by my youthful prescience. For among the books that I chose, with no knowledge whatever of what I was doing, were volumes by three members of the Nashville Fugitives—John Crowe Ransom's *Chills and Fever*, Donald Davidson's *An Outland Piper*, and Merrill Moore's *The Noise That Time Makes*. (There must have been a copy of Allen Tate's *Mr. Pope and Other Poems* there, too; I berate myself for not having found it.) I also brought home two books of poetry by William Alexander Percy and the collected poems of Cale Young Rice. In later years I realized that the books in that office must have been those submitted for the prize competitions of the Poetry Society of South Carolina during the 1920s. During the Depression the Poetry Society went defunct, and no doubt one of the attorneys in the firm had been charged with housing the leftover books. When after a time the need for additional office space arose, the books had to go. Whether the ones that I did not take home ended up anywhere short of the city dump, I have no idea.

I should like to believe that serendipity was involved in my good fortune that day. It would also be nice to think that even back then I went looking for books by southern poets, and that my nascent literary interests were already beginning to take form. The only trouble is that I am quite certain that, even though I lived in so self-conscious a community as Charleston, I had at that time no notion that any such thing as southern literature even existed. I had heard of the poet Henry Timrod, to be sure; not only had we been made at school to recite by heart the Magnolia Cemetery Ode, but there was a local hotel named after him. I knew that Poe had set "The Gold Bug" on Sullivan's Island across the harbor. But of other southern writers I knew nothing, and as for the twentieth century, I was acquainted with nothing whatever in the way of literature.

It was not until I was in graduate school that I began to think about novels and poems as being in any important sense southern. I think it was the experience of being out of the South and in Baltimore at Johns Hopkins, among articulate fellow students and a faculty who for the most part had no southern ties or interests, that made me become conscious in an intellectual way of my own regional origins and loyalties; it usually happens like that. One day I set out to review a group of five novels, all by southerners, for the

Hopkins Review. Whatever value that review had—surely it had none for anyone wishing to find out about the books being reviewed—consisted in its having been the occasion for making me begin to think consecutively and to some purpose about the subject. Three decades later I am still trying to do it.

How could anyone, even as naïve and brash as I was, have moved, at the ripe age of twenty-five and without ever having read so much as a book or even an essay on the specific subject, so confidently into the business of discussing literature *as* southern literature? What did I know about it? The point, as I see it, is that I was not merely undertaking an intellectual or literary inquiry; I was also investigating my own identity. I assumed that I might generalize about the South just about as well as I could about myself. Of course I knew what the South was; wasn't I a southerner? I didn't have to read books to explain *that*.

It is just there that the attraction of southern literature lies. One is dealing not with an idea, or a body of literary knowledge, but an experience; the South *is*. And *was*. The fascination with the literature is that it mirrors—more than that, it orders and articulates—a living human community. History, geography, politics, religion, economics, language: each of these aspects of human experience plays a part in the complex social organism known as The South, and each exists not in isolation but in an inescapable relationship with all the others, so that the result is *life*, seen and experienced not in fragmented, specialized form, but whole. The literary image, with its premium upon tangible, concrete representation rather than on the singling out of specific characteristics for purpose of analysis and comparison, is uniquely equipped to render that kind of experience. Moreover, one's relationship to that community is not dispassionate, but powerfully bound in with the exigencies and compulsions of one's own personality, so that to read a good southern novel or poem is to encounter aspects of oneself.

There was in my younger days a strong sense of community identity involved in being a southerner, with the result that the attempt to understand the region was also an attempt to understand oneself. It is often said nowadays that this is ceasing to be so. I do not believe it; I have had all too many students in classes in southern literature come up and tell me that they had recognized themselves in the novels and poems we were reading.

Genuine human communities, as opposed to economic societies, are rare commodities in the modern world. One tends to cleave to them. And I can see how in my own instance this was especially true. For not only was I a southerner, but a Jew, one who had been born into and grown up in a family with only perfunctory ties to a Jewish heritage. Perhaps it was because the Reform Jewish community in Charleston in my day was so small, and hardly even a community at all, that racial and religious origins and identity played a relatively small part in my childhood; I did not importantly define my relationship to the larger community along those lines. There was every reason, therefore, for me to want to attach myself to the community identity that *was* so abundantly available. And if I have had any special aptitude for understanding and revealing the ways of that community, it may well be because my own relationship with it was in certain ways oblique, so that I have been, to a degree at least, conscious of what was for others largely unconscious and automatically assumed.

Without subscribing to the wound-and-the-bow theory of art, I think there is something to the idea that there is always an inadequacy or shortcoming in one's life that makes one wish to recreate that life in language. It is not that art is neurosis (though many of the writers I have known would probably qualify); for there are many millions of neurotics, but mighty few good writers. The writer is able to do precisely what the merely neurotic person is prevented from doing: he has the power, as Lionel Trilling put it, to conceive, to plan, to work, and to bring his work to a conclusion. All the same, I think that there has to be an element that enforces a degree of separateness and impels its possessor toward a greater identification. As Willie Stark told Jack Burden, there is always something.

Of the southern writers I have known, it strikes me that in each instance there is something that served to set that author apart from the community in early years, so that there was not the more or less complete, unquestioning immersion in the patterns of the community that the writer's friends and neighbors enjoyed. I never knew Faulkner, but his position as the oldest son of a heavy-drinking father in a once-distinguished family fallen upon crass days has been amply documented by Joseph Blotner. Allen Tate's mother was a strong-willed woman with powerful pretensions to an aristocratic Virginia lineage, married to a businessman of more plebian origins who was a failure. John Ransom came from several generations of Methodist preachers; the family moved every two years. The fact that Eudora Welty's parents were not Mississippians but from Ohio and West Virginia is not, I think, without relevance to the marvelous insight with which she delineates the social complexity of the community. Flannery O'Connor's people were Roman Catholics in the Bible Belt; and so on. I do not think this is an accident, any more than it is mere happenstance that the most profoundly Irish of Irish poets was a Protestant rather than a Catholic, or that the greatest chronicler of French society during the years of the Third Republic was a half-Jew and a homosexual. For it seems to me that the impulse to write is the impulse to give order and definition to one's world, and such a desire can arise only out of need.

The powerful presence of the southern community has been such that any kind of oblique relationship to it has served to enforce the wish to understand it. Isn't it significant that the imagination of the midwestern writer—I think of Dreiser, Hemingway, Fitzgerald—has so often been directed outward, while that of the southern writer has generally insisted upon finding its direction within the community?

Another characteristic of the southern writers that has intrigued me is the extent to which so many of them seem to resist the idea that because they are writers, and often very learned ones indeed, they are intellectuals—persons whose life is primarily that of the mind, for whom ideas constitute the principal reality. This is by no means exclusively true of the southerners; one thinks at once of Ernest Hemingway. But it is very much a part of their public stance that they *not* be thought of as importantly different from their fellow nonliterary townsfolk. The author of *The Sound and the Fury* liked to insist that he was just a plain old Mississippi farmer. Thomas Wolfe raged against "lily-handed intellectuals"; *he* was descended from generations of mountain farmers and Pennsylvania farm workers, he often asserted. Indeed, part of the impulse that produced the Nashville Agrarian movement might be interpreted as the need to assert, on the part of writers and university scholars, a continuing identity with the plain folk. It is an interesting phenomenon, which has frequently baffled Frenchmen and New Yorkers, among others. I have speculated on its meaning elsewhere; it will suffice to say here that the powerful experience of the southern community, and the kind of self-definition it has offered, seems to have had the effect of making the writers feel somewhat uncomfortable with any kind of specialized, intellectual existence, and to want to assert membership in a social community not thus compartmentalized.

What is true for novelists and poets is, somewhat less obviously perhaps, true for critics. When I look at the essays in this volume, I note that what I seem to be most interested in is the relationship of the literary work to the community, or more than that, the link between the writer, in and through the work, and the community. With some chagrin I recognize that many of the issues that I have singled out for attention are those that have played a part in my own life, whether directly or by extension. I wasn't born into a once-distinguished Mississippi family, for example, and my father didn't drink, but when I look at my childhood in terms of the desire for status, I realize how very divided my ambitions were between sports, at which I wasn't very good, and writing, at which I was. It occurred to me once that the happiest situation I could conceive of would be to be watching a baseball game while listening to a Beethoven quartet! And as for the business about the discomfort with intellectual specialization and the need to insist upon an identity within the larger community, I confront the fact that the current chairman of the twentieth-century American literature group of the Modern Language Association is also the vice-president of the North State College Baseball League. As Don Quixote told Sancho Panza after the ride on Clavileño, I have said enough.

The danger with this kind of thing, of course, is that the critic reads his own needs into the work, instead of reading the work for what it has to say, in the way that T. S. Eliot declares that his preferences as a critic arose from his personal requirements as a poet.

On the other hand, and one can cite Eliot as an example, such criticism, when properly thought out, can be useful, in that the work of literature is approached in terms of its apprehension of life as well as its formal, literary relationships. In any event, it seems to me that what I say of myself is true to a degree at least for almost every southerner I know who has written importantly about southern literature, and that this is one of the attractions of the literature for us. We do indeed see ourselves in it; imaging as it does a palpable social complexity, bounded in a time and place and with its own complex representation of reality, even its own mythos and legendry, the best literature of the South offers a version, ordered and criticized, of our own situation, and the southern reader in particular is able to respond to it with considerable shock of recognition. To be sure, all great literature offers that, and by definition; but here the identification is so specific, so focused, on so many planes and angles of access, that one's engagement with it can become very personal and very compelling. I cannot otherwise account for the intensity with which some of us seem to go at it.

Someone once expressed amusement at the way in which the academic southern literature community—the group of scholars and critics who write most about southern literature—seems to mirror the virtues (and no doubt some of the vices) that its members insist upon finding in the southern community. That is, almost all the more active participants tend to be personal as well as professional friends, to seek out each other's company, to share numerous interests that go beyond their common intellectual concerns, and to spend much of their time talking to each other about sports, outdoor activities, and the like. I had not thought of it that way, but upon reflection it is quite true. They do tend to think of themselves as a group; and in the way they go about things I suppose there is something resembling a coterie, or perhaps a mutual admiration society. To an outsider I have no doubt that it has its aspects of smugness, even clannishness; an unkind soul might even grumble about an establishment. But it does exist. Not only that, but it flourishes. What strikes me about it is that it is really quite self-contained. One may call it insular, self-congratulatory, pretentious if one likes, but it is an old southern custom. It reminds me just a little of the way the old Virginians used to function, as noted by Joseph G. Baldwin in the *Flush Times*, when he quotes one of them as follows: " 'What, gentleman,' said the old man, with a sonorous swell—'what, burst up this glorious Union! and who, if *this* Union is torn up, could write another? Nobody except Henry Clay and J—— S. B——, of Culpeper—— and may be *they* wouldn't—and what then would you do for another?' "

Be that as it may, herewith is another gallery of literary southerners. The essays that follow are almost all of them occasional pieces, commissioned for the most part. The final essay was written to conclude a book for the Voice of America not long after the first man to be elected President of the United States as a southerner since James Knox Polk had taken office. It seemed time for a stock taking. For if an important part of the reason why the South was what it was, and thus southern literature had been what it was, lay in just those factors that had made it impossible for a southerner to be elected to national office, then was it all over? And what had it meant? What I ended up doing was trying to tell what it meant for me, and to use a novel by Walker Percy to show what it could mean for one of the most gifted of the novelists of my generation.

Some ten years or so ago, I made a decision not to write about the generation of southern novelists who came along in the 1960s and 1970s. My admiration for some of them is great indeed, and I am proud to say that several of the better ones have been my students. But I felt that if I tried to write about them, what I would inevitably end up doing was comparing them to their predecessors and judging their achievement in terms of that of previous writers. When I was explaining this once in response to a question from an audience, someone remarked that it seemed like "an elaborate cop-out" to him. Perhaps it is; but I have seen too many good literary critics make transparently foolish statements about the literature written by generations that followed their own.

So often one is asked, "Is the Southern Renascence continuing?" Of course it isn't—not in the sense that the younger southern writers are producing work that is essentially of the same sort as that of the writers who came onto the scene in the 1920s, 1930s, 1940s, and 1950s. Were such the case, the more recent work would have to be imitative and derivative. I don't think it is, for the most part. Yet the best of the new work impresses me as being recognizably southern, all the same, and I think that in the foreseeable future there will continue to be good southern writing, and also good critical writing about that writing. Temperamentally and intellectually, therefore, I do not hold with those of my friends who see, for the literature of the region we write about, only exhaustion and decline. The community identity is still there; the burr is still under the saddle. What is to come will be different, or else we have largely worked for nothing. I do not think we have.

Acknowledgments

The essays chosen for this collection were first written for various occasions and various kinds of audiences. Doubtless they bear the stylistic imprint of the occasion. I have left them pretty much as they are. Some are annotated, others aren't. Some are scholarly, others are informal.

"William Faulkner: The Discovery of a Man's Vocation" was originally prepared for delivery at the University of Alabama, and was first published in George Wolfe (ed.), *Faulkner: Fifty Years After "The Marble Faun"* (Tuscaloosa: University of Alabama Press, 1976). My thanks to Mr. Wolfe and Mr. Donald R. Noble.

"Scarlett O'Hara and the Two Quentin Compsons" was given at the University of Mississippi Conference on Faulkner in 1976 and first published in Evans Harrington and Anne J. Abadie (eds.), *The South and Faulkner's Yoknapatawpha: The Actual and the Apocryphal* (Jackson: University of Mississippi, 1977). I am grateful to Mr. Harrington for numerous kindnesses.

"Art and Artistry in Morgana, Mississippi" was written for the recent Eudora Welty lecture series at Anderson College, Anderson, South Carolina.

"Thomas Wolfe and the Place He Came From" was written for the Thomas Wolfe 75th birthday commemoration at the University of North Carolina at Asheville in 1975. It was first published in the *Virginia Quarterly Review*, LII (Spring, 1976). I am indebted to the editor of that review, Mr. Staige Blackford, for much help and encouragement.

"In Search of the Country of Art: Thomas Wolfe's *Of Time and the River*" was prepared for the Thomas Wolfe Festival at Saint Mary's College, Raleigh, North Carolina, in 1980.

"Allen Tate, 1899–1979" was written upon the occasion of Allen's death, at the request of George Core, editor, for *Sewanee Review*, LXXXVII (Spring, 1979). Writing it was a painful but cherished task; to Mr. Core I am deeply indebted for many favors.

"Flannery O'Connor's Company of Southerners: Or, 'The Artificial Nigger' Read as Fiction Rather Than Theology" was prepared for delivery at the annual Flannery O'Connor conference at Georgia College, Milledgeville, in 1976, and published in the *Flannery O'Connor Bulletin*, VI (Autumn, 1977).

"Carson McCullers: The Aesthetic of Pain" was prepared for a conference, subsequently canceled, at Columbus College, Georgia, and published in *Virginia Quarterly Review*, LIII (Spring, 1977).

"Trouble on the Land: Southern Literature and the Great Depression" was written for a conference on the 1930s at the University of Alabama in 1978 and published first in the *Canadian Review of American Studies*, X (Fall, 1979). My thanks go to Mr. Ralph Bogardus and Mr. Fred Hobson, of the University of Alabama.

"Shelby Foote's Civil War" was first published in Jack Salzman (ed.), *Prospects: An Annual Journal of American Cultural Studies*, I (New York: Burt Franklin, 1975).

"The Boll Weevil, the Iron Horse, and the End of the Line: Thoughts on the South" was originally written as the summarizing essay for a Voice of America forum on the South. It was published in the book that came out of that series, *The American South: Portrait of a Culture*, edited by myself, the overseas edition of which was published in 1979 by the United States International Communications Agency, and the American edition in 1980 by the Louisiana State University Press. I have chosen to include it in this collection despite its several appearances in book form because it seems to me an essential part of the intellectual and emotional inquiry that this volume, for better or worse, represents. When I begin an essay on southern literature I never know exactly where I am going;

this one turned out to be an attempt to understand what I was trying to find out in writing so obsessively about southern literature.

A GALLERY
OF SOUTHERNERS

William Faulkner: The Discovery
of a Man's Vocation

In April of 1958, William Faulkner delivered an address to the English Club of the University of Virginia which he entitled "A Word to Young Writers." In the course of his remarks he said that he had not for many years read the work of younger American writers, "perhaps for the same reason which the sprinter or the distance runner has: he does not have time to be interested in who is behind him or even up with him, but only who is in front." Of late he had been working to remedy this lack of acquaintance with contemporary literature, he said, and the book he liked best of those he had read thus far was J. D. Salinger's *The Catcher in the Rye*. His comments are so interesting that despite their length I wish to quote them in full:

> ... because this one expresses so completely what I had to say: *a youth, father to what will, must someday be a man, more intelligent than some and more sensitive than most*, who (he would not even have called it by instinct because he did not know he possessed it) because God had put it there, loved man and *wished to be a part of mankind*, humanity, who tried to join the human race and failed. To me, his tragedy, was not that he was, *as he perhaps thought, not tough enough or brave enough* or deserving enough to be accepted into humanity. His tragedy was that when he attempted to join the human race, there was no human race there. There was nothing for him to do save buzz, frantic and *inviolate*, *inside the glass wall of his tumbler* until he either gave up or was *himself by himself*, by his own frantic buzzing, *destroyed*. One thinks of Huck

Finn, another *youth already father to what will some day soon now be a man*. But in Huck's case all he had to combat was *his small size*, which time would cure for him; in time he would be *as big as any man he had to cope with*; and even as it was, all the adult world could do to harm him was *skin his nose a little*; humanity, the human race, would and was accepting him already; all he needed to do was *just to grow up in it*.

That is the young writer's dilemma as I see it. Not just his, but all our problems, is to save mankind from being desouled *as the stallion or boar or bull is gelded*; to save the individual from anonymity before it is too late and humanity has vanished from the animal called man. And who better to save man's humanity than the writer, the poet, the artist, since who should fear the loss of it more since the humanity of man is the artist's life blood.[1] (Italics are mine.)

I want to examine the way that William Faulkner saw his vocation of writer, and how, as I see it, he came to look at it as he did. I might have entitled this inquiry "A Portrait of the Artist as a Young Man," except that the title has already been usurped, and also that it implies the existence of a kind of *Kunstlerroman*, and Faulkner never wrote one of those. In any event, I should like to ask you to keep in mind those remarks about *The Catcher in the Rye*, for we shall return to them a little later on. For now, I want to consider several of Faulkner's own works.

It is well known that at the beginning of *Absalom, Absalom!* when Miss Rosa Coldfield attempts to justify to Quentin Compson her insistence upon holding him there in her parlor to listen to her story, she suggests that he might want to write about it some day: "So I dont imagine you will ever come back here and settle down as a country lawyer in a little town like Jefferson, since Northern people have already seen to it that there is little left in the South for a young man. So maybe you will enter the literary profession as so many Southern gentlemen and gentlewomen too are doing now and maybe some day you will remember this and write about it."[2] There is no satisfactory explanation for that passage's presence in the novel, at that point in the narrative, if it were not a way of informing us, as it were, that we are presently reading that story. I do not mean by this, of course, that Quentin himself wrote the book in the way that, say, the mature Stephen Dedalus wrote about himself and Bloom in *Ulysses*—to say the least, it would have had to have been posthumously published—but rather that in his role in *Absalom, Absalom!* one of Quentin's functions is to serve as symbol of the twentieth-century writer growing to manhood in the South, as William Faulkner saw that writer—*i.e.*, himself. It is for this reason that Quentin is made to feel the obligation he cites somewhat later on, *"Tell about the South. What's it like there. What do they do there. Why do they live there. Why do they live at all,"* and also why he is made to tell his Canadian friend Shreve that in order to understand the meaning of the South he would have had to have been born in the South.[3]

We do not think of Faulkner as an autobiographical novelist, even though Joseph Blotner's magnificent biography demonstrates how much more direct and detailed was Faulkner's use of his own family and personal experience in his fiction than most of us had hitherto suspected. His friend Robert Farley's remark that "the reason why Bill's characters are so real is because they were real" is doubtless an overstatement by an Oxford friend who recognized distinctive traits of people he knew in Faulkner's fiction and did not perceive the extent to which they were that: materials used in a larger imaginative creation that was based on the authority not of life but of art.[4] But if there was any doubt whether Faulkner was writing out of his own experience, Blotner's exhaustive portrayal of Faulkner's family background and his first twenty-five years surely dispels it.

William Faulkner, as we know, intended almost from the beginning to be a writer like his great-grandfather, the author of the *White Rose of Memphis*. The extent of his dedication to that kind of career, and his conviction that he would succeed in it, was massive and total. We know that the portrait of Colonel Sartoris in *The Unvanquished* is closely modeled upon that of Colonel William Clark Falkner as Confederate soldier, lawyer, politician, railroad builder, and entrepreneur.

There is, however, one notable difference, which I think, given Faulkner's admiration for his great-grandfather, ought to be remarked. I do not believe that it is ever suggested—and if it is, then certainly not importantly—that the Old Colonel, for all his many accomplishments, was an imaginative writer. He is portrayed as the man of action, of violence, the brave and impulsive soldier and the political and economic tycoon. There is the great moment in "An Odor of Verbena" in which the Old Colonel recognizes what he has come to, as a tragic hero should, and declines to continue the sequence of bloodshed that has become central to his life by killing once again, but that is about as close as Faulkner ever comes to giving him the kind of introspectiveness that one might expect of a literary man. Nothing about his characterization as a Sartoris would indicate the capacity for writing an epic poem, a play, three novels, and a travel book, as Colonel W. C. Falkner himself did.

It is not difficult to explain this omission on literary grounds, of course. The demands of characterization and of the economy of plot were doubtless such that to make the Old Colonel into a literary man would have necessitated a complication all out of proportion to the advantages to be secured. More than that, however, the point about the Colonel and of all the Sartorises, as they figure in the Yoknapatawpha mythos, is that they are the dashing, reckless men of action, the gallant patricians who live perilously and die gloriously. As such they lie at the heart of Faulkner's view of southern history and his sense of decline and fall; they exemplify the old-time heroic possibility of direct, uncomplicated action that the conditions of modern life no longer provide, and Faulkner's attitude toward them, as we know, is compounded both of admiration and a certain amount of skepticism. Thus the Civil War Bayard Sartoris dies heroically and gallantly in attempted capture of Union Army anchovies.

The fact remains, however, that Faulkner did not, at this point in his literary career, conceive of his old-style aristocratic hero, his man of action, as possessing or desiring to possess the sensibilities of a writer—which is to say, of one addicted to introspection, self-scrutiny, nuances of feeling. And if we think about all of the Yoknapatawpha novels up through *Go Down, Moses*, we will quickly perceive that this generalization holds good throughout. Thomas Sutpen, of course, is the best example: in his characterization there is the explicit premise that he is able to do what he does, build his house and get his dynasty, *because* of his utter lack of introspection or awareness of the humanity of others.

It will be recalled what Quentin's father says about the heroes of an older time: "people too as we are, and victims too as we are, but victims of a different circumstance, simpler and therefore, integer for integer, larger, more heroic and the figures therefore more heroic too, not dwarfed and involved but distinct, uncomplex who had the gift of loving once or dying once instead of being diffused and scattered creatures drawn blindly limb from limb from a grab bag and assembled, *author* and victim too of a thousand homicides and a thousand copulations and divorcements."[5] (Italics are mine.)

The latter description, it must be admitted, fits Quentin Compson a good deal less appropriately than it does another Faulkner character, Horace Benbow of *Flags in the Dust*. In that novel, to a considerably more obvious extent than the severely cut version published as *Sartoris*, Faulkner makes an explicit comparison between the man of action, represented by Bayard Sartoris, and the man of sensibility, represented by the lawyer and the dilettante Horace Benbow. Both return to Jefferson after the First World War, but where Bayard has been a combat aviator who has dueled with Richthofen's Flying Circus in the sky and seen his brother go down to his death, Horace Benbow has been a YMCA worker. Arriving home in his khakis—a uniform, yet not that of a real soldier—he is viewed contemptuously by a Marine who "remarked the triangle on Horace's sleeve and made a vulgar sound of derogation through his pursed lips."[*][6]

Horace Benbow has brought back from France a treasured possession, a glassblower's apparatus, with which he can fashion vases. Here is a description of Horace as blower of glass: "But Narcissa had finally persuaded him upon the upper floor of the garage and here he had set up his furnace and had had four mishaps and produced one almost perfect vase of clear amber, larger, more richly and chastely serene and which he kept always on his night table and called by his sister's name in the intervals of apostrophising both of

* William Faulkner himself returned home in the uniform of a Royal Air Force pilot, though he had been only a cadet and never flown, and limped from a wound that he never suffered. He wore a Sam Browne belt and wings on his tunic, and an overseas cap, which in his brother John's words "was only issued to our men if they had served overseas." He was thus saluted by American soldiers about town, since "to them it meant he had been overseas and they saluted an overseas man. They turned up their noses at our own officers who had not been over and refused to acknowledge them in any way."[7]

them impartially in his moment of rhapsody over the realization of the meaning of peace and the unblemished attainment of it, as Thou still unravished bride of quietude."[8]

The similarity of that description of the vase to the famous urn in "The Bear," in which Faulkner has Carothers McCaslin quote the poet Keats to apostrophize the timelessness of art—"he was talking about Truth"—is I think quite remarkable. The relevance to Quentin Compson's situation vis-à-vis his sister Caddy in *The Sound and the Fury* is also obvious. I shall return to the latter; for now I would point out that in this novel, the first of all the great novels of Yoknapatawpha, Faulkner sets up a contrast, a dichotomy even, between the Sartoris man of action who lives violently in time, and the Benbow man of sensibility who is ineffectual in the everyday world but who dreams of loveliness and creates works of art, "rich and chastely serene," that outlast time, though at the price of forever unconsummated love.[9] The distinction in *Flags in the Dust*, I think, is mostly in favor of the man of action, Bayard Sartoris, but at the same time—and what a crime it was to have removed most of the Horace Benbow material from the manuscript published as *Sartoris*—it was when Faulkner could get the kind of sensibility and use of language that in *Flags in the Dust* he ascribes to Horace Benbow fully deployed in his storytelling that he was able to create his major work. In *Absalom, Absalom!* we see a man of action as central figure, but perceived and interpreted through use of the sensibilities of Quentin Compson. A tension is achieved in the interplay of these two kinds of sensibility that is very close to the kind of tension between life and art that Faulkner is getting at with his use of the Grecian urn and Keats's poem.

There is also an interesting conjunction of ideas here. The idea of art and timelessness, on the one hand, is joined to the idea of chastity, of sexual virginity, on the other. The "vase of perfect amber" that Horace creates he calls by his sister's name; each is "Thou still unravished bride of quietude." C. Hugh Holman has pointed out that in *Light in August* the connection is made explicit: when Joe Christmas confronts the fact of Bobbie Allen's menstruation, "he seemed to see a diminishing row of suavely shaped urns in moonlight, blanched. And not one was perfect. Each one was cracked and from each crack there issued something liquid, deathcolored, and foul."[10]

In *Flags in the Dust* what happens to Narcissa is that she marries Bayard Sartoris, but though in so doing her chastity is technically violated for the first time, we know also that it is not much more than a technicality, so far as anything more than what in *The Sound and the Fury* is described as being to Caddy Compson a "frail physical stricture which to her was no more than a hangnail would have been" is concerned.[11] For Narcissa has been for some time receiving anonymous letters that are full of foulness. When she tells Miss Jenny Du Pre that the letters make her feel filthy, Miss Jenny retorts, "How can this thing make you feel filthy? Any young woman is liable to get an anonymous letter. And a lot of 'em like it. We all are convinced that men feel that way about us, and we can't help but admire one that's got the courage to tell us about it, no matter who he is." But Narcissa does not destroy the letters; she keeps them. They are stolen from her, and, as Cleanth Brooks points out, in a later short story, "There Was a Queen," Faulkner describes how she gets them back: by sleeping with the government agent who has them.[12]

Horace, of course, cannot sleep with Narcissa, for they are brother and sister, and this is the situation with Quentin and Caddy Compson in *The Sound and the Fury*. But where Quentin, a youth in his teens, is a virgin, Horace, an older man, is not. He has slept around a bit—but not until Narcissa is engaged to Bayard Sartoris does Horace move toward marriage himself. In both novels there is the suggestion of incest, but it has always seemed to me that if so, it is a very special kind of incest, since in both instances what the brother most cherishes in the sister is the technical virginity, the chastity. In Quentin's case the chastity of Caddy serves at least two functions, and I think it is important to recognize both of them.

In one instance, as we know because Faulkner explicitly tells us so, Caddy's maidenhead symbolizes for him "some concept of Compson honor"—her sexual purity means that an unblemished ideal of aristocratic role is still intact. And Faulkner censures Quentin for this; it is ultimately selfish, making a fetish of Caddy's symbolic virginity in order to feed self-love, a concept of family role devoid of real love and understanding for his sister, who has been violated not by a lover named Dalton Ames but by a family incapable of genuine love and trust.

But there is another way of looking at Quentin's view of Caddy's chastity and his grief over its loss, and if we do not see it, too, we will miss much of its significance. Some years ago a very fine student of mine, a woman in her middle years who had raised several sons, wrote a paper on *The Sound and the Fury* in which she showed that while the particular sordid circumstances of the Compson family situation may have driven Quentin to suicide, in many respects the actual problems he confronted were neither unnatural nor necessarily hopeless, but merely those of many a young adolescent. Growing up as Quentin did in a double-standard society, in which the proof of masculinity was strongly equated with sexual prowess, much of Quentin's anguish comes from his emotional immaturity, which has left him still virginal at a time when many of his contemporaries have become sexually active. Under these circumstances his strong feeling for his sister exists in part *because*, overtly at least, no sexual role is either permitted or demanded of him. Caddy is "safe": in his relationship with her he feels no challenge to prove his masculinity. But as Caddy grows into womanhood and becomes sexually active, this line of self-defense is gone, and his own failure to "be a man" is doubly painful.*[13] His memories of his interview with Caddy in this sense are rending:

> poor Quentin
> she leaned back on her arms her hands locked about her knees
> youve never done that have you
> what done what
> that what I have what I did

* Jackson J. Benson, in an interesting essay entitled "Quentin Compson: Self-Portrait of a Young Artist's Emotions," goes ahead to draw a detailed parallel between Quentin's state of mind and William Faulkner's relationship with his childhood sweetheart Estelle Oldham, and he likens Caddy's marriage to Herbert Head with Estelle's to Cornell Franklin, so far as the emotions felt by Quentin are concerned; Quentin's departure for Harvard is equated with Faulkner's departure to stay with Phil Stone in New Haven at the time when Estelle was to be married. This may well be so; my argument, however, is that, viewed apart from the decline and fall of the Compson family, Quentin's anguish over his sister's sexual activity can be understood as the normal response of a rather sensitive, introverted, sexually immature adolescent to a situation that seems to him to confirm his own fears of being insufficiently masculine.

yes yes lots of times with lots of girls
    then I was crying her hand touched me again and I was crying against
    her damp blouse then she lying on her back looking past my head into
    the sky I could see a rim of white under her irises I opened my knife[14]

What I would stress is that Quentin's relationship with his sister *is* strongly sexual, but entirely latently and implicitly so, and the reason why it exists as it does is that Quentin has been able to engage in it without feeling any social imperative to make it into one that is explicitly sexual. It is when this self-defense is destroyed by Caddy's promiscuity, so that Quentin can no longer feel that Caddy is "pure" like himself, that he becomes desperate.

Earlier I quoted at some length from Faulkner's praise of Salinger's *The Catcher in the Rye*. In that novel, when Holden Caulfield learns that his prep school friend Stradlater, who is very much the ladies' man, has spent several hours in a parked car with Jane Gallagher, he goes berserk, leaps upon Stradlater, and begins hitting him, only to be easily overcome by the much stronger Stradlater and get his nose bloodied in the process. Holden himself doesn't know why he attacks Stradlater, but clearly it is because Jane Gallagher had been for him the one girl whom he could love without feeling a role-impelled necessity to attempt overt sexual advances; the knowledge, therefore, that Jane has reached the age at which she must be seen as a legitimate sexual object destroys this refuge for Holden. By "giving her the time" Stradlater has rebuked Holden's imagined failure in masculinity and shown him a world in which relationships with women *must* be sexual. All that seems left to him is his own little sister, a child, and Holden dreams of protecting little children from falling over the cliff into adult sexuality. It is against this knowledge, and in rage against his own imagined sexual cowardice, that Holden strikes out so obsessively when he attacks Stradlater.

The situation is most reminiscent of Quentin Compson's apparently unmotivated attack on Gerald Bland for boasting of sexual conquests; afterwards his friends attempt to understand why Quentin acted as he did. Gerald had been bragging, they remember:

You know: like he does, before girls, [Shreve McCannon says] so they
    dont know exactly what he's saying. All his damn innuendo and lying
    and a lot of stuff that dont make sense even. Telling us about some

wench that he made a date with to meet at a dance hall in Atlantic City and stood her up and went to bed and how he lay there being sorry for her waiting on the pier for him, without him there to give her what she wanted. Talking about the body's beauty and the sorry ends thereof and how tough women have it, without anything else they can do except lie on their backs. Leda lurking in the bushes, whimpering and moaning for the swan, see.[15]

Shreve and Spoade interpret Quentin's attack on Gerald as a defense of female honor; "the champion of dames," Spoade calls Quentin. "Bud, you excite not only admiration, but horror."[16] But what has motivated Quentin's quixotic assault upon the much more powerful Gerald is less that than fear that Gerald's view of the world is right and that sexual promiscuity is inescapable. "Have you ever had a sister?" Quentin asks of Bland just before his assault.

I have sought to show a convergence, in Faulkner's fiction, of the idea of sexual virginity and artistic talent, to suggest that with Quentin Compson in particular, Faulkner created a character who felt keenly what he feared was a lack of masculinity on his part, and to propose a link between this kind of character and what Faulkner felt was the artistic temperament, in contrast to the masculine man of action. With this in mind, let us now turn back to the passage in which Faulkner expressed his admiration for J. D. Salinger's novel.

If we examine the imagery we find that the contemporary artist is likened to Holden Caulfield, "more intelligent than some and more sensitive than most," wishing to be "a part of mankind," but fearing himself insufficiently tough or brave. He is also, I think, just a bit reminiscent of Quentin Compson, "frantic and inviolate," destroyed by himself. There is also the image of "the glass walls of his tumbler"—which suggests not only the "minute fragile membrane" but also that "perfect vase of clear amber, larger, more richly and chastely serene" which Horace Benbow kept by his bed table and called by his sister's name—again the equation of the artist with virginity. We then get Huck Finn, who was handicapped only by his small size; however, Huck would eventually become "as big as any man he had to cope with," and all the adult world could do to him was to "skin his nose a little," for he would grow up in it. There we have the same bloodied nose, and we are reminded that, in Blotner's words, William Faulkner was "five feet five and a half inches tall and he would never be any taller. No smart dress suit or bench-made shoes could conceal the fact that the oldest of the three grown Falkner boys was also the smallest. He was built on the Old Colonel's lines, but his grandfather, his father, and his younger brother Jack were all six-footers."[17]

Faulkner says that the role of this Holden-Quentin-Huck-like artist is to save mankind from being "desouled as the stallion or boar or bull is gelded"—in other words, it is his artistic sensitivity and spirituality that will prevent the desexing of man, which Faulkner equates with the loss of one's soul. The mature artist, that is, once he grows up to his full size, is as much a man as the Sutpens and the Sartorises, since without him these will become mere animals. The adolescence of the artist, therefore, comes before he is able to assert his masculinity in his own way and before he realizes that his manhood is to be proved in different terms than for others whom he might at the time think are more masculine than he because tougher and physically braver than himself. When he grows to his full maturity as an artist, he will no longer doubt his own masculinity but instead cherish his unique, saving gift.

Faulkner once said an interesting thing about *Absalom, Absalom!* Writing to Malcolm Cowley, he insisted that it was the character Quentin, not the author Faulkner, who was brooding over the situation of Thomas Sutpen. If we think of Quentin as the artist when young, we can see its relevance to the remarks on Salinger. He then went on to declare that "He [Quentin] grieved and regretted the passing of an order the dispossessor of which he was not tough enough to withstand." And he continued, "but more he feared the fact (because he hated and feared the portentous symptom) that a man like Sutpen, who to Quentin was trash, originless, could not only have dreamed so high but have had the force and strength to have failed so grandly."[18] He was telling Cowley several things about Quentin's attitude toward Sutpen. One is that Quentin marvels at Sutpen's sheer strength, as contrasted with his own lack of toughness; the other is that Quentin fears what the example of Sutpen, a commoner, means for the survival of the old southern aristocracy whose descendant he was. That a nonaristocrat, a man without a family background, could have done and been what Sutpen did and was is appalling, because it is the rise of the nonaristocratic, plain-folk South in Quentin's time that meant the end of the role of leadership of the older families—the Compsons were being dispossessed by these people, and as a Compson he was not sufficiently tough to resist effectively. Sutpen, in other words, though a nobody, was capable of the dream of dynasty and the strength to achieve it.

What had happened, then, to the old leadership, that it could be dispossessed? Very simply, it had become weak, self-conscious, decadent. It had become Quentin. It was no longer possible to be a Colonel Sartoris, and it was inconceivable that a Colonel William C. Falkner, man both of action and of letters, could be made believable in a novel. Either their latter-day exemplars retain their old recklessness and thoughtlessness—in which case they are like the young Bayard Sartoris of *Flags in the Dust*, born into the wrong time and driven to wild deeds of useless self-destruction—or else they lose all capacity for leadership and action and become author and victim both of petty crimes, sins, failures—*i.e.*, Horace Benbow.

To their place of leadership rise the lower orders, the Thomas Sutpens, the Flem Snopeses, and their kind. Significantly, as Blotner tells us in his biography, Flem Snopes and Thomas Sutpen evolved out of a single character in an early short story.[19] The taking over of Colonel Sartoris' bank by Flem Snopes is the result of this transaction. And we know too, as Blotner tells us, that the real-life Young Colonel, J. W. T. Falkner, had pretty much the same thing happen with him and his bank. And Faulkner needed to look no further than the Young Colonel's onetime law partner, Lee Russell, for a model of some of Flem Snopes's talents at elevating himself, and to compare such contemporary Mississippi political figures as Russell and Theodore (The Man) Bilbo to the likes of his own great-grandfather, William C. Falkner, to conclude that not only was the bottom rail now on top, but the day of honor and patrician dignity in public life had passed away.

But before we write off Faulkner's view of decline and fall as merely another patrician version of the Death of the Gods, an *Education of Henry Adams* for the Deep South such as might have been composed by a Will Percy or a Thomas Nelson Page, we had better think a little more about *Absalom, Absalom!* and about what Faulkner said about it. Specifically, we might keep in mind the distinction Faulkner was insisting on to Malcolm Cowley between himself and Quentin Compson. He agreed that it was the South that was the subject of Quentin's meditations, but "I think though you went a step further than I (unconsciously, I repeat) intended. I think Quentin, not Faulkner, is the correct yardstick here. I was writing this story, but he not I was brooding over a situation." And he went on, after remarking Quentin's grief over realizing that a Sutpen, a common man, could have dreamed so high and been strong enough to fail so grandly, to say that "Quentin probably contemplated Sutpen as the hypersensitive, already self-crucified cadet of an old long-time Republican Philistine house contemplated the ruin of Sampson's portico. . . . He grieved and was moved by it but he was still saying 'I told you so' even while he hated himself for saying it."[20]

Faulkner was not, I think, merely making a point about authorial objectivity, though doubtless that was involved. It is true that, if the characterization of Quentin Compson was in part drawn from Faulkner's own youth, one can understand why he might be reluctant to have Cowley or anyone else say that Quentin spoke for Faulkner. Rightly so; for though there was some of the youthful Faulkner in the makeup of Quentin Compson, there was also a great deal about William Faulkner that was not in the characterization. I think of the Faulkner who played football and baseball, took part in dramatics, drew and painted, and by the time he was Quentin's age was already a hardworking young writer. The concerns of this young man, so fully described in Blotner's biography, do not find expression in the characterization of Quentin Compson.

Furthermore, though the Falkners were among the aristocracy, such as it was, of the community and furnished the models for both the Sartorises and the Compsons and though Faulkner himself tended to be something of a snob in his earlier years, it is also true that the advent of the early Falkners and Thompsons into the Mississippi country in the 1820s and 1830s exhibited a good deal of Thomas Sutpen's energy and even his ruthlessness. It is significant, I think, that nowhere in his Yoknapatawpha fiction did Faulkner attempt to do much with the early Compsons and Sartorises in the Mississippi territory. For the most part they come into the fiction already established on the land, though on occasion there are references made to how they got there. Dramatically it is Sutpen's setting up his house in the wilderness that covers that phase of the Yoknapatawpha saga. It seems to me that something of Thomas Sutpen's strength, ruthlessness, and dream of dynasty can be seen in the life and character of Faulkner's admired great-grandfather Colonel William C. Falkner, too.

The description of Quentin as a "self-crucified cadet of an old long-time Republican Philistine house contemplat[ing] the ruins of Sampson's portico" is also revealing. Whatever might have been his affinity for lost causes, we cannot assume that Faulkner's ultimate loyalties lay with the Biblical Philistines rather than the Israelites. Quentin, Faulkner was saying, was something of a snob, perhaps because Faulkner recognized that he too had been something of a snob. However crude and ruthless and unjust Thomas Sutpen may have seemed to Quentin and to us, he did indeed dream high and work mightily and bravely for his dreams, as Faulkner insists. To assume that Faulkner's sympathies were primarily with Quentin in the matter is a mistake. Sutpen was a tragic hero—not on the Christian but on the classical Greek model—and it is impossible, however much he repels and dismays us, not to feel admiration as well. What I am suggesting, therefore, is that in insisting to Cowley that it was Quentin, and not himself, who was doing the brooding over the Sutpen story, Faulkner was making the point that the patrician disapproval and dismay that came naturally to Quentin Compson was not by any means his own considered attitude toward a man like Sutpen. He may have recognized within himself some of that attitude and put it into the characterization of Quentin, but he was also clearly aware of the limitations of Quentin's attitude, and that too was part of the story he had to tell. In writing about Quentin and his patrician horror over Thomas Sutpen, Faulkner was also sketching the futility of the decline and fall attitude, and he was attributing Quentin's hypersensitivity and overwrought temperament *to* his patrician identity, with the obvious implication that Quentin was the one who exemplified the decline and fall, not Faulkner.

So it will not do to say that William Faulkner saw in the decline and fall of the Compsons and Sartorises the death of all that was best about the South. Instead, he made it very clear in *Absalom, Absalom!* that such qualities as imagination, great ambition, force and strength of character were by no means the property of the well-born alone, and he portrayed Quentin's appalled recognition that a Sutpen, a man of no breeding, could possess such characteristics as a sign of Quentin's incapacity for coping with the modern world.

Yet the depiction of Quentin's character is sympathetic. Faulkner did not undervalue Quentin's sincerity, his high-mindedness, his powers of sympathy and of understanding. Though he portrayed them as going to waste in *The Sound and the Fury* for want of any capacity for adapting them to the world that Quentin was living in, the general portrait of Quentin is compassionate. I have always felt that Quentin's suicide was the crucial event in *The Sound and the Fury*; the family disintegration that follows is the result of that suicide. Had Quentin been able to live and function in the world, then the other sad events—Caddy's separation, Mr. Compson's death from drinking, Benjy's gelding and incarceration in the state asylum, Caddy's daughter's wretched childhood and her flight into nowhere—might not have taken place. Jason's ascendancy is possible only because the one Compson who could have stood up to him was dead. What was wrong with the world was that a Quentin Compson could not survive in the society in which he found himself.

How might have Quentin survived? It is customary to say only by turning into a Snopes—*i.e.*, becoming Jason Compson. But there was another way, which was, by being more than Quentin was, which is to say, by adding to that capacity for sympathy and honor and kindness the kind of toughness and good sense that we see in Faulkner's own character. If we equate Quentin's general background and station with that of the young William Faulkner, then we realize, from reading Blotner's biography and from the evidence of the novels themselves, what the young William Faulkner had that Quentin Compson lacked—the Sutpen-like dream of greatness, which for him took the form of a sense of vocation, the desire to be an author, and the imagination and self-knowledge that could make that dream a reality. Faulkner conceived of his role (whether consciously articulated or not does not matter) as that of the artist, which is to say, of recreating in language the life, and the meaning of the life, that he saw around him. The great-grandfather he so admired had been writer and man of action; but his literary ambition was not so dominant, and the novels and poems that he wrote had not lasted. His great-grandson saw himself as giving to his writing the importance and energy that William C. Falkner had brought to railroad building, politics, and to his military career. This was his bent, his métier; clearly his talents and his sensibilities were not suited to the pursuit of financial or political or military success. What he could do—he said it again and again, throughout his life— was what a latter-day member of the Falkner family of Mississippi might do in his own time and place: write books that might lift men's hearts.

Floyd Watkins, in an excellent review of Blotner's biography, makes a significant point about Faulkner's early life. Noting the extensively delineated portraiture of the ordinary, nonaristocratic whites that the "semi-aristocrat" Faulkner provides throughout his novels, he declares that "somehow Faulkner got to know these people better than his friends knew them and better than any other major Southern writer ever has, but Blotner develops only brief accounts of how Faulkner played with farm children, saw country people when they came to town, dealt with them on his farm, hunted deer with them."[21] This is quite true, but I believe that part of the answer is that being a member of one of the First Families of northern Mississippi was a great deal different from having similar credentials as a member of, say, the First Families of the Mississippi Delta, perhaps. There was nothing like the same kind of social distancing involved; Faulkner, after all, grew up in a small southern town, went to its public schools, played football and baseball, engaged in various youthful exploits, and in general cannot be said to have known a boyhood that was importantly different or more socially fastidious than those of most of his townsfolk. It is true that Old Colonel J. W. T. Falkner liked to make a distinction between political and business relations on the one hand, and social relations on the other, as Blotner makes clear, but it is also made clear that his sons and grandsons made no such rigid distinction. Though the Falkners came out of good and honored lineage, to judge from Blotner's biography their lives were not notably different from that of the small town, middle-class upper South in general, and they knew relatively little of the kind of social exclusiveness that might have been the case had they possessed similar social standing in the Tidewater South. So I am not sure that I agree with Watkins' assertion that how Faulkner came to know the "plain folk" so well "remains a mystery."[22] He knew them because he grew up with and among them and for the most part their experiences were his own as well.

Quentin Compson is a patrician, no doubt of that. So are the Sartorises. And I have already suggested that in certain ways the young Faulkner was something of a snob. But there is really no contradiction here. Earlier I noted that only part of the life and personality of the young William Faulkner got into the characterization of Quentin Compson and that the part that did get in was the sensitive, attenuated, impractical, lonely dreamer, traits which I have sought to show that Faulkner associated with the personality of the youthful artist. The early pages of Blotner's biography contain many references to this young man, small for his age, wearing shoulder braces, writing poems and stories, drawing sketches, listening to Estelle Oldham play the piano, absorbed with Melville's *Moby Dick* and Shakespeare and Bunyan, spending much time with his older friend Phil Stone and reading Swinburne, Keats, Conrad Aiken, and as he grew into his middle and late teens growing more aloof and distant from his fellow townsfolk, until he acquired his nickname, "Count No-Count."

What was it that set the young William Faulkner apart from his Oxford friends and companions? We may answer that it was because he was *William Faulkner*, who was destined to be, and wanted to be, a great writer. One feels sure that the mature William Faulkner who created the characterizations of Quentin Compson, Horace Benbow, Ike McCaslin, and Darl Bundren realized that, too. But whether the young Faulkner was convinced of it is another matter. I have already shown how Faulkner equated the artistic sensibility with weakness, lack of physical courage, and sexual awkwardness and virginity. The rending scene comes to mind in which Quentin confronts his sister's seducer, Dalton Ames, desiring to play the traditional role of brother-protector, only to faint dead away: "I knew that he didnt hit me that he had lied about that for her sake too and that I had just passed out like a girl."[23] The scene is remembered, agonizingly, by Quentin later. If we compare the remark to what Faulkner much later wrote about Holden Caulfield: "To me, his tragedy was not that he was, as he perhaps thought, not tough enough or brave enough or deserving enough," the connection seems clear. "As he perhaps thought"—*i.e.*, because he did not yet realize that his gift of sensibility and understanding was ultimately no less masculine and respectable than physical size and strength and prowess in the hunt, or in the back seat of a parked car, even.

The probability is that as a young man Faulkner did indeed fear for his courage and masculinity and feel a certain amount of shame over his emotional complexity, and *he equated these with his aristocratic heritage.* They were what had been handed down across four generations from his great-grandfather, and also from his mother. His great-grandfather had been novelist, poet, and playwright, but also man of action, railroad builder, Confederate hero, politician. But over the course of four generations of decline and fall, the latter qualities had been bred out of the blood—so that the oldest son of the current generation of the Falkner family was, like Quentin Compson, something of a "hypersensitive, already self-crucified cadet" who had lost the rough, animal force and aggressiveness that the family had once exemplified and could only look backward and regret "the passing of an order the dispossessor of which he was not tough enough to withstand." Or so he "perhaps thought" at the time. To be concerned, as he was, with putting words on paper to express a craving for beauty both lost and distant (in properly world-weary fashion, to be sure) was hardly the accepted pursuit of a man among men. By dint of his time and place, he, a Falkner of Mississippi, had become a sybarite, a decadent.

Thus the young Faulkner, or an important part of the young Faulkner. The aloofness and "hypersensitivity" were made into a self-protective shield, a mechanism for defense, after the fashion of the young artist anywhere and anytime. The quasi-aristocratic status became a kind of chalice to be borne through a throng of insensitive foes, at once the curse and the glory of his uniqueness.

But not for the mature Faulkner, the artist who wrote the novels about Quentin and Horace Benbow and Thomas Sutpen and the whole universe of great characters who inhabit Yoknapatawpha country. As early as 1920, a year after he returned from the war, we find him reviewing William Alexander Percy's *In April Once* for the University of Mississippi student newspaper and remarking with some sarcasm that "Mr. Percy—like alas! how many of us—suffered the misfortune of having been born out of his time. He should have lived in Victorian England and gone to Italy with Swinburne, for like Swinburne, he is a mixture of passionate adoration of beauty and as passionate a despair and disgust with its manifestation and accessories in the human race."[24] This was very appropriate criticism of Percy, and like so much criticism by young authors it involved the heaping of some scorn upon an aspect of himself that he recognized. Faulkner's own poetry of the period is filled with just such *fin de siècle* sentiments, by Dowson out of *The Rubaiyat*.

The point is, however, that though Faulkner might be playing a role, he had the good sense to recognize that it was a role and felt dissatisfaction with it. A little later he would refer to his early addiction to poetry as part of "a youthful gesture I was then making, of being 'different' in a small town."[25] We find the same censure, much more strongly pronounced this time, in another piece written for the *Mississippian* somewhat more than a year later. This time Faulkner was discussing American drama, and he declared that American playwrights were not making proper use of the American language. "Our wealth of language and our inarticulateness (inability to derive any benefit from the language) are due," he said, to our overreliance upon action: "As a nation, we are a people of action (the astounding growth of the motion picture industry is a proof); even if our language is action rather than communication between minds." This failure to explore language other than in terms of its immediate utility, he concluded, "is the Hydra we have raised, and which we become pessimists or idiots slaying; who have the fundamentals of *the lustiest language of modern times;* a language that seems, to the newly arrived foreigner, a mass of subtleties for the reason that it is employed *only as a means of relief, when physical action is impossible or unpleasant,* by all classes, ranging from the Harvard professor, through the gardeniaed aloof young liberal, to the lowliest pop vendor at the ball park."[26] (Italics are mine.)

What he was saying here was implicitly what he would tell the

English Club at the University of Virginia almost four decades later: that the role of the writer was to save men from being desouled by asserting in language the virtues without which men are only animals. The American writer must use his language to go beyond the materialistic and the practical world of action into the human values, what in his Nobel Prize speech he would denote as "love and honor and pity and pride and compassion and sacrifice," without which the writer would be writing not of the heart but of the glands alone.

Note his imagery. The true use of language is now portrayed in sexual terms—"the lustiest language of modern times." As employed merely on utilitarian grounds, however, it is used "only as a means of relief, when physical action is impossible or unpleasant"— as if it were a kind of masturbatory compensation. He would seem to be suggesting that he had had just about enough of wan pastorals and lamentations for departed beauty, which he characterizes as "the manners of various dead-and-gone stylists—achieving therefrom a vehicle which might serve to advertise soap and cigarettes." Nor would he pursue the false heartiness of "slang and our 'hard' colloquialisms," since that was to ape the poverty of the inarticulate.[27] (He would soon skillfully employ just such language, however, in *The Sound and the Fury* in order to portray precisely the soullessness he despised: *i.e.*, the Jason section.)

It was at this period in his life, of course, that he had gone down to New Orleans and struck up his acquaintanceship with Sherwood Anderson, and when he was beginning to discover prose for his medium. The friendship with Anderson has been well chronicled, by Faulkner among others, and there is no need to go into it here, except to make this point: that in Anderson Faulkner found a writer he could respect both for his dedication to his art and for the sturdy courage of his commitment. Anderson's background, Faulkner wrote of him much later, "had taught him that the amount of security and material success which he had attained was, must be, the answer and end to life. Yet he gave this up, repudiated and discarded it at a later age, when older in years than most men and women who make that decision, to dedicate himself to art, writing."[28] This was no pale, wan fugitive from the crude actuality of everyday life, nor yet another slick commercial manipulator of popular taste; this was the author of *Winesburg, Ohio*, and though Faulkner soon came to sense Anderson's limitations and weary of his unflagging naïveté he had never ceased to admire him, and he closed his tribute to his early benefactor by describing their last meeting. The physical imagery is interesting: "Again there was that moment when he appeared taller, bigger than anything he ever wrote. Then I remembered *Winesburg, Ohio* and *The Triumph of the Egg* and some of the pieces in *Horses and Men*, and I knew that I had seen, was looking at, a giant in an earth populated to a great— too great—extent by pigmies, even if he did make but the two or perhaps three gestures commensurate with gianthood."[29]

Knowing Sherwood Anderson, therefore, confirmed Faulkner's pride in his choice of vocation. But Faulkner was already coming to see that the life of writing that he had elected for himself was not a way of escaping his experience by using pretty words to gild the tawdriness of the everyday world. He was discovering that it was in that everyday life, and in how he felt about it, that the meaning that he had hitherto attempted to abstract into poetry was to be found and that the way to give form to his experience was to immerse himself in what he knew and saw, and to recreate it in language that could define it. To do that would be the most difficult of tasks, and no job of a weakling or a coward. Truly it would require the strength of a giant, but not as such strength was measured in the market-place or the athletic field or the courthouse square. The strength needed for this task would be found in the courage of man's meta-phors and the boldness of his imagination, and the mark of success would not be in winning the girl or building the railroad or even selling copies of books, but telling a story so well and so firmly that nothing important would be left out.

A man's work indeed, as he had seen from the work by other good men he had read. "I read 'Thou still unravished bride of quietness,'" he wrote in 1922, "and found a still water withal strong and potent, quiet with its own strength, and satisfying as bread. That beautiful awareness, so sure of its own power that it is not necessary to create the illusion of force by frenzy and motion. Take the odes to a night-ingale, to a Grecian urn, 'Music to hear,' etc.; here is the spiritual beauty which the moderns strive vainly for with trickery, and yet beneath it one knows are entrails: masculinity."[30]

It was no task for a sentimentalist or a dilettante. As he wrote of the southern writer, "It was himself that the Southerner is writing about, not about his environment; who has, figuratively speaking, taken the artist in him in one hand and his milieu in the other and thrust the one into the other like a clawing and spitting cat into a croker sack. . . . The cold intellect which can write with calm and complete detachment and gusto of its contemporary scene is not among us; I do not believe there lives the Southern writer who can say without lying that writing is any fun to him. Perhaps we do not want it to be." To see himself in the life around him, and the life around him within himself, was not an easy vocation. There was so much temptation, as he noted, to retreat from it through a savage indictment of everything, or else to escape into what he called "a make believe region of swords and magnolias and mockingbirds."[31] So much of the South's literature had consisted of just such sentimental escape; and such new naturalism as had penetrated the South—T. S. Stribling, perhaps—seemed only another phase of it. Each course was evasive; each was rooted in the desire to perceive less or other than what was there. But if one wanted to tell the truth in language, one would have to face up to it.

This is a vocation worthy of a Falkner of Mississippi. The South was changing. Everywhere around him he saw force and passion, sound and fury. Yet only the externalities were different. How to identify in the shapes and forms now before him the human meanings and values that were visible in the past because of their familiar contours, but which needed to be made recognizable in their new manifestations, if the life of his own day were to be something more than mere action without purpose, motion without direction, passion without fulfillment?

Why, by telling a story, by writing about it. Art, he told the young people of Japan many years later, "is the strongest and most durable force man has invented or discovered with which to record the history of his invincible durability and courage beneath disaster, and to postulate the validity of his hope."[32] Faulkner moved, once he found his medium, from strength to strength, and with the discov-

ery in the late 1920s of his real subject matter, he was launched
upon a career that he must have known could be set next to that of
the Old Colonel his great-grandfather's and not suffer in the comparison.

William Clark Falkner had been a man of action who was also, to
the extent that he was novelist and poet, a man of sensibility. His
grandson, "Count No-Count," would write novels, beginning with
Flags in the Dust, in which those two modes would be contrasted,
compared, and played off against each other in a kind of moral dia-
lectic. His greatest books would each one of them embody something of that tension: he would explore the urge toward definition
and the resistance to being defined in all manner of guises, of which
Quentin Compson's *I dont hate it! I dont hate it!* is but one. And
for as long as this division seemed important to him, his art would
flourish. It is only when it ceases to seem a contradiction—when
the garrulous, poeticizing Heidelberg-trained attorney who is also
the respected county attorney and solver of mysteries moves onto
centerstage—that his art falters, and he attempts, just as he said
about Sherwood Anderson, to let style alone carry the burden. But
by that time he had said most of what he had to say.

Scarlett O'Hara and the Two Quentin Compsons

In the year 1936, which happened to be the seventy-fifth anniversary of the outbreak of the American Civil War, there were two works of fiction published which dealt importantly with that war, and which are still very actively in print today. One of these novels is by all odds the best-selling popular historical novel ever published in America; the sales of *Gone with the Wind* have run into the tens of millions. The other, though it has never achieved the general popularity of Margaret Mitchell's novel, is the book which many consider the finest historical novel ever written by an American, and one of the great works of modern literature, William Faulkner's *Absalom, Absalom!*

My guess would be that for every person who has read *Absalom, Absalom!*, fifty have read *Gone with the Wind*. I have run into people who go through Miss Mitchell's novel almost annually—all 917 printed pages of it—and who could no more accept the suggestion that it has faults or blemishes than that the Holy Scriptures err. Such devoted readers grow angry at any criticism of their favorite novel: it is the work of nit-pickers, or even worse, of college professors.

Quantity, of course, is no reputable index either of a book's literary merit or of its capacity for lasting beyond its immediate occasion; otherwise the year of 1850, for example, would be literarily memorable not for the publication of Hawthorne's *The Scarlet Let-*

ter but of Ik Marvel's *Reveries of a Bachelor, a Book of the Heart,* which outsold it many times over, while it would be Maria Cummins' *The Lamp-Lighter,* now remembered only as the subject of a wicked stylistic parody by James Joyce, and not Thoreau's *Walden,* which would cause us to look back with interest at the publishing season of 1854. All the same, I do not believe that *Gone with the Wind* was or is no more than a mere popular amusement; it has endured for four decades, and for all its literary clumsiness it is an important work of the imagination, with genuine insight into its time.

Of the literary excellence of Faulkner's *Absalom, Absalom!* there now seems little question. Yet at the time of its first publication it was only modestly noticed and even more modestly read; by the 1940s, it was out of print, and remained so until "discovery" of Faulkner by the academic literary community in the 1950s. The response of two of the more influential middlebrow critics to the publication of the two novels in 1936 is illustrative. A well-paid lightweight such as the late J. Donald Adams could declare of Miss Mitchell's novel in the New York *Times* that "in narrative power, in sheer readability," it was "surpassed by nothing in American fiction."[1] Meanwhile in the *New Yorker* the somewhat more sophisticated but certainly no more intelligent Clifton P. Fadiman could unleash a tirade against *Absalom, Absalom!* Missing the chief structural point of the story, the search for the meaning of the past, Fadiman could assert sarcastically that Faulkner "gets quite an interesting effect, for example, by tearing the Sutpen chronicle into pieces, as if a mad child were to go to work on it with a pair of shears, and then having each of the jagged divisions narrated by a different personage." He concludes with the following ringing insight into twentieth-century American literature: "Seriously, I do not know what to say of this book except that it seems to point to the final blowup of what was once a remarkable, if minor talent."[2]

Absalom, Absalom! sold very poorly. William Faulkner found, shortly after it was published, that he would have to go back out to Hollywood, which he hated, to work as a screen writer in order to pay his bills and buy a little time for writing fiction. It was not until the 1950s, when he had won the Nobel Prize and his books were being reissued in the hundreds of thousands, that he was able to support himself on his literary income and so could abandon his stints in Hollywood and concentrate on the one thing he wanted to do in his life: write good fiction. By contrast, Margaret Mitchell made vast sums for *Gone with the Wind*; the screen rights alone brought her fifty thousand dollars. One of the provisions in her contract with David O. Selznick was that under no circumstances would she be expected to go out to Hollywood or have anything to do with the conversion of the novel into film. The public prominence into which the novel and then the movie forced her was such that she declared emphatically that she was through with writing fiction forever, and glad of it. In later years she appears to have changed her mind, but not to the extent of ever actually beginning another novel. When she died on August 16, 1949, after being struck by an automobile, she was a one-book novelist: a single book that has been translated into twenty-five languages and sold in the tens of millions.

If Margaret Mitchell ever read William Faulkner, I do not know of it; if nothing else she must have encountered his stories in the *Saturday Evening Post*. Faulkner would seem to have left no comments on *Gone with the Wind*. At the time of its publication he said he hadn't read either it or *Anthony Adverse* because of their inordinate length: "No story takes 1000 pages to tell," he said. Faulkner was not a notably jealous man, but it must have galled him to realize that a book such as *Absalom, Absalom!*, which he told a friend was "the best novel yet written by an American," should have so poor a sale, while another southern novel with roughly the same southern subject matter was so extravagant a best seller.[3] Faulkner didn't write merely for money, but at the time he needed money very badly indeed.

No matter; the two novels have had different audiences, will doubtless continue to do so. Faulkner's fiction is "highbrow" fiction, written in the tradition of Dreiser, Hawthorne, Melville, James; Miss Mitchell's novel is and was intended to be "middlebrow" literature, of a piece with *Anthony Adverse, To Have and To Hold, Ben Hur, The Last Days of Pompeii*, and so on. So we have treated them, and with some justification. As well compare the painting of Pablo Picasso with that of Norman Rockwell, or the mind of the late Sigmund Freud with that of Dr. Joyce Brothers, Ph.D., or the theology of Karl Barth with that of the Reverend Billy Graham.

Yet is it so simple as that? I think not. My hunch is rather that these two novels, published in the same year by two southern novelists, and dealing with the same period of southern history, not only make an interesting comparison, but that each emerges from such a comparison with considerable honor. Moreover, there are certain startling similarities in *Absalom, Absalom!* and *Gone with the Wind*, and we might well consider what they signify about the time and place from which both novels sprang—the Deep South of the Depression 1930s, with the Confederate veterans almost all dead by then, and the onetime agricultural region a full working partner in an industrializing, urbanizing American society, though still with enough significant differences to keep it politically the Solid South.

Consider, first of all, the personality of the central protagonist of each novel, and that protagonist's relationship to the community. Thomas Sutpen is a strong, ruthless, single-minded man, intent upon setting up his dynasty, and with neither an interest in or even an awareness of the feelings of those with whom he comes into contact in his relentless drive for his goal. Scarlett O'Hara is similarly quite contemptuous and heedless of the manners, mores, and feelings of her fellow Atlantans in her quest for success. She horrifies her friends and enrages her foes as she flouts the conventions of well-bred Atlanta society both during and after the war; nothing— her family, her honor, her sex, her several husbands' needs or wishes—is allowed to stand in her way. Both Sutpen and Scarlett are hard-headed, tough-minded self-seekers, who refuse to allow the niceties of social custom to retard their consuming ambition. Neither of them is remotely concerned with public opinion; both view the human beings they encounter merely as commodities to be expended in pursuit of their objectives.

When the Civil War comes to Georgia, Scarlett O'Hara resents it because it will interfere with her social life; and when as a young war widow she is expected to remain in mourning she uses southern patriotism, about which she has no feelings at all, as an excuse to permit her to go out in public, dance with Rhett Butler, and resume her prematurely blighted social career. Thomas Sutpen rides off to war as a Confederate officer, but there is never any doubt about why he is in the army: he wishes to protect his investment. When after the war he is urged by his neighbors to join in night-riding activities he tells them he is too busy; the proper course of action for the South, he says, is to get back to work and restore its fortune—admirable advice in this instance, but given not from a feeling for the welfare of the South but because he doesn't wish to be diverted from his sole and consuming private goal. Sutpen has no wish to get involved in overthrowing the Yankee-enforced Reconstruction government; any government that will keep things sufficiently orderly so that he can concentrate upon his design is presumably acceptable to him. Similarly, Scarlett O'Hara doesn't care for the Klan because it means disorder, and for all her troubles with Yankee bummers and Scalawag politicians while she was trying to save Tara, she is quite willing to socialize with the recent enemy after the war if it will promote her lumber business.

Both Thomas Sutpen and Scarlett O'Hara, in short, live and function within a complex and sharply drawn community, yet they are not members of that community in any true sense. They are almost completely passionless concerning the things about which the community feels most strongly, and for identical reasons: they have their own private goals, and will expend no passion or emotion on anything that does not advance those goals. Though nominally citizens they are outsiders, and moreover, their single-mindedness and their ruthless acquisitiveness embody just those elements which will eventually destroy the societies in which they live and flourish.

Of the last comment, more later; for now I should like to note certain interesting similarities in the class stratification in the two novels. Here, because of chronology, it is appropriate to shift the comparison with Thomas Sutpen from Scarlett O'Hara to her father Gerald, who is roughly Sutpen's age. Sutpen, of course, is a parvenu, a man of no breeding, who as a poor white youth in Tidewater Virginia aspires to the status of a planter-aristocrat and will not rest until he can secure the big house with the formal gardens and the family that will give him his dynasty. Though the northern Mississippi country he seeks out in order to secure his land and begin his dynasty has itself been settled by whites only for a very few years, there are already men upon the land who have made themselves into something of a local squirearchy: the Compsons, Benbows, Sartorises, De Spains. Members of these families, if they did not trace their lineage back to the grandees of plantation Virginia, could even so say as Rosa Coldfield did, that "our father knew who his father was in Tennessee and who his grandfather had been in Virginia and our neighbors and the people we lived among knew that we knew and we knew they knew we knew."[4]

When Sutpen gets his ten miles of bottom land and brings in the slaves and builds his mansion—the source of his wealth being highly suspect—he then seeks respectability, and goes to town in search of a wife who can provide him with that status as well as be the mother to a son and heir. His choice of Ellen Coldfield, as we are told, is deliberate and unerring, and though it shocks the town to learn that this daughter of a Methodist elder has accepted him, the eventual result is that together with Sutpen's land and money, her presence as mistress of Sutpen's Hundred is sufficient to give Sutpen the status he requires. There is, in any event, no question of the right of his son Henry to be considered—to use the words of the letter that Quentin Compson and Shreve McCannon imagine the New Orleans lawyer as addressing to Henry Sutpen, Esquire, at the University of Mississippi—a "young gentleman whose position needs neither detailing nor recapitulation in the place where this letter is read."[5]

In very much the same situation, the Irish immigrant Gerald O'Hara "with a ruthless singleness of purpose . . . desired his own house, his own plantation, his own horses, his own slaves." Upon discovering that the tidewater region of Georgia "was too firmly held by an entrenched aristocracy for him ever to hope to win the place he intended to have," he seeks out the new lands of northern Georgia. He wins a plantation in a carefully arranged poker game, buys his slaves, and builds his mansion. Next he too recognizes the need for a wife, who "must be a lady and lady of blood," and so goes back to Savannah and wins the hand of his Ellen—a Robillard, of an old French family.[6] Their children, growing up among Wilkeses, Calverts, Tarletons, and Fontaines, are indisputably of the resident gentry; they belong to what the slaves are made to refer to as "the Quality," and they look down upon the Poor White Trash.

Now of course there are important differences between Thomas Sutpen and Gerald O'Hara, and so far as qualities of human warmth go, these are all to the advantage of O'Hara. However intense his ambition, he is affable and generous, kind to his slaves, and despite his roughness of manner and style is generally accepted and liked by his neighbors. There is nothing in Gerald O'Hara's makeup comparable to the passion for abstract perfection of design, devoid of human considerations, with which Thomas Sutpen pursues his dream. When O'Hara goes in search of a bride it is for a wife he can love and cherish, not merely a breeder of children who will perfect a design; human love, not dynastic perpetuation, is what produces his children and characterizes his conduct as their father.

We can see the difference in the houses the two men build; the mansion at Sutpen's Hundred, designed by an imported French architect, rises in the Mississippi wilderness as an empty symbol of planter magnificence, a palace, for which the necessary dynastic occupants must then be secured. By contrast Gerald O'Hara's Tara is an ample, rather plain affair of no particular style, added to as the family's needs require. Thomas Sutpen lives *in*, but is not *of*, the community of Yoknapatawpha. Gerald O'Hara, the Irish-born immigrant, becomes a member of the north Georgia community, and shares its loyalties, hatreds, loves, and sorrows. Not Gerald O'Hara but his daughter Scarlett stands aloof from the human beings around her.

Thomas Sutpen's dynastic ambitions fail when his unacknowledged son by his first wife, Charles Bon, is shot to death by Henry Sutpen, his son by his second wife, in order to prevent Charles, who is presumably part black, from marrying his half-sister Judith Sutpen. Despite Henry's admiration and love for Charles Bon, he proves obedient to the community's racial mores; we recall that when Henry urges Charles not to go through with the marriage plan because he is Judith's and his own brother, Charles replies, "No I'm not. I'm the nigger that's going to sleep with your sister."[7] The issue is stated succinctly: Faulkner deliberately has a Confederate soldier use an anachronistic expression, characteristic of the South of Faulkner's own day. In shooting his brother, Henry does his father's bidding, but not in any attempt to further Thomas Sutpen's abstract design of perfection; rather he acts out of the racial prejudices of his community, which decree that racial "purity" comes before all else.

There is little or no evidence that his father shares any such personal racial prejudice. Thomas Sutpen twice destroys his plans for dynastic continuity when he learns that its absolute perfection of design would be tarnished by the likely presence of black blood. Yet when the dynasty is not involved, he displays no racial prejudice whatever, raising his daughter by a slave right there in the house with his family, and even engaging in public fist fights with his slaves. His insistence upon an immaculate racial heritage for his children is abstract: because in the *society* (not the *community* as such) in which his design is to be executed, black ancestry is held to be a flaw, he cannot tolerate it. By contrast his son Henry shares the community ethos, kills the man he admires most in the world because finally, as Charles himself tells him, "it's the miscegenation, not the incest, which you cant bear."[8] The crime is the same; the motives for it are importantly different.

In *Gone with the Wind* Scarlett O'Hara is no dissenter from community standards on racial matters, nor for that matter is Margaret Mitchell; but otherwise it is she, and not her father, who pursues a design for success without reference to its relationship to the community. The ostensible reason for Scarlett O'Hara's single-minded quest for financial fortune is the destitution she experienced at Tara during the final months of the war; she is determined to save Tara at any cost, and has recurring nightmares of being hungry and cold and of fleeing from some nameless terror. This explanation has always seemed rather unconvincing to me. Well before the wartime ordeal at the devastated plantation home, she has demonstrated that she is deeply out of sympathy with the social and familial status quo, abidingly unhappy with her lot, contemptuous of the patriotic feelings of the community, and unwilling to acquiesce in the traditional standards set for the southern lady of her station and her time.

Supposedly this is because she is in love with a man she cannot have. But what is Ashley Wilkes's appeal for her? It is not Ashley's actual personality; when finally she realizes what he is really like, she does not want him. He seems to be a kind of symbol of well-born grace, culture, sophistication, aristocratic bearing: the perfect southern gentleman. " 'He never really existed at all, except in my imagination,' " she realizes at the end. " 'I loved something I made up, something that's just as dead as Melly is. I made a pretty suit of clothes and fell in love with it. And when Ashley came riding along, so handsome, so different, I put that suit on him and made him wear it whether it fitted him or not. And I wouldn't see what he really was. I kept on loving the pretty clothes—and not him at all.' "[9] She realizes then that she had wanted him only because she could not have him, and that if ever she had gotten him she would no longer have desired him. Ashley Wilkes, as he existed for her in the long years before Melanie's death, was thus in his own way an abstraction, an ideal design as unanchored in real life as Sutpen's dream of dynasty.

Why such an abstraction? Because, I would think, Ashley Wilkes symbolizes the dream of the Old South: the ideal of plantation perfection. Even the home he will someday inherit, Twelve Oaks, partakes of the ideal for Scarlett: "They topped the rise and the white house reared its perfect symmetry before her, tall of columns, wide of verandas, flat of roof, beautiful as a woman is beautiful who is so sure of her charm that she can be generous and gracious to all. Scarlett loved Twelve Oaks even more than Tara, for it had a stately beauty, a mellowed dignity that Gerald's house did not possess." And after Sherman had come through, it is precisely the sight of the gutted and ruined Twelve Oaks that directly triggers the vow she makes that " 'As God is my witness, as God is my witness, the Yankees aren't going to lick me. I'm going to live through this, and when it's over, I'm never going to be hungry again. No, nor any of my folks. If I have to steal or kill—as God is my witness, I'm never going to be hungry again.' "[10]

The loss of the war, the destruction of the plantation way of life, the coming of the Yankees, the carpetbaggers, and the Reconstruction supposedly represent deprivation, the loss of the beauty and comfort that might have been, the end of a golden age; and Scarlett O'Hara's subsequent career as businesswoman and entrepreneur in postwar Atlanta is depicted as the response of one who, determined not to be borne down to destruction by living in the past, squares her shoulders and makes the most of a new and more elemental world. As she says of the women of postwar Atlanta, " 'The silly fools don't seem to realize that you can't be a lady without money!' "[11] For Ashley Wilkes it may be the Götterdämmerung; Scarlett will live in the present.

The novel, Miss Mitchell once said, is about the theme of survival; because Scarlett has Gerald O'Hara's toughness within her bones, she will not be defeated by the cruel circumstance in which she finds herself, but will make the best of it. Isn't the truth rather that the debacle of the war and the breakdown of the old plantation society serve to liberate Scarlett? They enable her to do what she could never have thought of doing in the antebellum plantation society: live a life of her own, own property, go into business, make money. The notion that what Scarlett does after the fall of the South is merely a matter of making the best of a disadvantaged situation is neither psychologically nor historically convincing. She does not *wish* to be a Lady. If we think of the Scarlett of Tara and compare her with the Scarlett who is married first to Frank Kennedy and then Rhett Butler, and is making money and thriving in Reconstruction Atlanta, we can only recognize how far more satisfactory she finds the postwar South than the old. She even says as much to Ashley Wilkes: " 'I like these days better.' "[12] Supposedly she doesn't really mean that, but given the energy, the determination, and the desire for material advancement that characterize her every action, it is difficult to see why not, or to imagine what charms the antebellum life would ever have held for her that could come close to equaling the active entrepreneurial existence she leads in postwar Atlanta. It is not without significance, I believe, that one of the more memorable scenes in the opening chapters of the novel, as Scarlett prepares to attend the festivities at Twelve Oaks, is that in which she is laced up into a whalebone girdle; her body as well as spirit rebels against the constricting role of the plantation belle.

Margaret Mitchell went to considerable length to identify Scarlett O'Hara with the city of Atlanta. For Atlanta, too, the coming of the war meant opportunity rather than misfortune. As the chief rail junction connecting the east with Tennessee and the gulf states, the city swiftly expanded in size and population, developed manufactures, and attained a boom-time prosperity until its defenses fell and Sherman's army burnt and pillaged it. The setback was only temporary; Atlanta rose from its ashes like a fully certified phoenix, and was very soon the commercial and manufacturing capital of the New South. The antebellum political domination of agricultural interests was broken by the war, and Atlanta most of all the cities of the New South took advantage of it. It was unhampered by the conventions and attitudes of the old tradition; it could make money and grow in size and strength without any of the aristocratic disdain for trade that had been part of the antebellum social stance. Atlanta had what it took to survive and flourish in postbellum America; it had less to forget, it was open to the methods and ethics of industrial society, it recognized that—to echo Scarlett—to be a lady or a gentleman takes money, and it put what it considered first things, which is to say financial things, first.

The implications of Scarlett O'Hara and her career for the community in which she is reared and thrives are, I think, quite far-reaching. But before we explore them, I should like to turn again to *Absalom, Absalom!* and Thomas Sutpen. Faulkner's protagonist, as we know, runs roughshod over the customs and attitudes of antebellum Mississippi. Indeed, Miss Rosa Coldfield's outrage is well known. As Quentin Compson thinks while listening to the old woman telling him about Sutpen's career, *"It's because she wants it told . . . so that people whom she will never see and whose names she will never hear and who have never heard her name nor seen her face will read it and know at last why God let us lose the War: that only through the blood of our men and the tears of our women could He slay this demon and efface his name and lineage from the earth."* Miss Rosa is, of course, to say the least rather biased. But Quentin Compson's father is considerably less personally involved with Sutpen's personality, and he remarks almost the same thing, if with less demoniac imagery. Speaking of Miss Rosa Coldfield's father and his withdrawal from all contact with the life of the community of Jefferson when the war broke out, he advanced, as Quentin tells Shreve, this interpretation of Coldfield's action: "He knew that he would either be killed or die of hardship, and so he would not be present on that day when the South would realize that it was now paying the price for having erected its economic edifice not on the rock of stern morality but on the shifting sands of opportunism and moral brigandage."[13] Now that is what Quentin says that his father said about Goodhue Coldfield's view, not what William Faulkner necessarily thought: but surely the comment describes, in quite accurate moral fashion, the social implications of Thomas Sutpen's career. There seems little doubt that this is one of the meanings (not the only one) of Thomas Sutpen's story, and it is no accident that the language that Quentin is made to use is that of the teller of the tale, the central rhetorical and moral consciousness wherein the events of Faulkner's novel and the interpretation of those events are presented.

But Thomas Sutpen is not a "typical," or even a "representative" antebellum southern figure. There is little doubt of that. The abstract nature of his design, the contempt for the community he inhabits, the utter ignorance and lack of feeling for tradition, his very pragmatic attitude toward race (*he* doesn't share in the prejudice, but because the society is prejudiced he must shape his design so as to keep his dynasty pure white)—surely none of these attributes is characteristic of the Old South. Whatever else may be said of the antebellum planter, lack of community passion was not one of his shortcomings! Sutpen, as Cleanth Brooks insists, scarcely makes a uniquely southern figure: "Thorstein Veblen would have understood Sutpen's relation to traditional culture. Sutpen is on all fours with the robber baron of the Gilded Age building a fake Renaissance palace on the banks of the Hudson."[14]

Brooks is led to emphasize Sutpen's relation to American, and not peculiarly to southern, society, in response to various glib assertions by critics that Sutpen's rise and fall is somehow an allegory of the rise and fall of the Old South, with the easy equation of Sutpen's rejection of Charles Bon with the South's employment of Negro slavery. The point is well taken, and I share Brooks's impatience with that kind of superficial generalization. But there is more to the problem than the question of Sutpen's "typicality," I think. One cannot separate *Absalom, Absalom!* from its relation to southern history simply because its protagonist is not "typically" or "representatively" southern. The issue is rather that in the antebellum South a Thomas Sutpen *was* possible, and it is this that so appalls Quentin Compson. Brooks's point, that Sutpen's career has its counterparts in the robber barons of the Gilded Age, only demonstrates its universality. In any society, one might say, there are such men (and women, if we are to believe Miss Mitchell) who can bend it to their personal desire, exploit its institutions, seize upon its openings, capitalize upon its weaknesses for their own purposes. Given the antebellum South as it was, with its attitudes toward land, its structure of caste, its reliance upon human slavery, this is what the ruthless ambition of a Sutpen could do, and the cost in human degradation that such an ambition could exact. Such is Faulkner's story, or part of his story.

Indeed, there is a rather striking parallel to Sutpen's particular career, I think, in the history of the Mississippi from which William Faulkner's imagination sprung. For as historians know very well, antebellum Mississippi settlement and development was not a matter of the slow evolution, over several centuries, of an ordered plantation society. It happened almost at once. When the Indian lands were opened up in the 1810s, 1820s, and 1830s, men came pouring in from the older South to seize the chance to raise cotton and grow rich. There are numerous instances of planters from Virginia and South Carolina transporting their entire establishments from the exhausted soil of the east to the new land, and setting up not merely farms and homes but ornate mansions in the cleared wilderness. More often the newcomers were not established planters seeking greater advantage, but men on the make, middle-class farmers and others who coveted, in the new land to the west, the opportunities denied them in the more settled seaboard South, and emigrated to the Mississippi country with the definite purpose of acquiring land, buying slaves, raising cotton, and becoming gentlemen-planters. The older aristocracy of the east called them "cotton snobs," the planter equivalent for newly rich opportunists in search of social status. Surely there was an important element of preconceived design, of abstraction, in the way in which the old Southwest was transformed almost overnight from wilderness to a society of white-columned mansions, plantation lords and ladies, broad acres of cotton worked by hundreds of slaves. And just as surely it was the ownership and exploitation of human beings as property which made such a life possible, and ultimately brought it down to defeat and ruin when the war came. And if so, is not Thomas Sutpen, in what he was and what he exemplified, only an intensified delineation of the potentialities within the society itself?

Were there any Thomas Sutpens in Margaret Mitchell's antebellum Georgia? To ask the question is to answer it; there are always Thomas Sutpens, and always will be, for there is something of the self-serving user of other persons in all of us, which is what gives *Absalom, Absalom!* the profound historical insight that it displays. We have seen how within the much more benevolently limned characterization of Gerald O'Hara there are elements of Sutpen's single-mindedness, his desire for status and dynasty, just as in Gerald's daughter Scarlett there are ruthless ambition, opportunism, contempt for tradition, barely masked aggressiveness.

The difference between Thomas Sutpen's antebellum Mississippi and Gerald O'Hara's antebellum Georgia lies in the willingness of William Faulkner to recognize the moral implications that Thomas Sutpen's career held for his society. By contrast, the depiction of plantation Georgia in *Gone with the Wind* is romantic, uncritical, eulogistic. Slavery is a benevolent institution, only poor whites and Yankee overseers are ever immoral or ambitious, life is beautiful, Eden is retold. There is no evil in Margaret Mitchell's antebellum southern garden; it comes from outside with Sherman's army. In Floyd Watkins' apt description, "There is no mention of sweat, of exhaustion, of the arduousness of field work. *Gone with the Wind* is a world without sweat, except for that caused by the Yankees."[15] The only hint that the antebellum society might contain within itself the possibility of self-destruction lies in its naïveté, as seen in its facile assumption that any southern boy will be able to whip ten Yankees, that southern independence can be secured merely by a declaration to that effect, and so on. From the standpoint of recorded history, Margaret Mitchell's depiction of prewar plantation society is romanticized and false. Miss Mitchell liked to think of herself as an historical realist, but when it came to antebellum life she was as whole-souled a perpetuator of the plantation myth as Thomas Nelson Page or Stark Young at their most eulogistic.

But with wartime and postwar Georgia it is another matter. Any reputable historian can attest to the one-sidedness of Margaret Mitchell's depiction of the Reconstruction in Georgia; she accepts uncritically all the folklore of the Reconstruction, depicts the Ku Klux Klan as a noble institution of the best people chiefly concerned with discouraging black sexual assault upon white women, portrays the Reconstruction government as being made up exclusively of scheming carpetbaggers and deluded blacks, magnifies the political disqualification of white Georgians, fails to recognize the extent to which ex-Confederates and other southerners of good family and social status took part in Reconstruction politics and finances and yet managed to retain and even enhance their positions when the Reconstruction government was ousted. As one Georgia editor admitted soon after the Reconstruction ended, "It is a mortifying fact that the extravagance of Bullock's administration—we say nothing as to the corruption—benefitted about as many Democrats as Republicans."[16] Anyone familiar with the postwar career of Governor Joseph C. Brown, the commercial and financial alliances developed among such leading Georgians as John B. Gordon and Alfred Colquitt, the way in which "carpetbaggers" such as H. I. Kimball and even Governor Rufus Bullock himself were received into the best society of post-1876 Atlanta, will recognize the element of falseness in Margaret Mitchell's supposedly realistic depiction of post-1865 Atlanta.

Yet despite the one-sidedness and the mythology of Miss Mitchell's elaborate documentation, in an ultimate sense her presentation is both remarkably accurate and deeply moving, for the simple reason that Scarlett O'Hara is what matters, and in the vicissitudes and triumphs of her career as entrepreneur and opportunist, we have a notable glimpse into the times. The most profound statement in *Gone with the Wind*, I think, is the one which I have several times quoted. Let me place it in context. Scarlett O'Hara, back in Atlanta after the desperate days at Tara at the close of the war, attends a dance. The ladies and gentlemen of Atlanta society, resuming the social regimen amid diminished circumstance, seem to Scarlett to be different from her. "'Everything in their old world had changed but the old forms,'" she thinks. "'The old usages went on, must go on, for the forms were all that were left to them. . . . No matter what sights they had seen, what menial tasks they had done and would have to do, they remained ladies and gentlemen, royalty in exile—bitter, aloof, incurious, kind to one another, diamond hard, as bright and brittle as the crystals of the broken chandelier over their heads.'" Scarlett realizes the difference, as she sees it, between them and herself. She cannot bravely ignore loss and misfortune, cannot wear a mask to disguise her feelings, "survey the wreck of the world with an air of casual unconcern." Not until she has once again acquired the comfort, the wealth, the material possessions of the prewar days will she rest easy: "She knew that she would never feel like a lady again until her table was weighted with silver and crystal and smoking with rich food, until her own horses and carriages stood in her stables, until black hands and not white took the cotton from Tara." And then, "'Ah!' she thought angrily, sucking in her breath. 'That's the difference! Even though they're poor, they still feel like ladies and I don't. The silly fools don't seem to realize that you can't be a lady without money!'"[17] Whereupon she goes in pursuit of Frank Kennedy, her sister's suitor, and secures him and his money for her own. Her career as sawmill operator, lumber salesman, investor, and entrepreneur follows.

The attitude may be materialistic, but historically it is also remarkably accurate, and in it lie the psychological strength and the historical insight of *Gone with the Wind*. The statement has often been made, by the author herself among others, that Scarlett O'Hara does what she does in order to survive, with the implication that had it not been for the need to sweat and scheme in order to survive, she would have been better off, happier, more contented. I have earlier suggested that rather the reverse is more like the truth: she was deeply dissatisfied under the old regimen, and the effect of the war and the destruction of the plantation system was to liberate her from the constriction of her traditional role as southern lady. And I have noted that in linking Scarlett with the spirit of postwar Atlanta, Miss Mitchell was quite accurate.

What Scarlett O'Hara does in postwar Atlanta—marrying for

money, becoming a hard-nosed businesswoman, collaborating with the carpetbag-scalawag government, employing convict labor to work her mill, marrying the wealthy Rhett Butler when Frank Kennedy dies and building an ostentatious Victorian mansion, and so on—is, though perhaps exaggerated at times, no more and no less than what the South as a whole did in the late nineteenth century, and is still doing in the twentieth century. It is what a middle-class, democratic, capitalistic society always does: try to make money and improve its position. Like Thomas Sutpen, Scarlett O'Hara is not peculiarly southern, but American *and therefore Southern*. She does not merely do those things; she enjoys doing them. One couldn't and can't be a lady—in Scarlett's definition—without money, because being what Scarlett means by a lady depends upon leisure, which is possible only when there is someone else to do the physical labor. When Scarlett refers to being a lady, she is not talking about morality, codes of honor and virtue, grace and courtesy and the like; she is talking about social status. And not merely Scarlett but Margaret Mitchell is aware of the inescapable relationship between leisure and money, between position and power—between, in short, worldly success and worldly ambition. And however the reader of *Gone with the Wind*, like the author, may be appalled at times by the price that must be paid to achieve success, there is no doubt that in a post-Edenic world such a price is always going to be paid, regretfully perhaps but willingly. Scarlett O'Hara has no choice, really, just as historically Atlanta and the South had no choice after Appomattox but to seek fulfillment on the terms offered it, which were those of postwar industrial America.

But there is always a bit of remorse that goes along with such a transaction: Americans (like other people) do what they must to make a good living and to achieve success, are pragmatic and reasonably efficient, yet at the same time tend to feel somewhat guilty over their efficiency and practicality, and look with a certain amount of wistful regret at the vanished grace and leisure of earlier and simpler days. This has historically been one of the charms of the plantation image in our literature: the idea of an ordered, leisured, settled life, free of striving and the pursuit of the almighty dollar, with time for relaxation and enjoyment of one's days. It has been a staple of southern literature at least since Kennedy's *Swallow Barn*. Thomas Nelson Page rang the changes on it; consider the opening paragraphs of "Marse Chan," in which a postwar gentleman rides along a Tidewater Virginia road, notices the run-down and decaying mansions of the old regime set back half-hidden from the road, and remarks as follows: "Distance was nothing to this people: time was of no consequence to them. They desired but a level path in life, and that they had, though the way was longer, and the outer world strode by them as they dreamed."[18]

But it *is* the past, it *is* a dream, not reality: and Margaret Mitchell shows her Scarlett O'Hara as preferring the present, doing what she must do because she believes in real life and not in playing a role in a game of charades. Historically she represents the spirit of enterprise, of ambition, of practical achievement; she is what the South felt that it *had to be* after 1865, and what Atlanta in particular wanted to be and did so well. But she is not happy. She does not recognize who it is that she loves, and when finally she does, it is too late, for she has driven him away: "Captain Butler—be kind to him. He loves you so."[19] Only he doesn't any more. So it is right; if the moral of the story is to come out right, the price must be paid, and yet is very sad. This is melodrama, but melodrama of a very high sort, for psychologically it is authentic, and historically quite accurate, ten thousand postwar eulogies to the Days Befo' De Wah and invocations of the Purity of Southern Womanhood to the contrary notwithstanding.

The difference between *Gone with the Wind* and *Absalom, Absalom!* is that William Faulkner realized, both in dismay and fascination, what Margaret Mitchell could face only partially and intermittently: that it is not history that makes human beings, but that human beings *are* the history. To put it another way, it was the Fall of Man, not the fall of Atlanta, that was responsible for Scarlett O'Hara's career. Thomas Sutpen pursued his design and wreaked his destruction in the Old South, but historically he could as appropriately fit into the history of the New South: his name could as appropriately have been Duke or De Bardeleben or Candler or Cannon or Reynolds (or for that matter, Carnegie or Rockefeller). In Faulkner's Yoknapatawpha County there is no golden age; there are only men in history. Or to express the difference between the two novels still another way: there is no Quentin Compson in *Gone with the Wind*. There is no point of historical consciousness from which to view the past *as the living past*, and in so doing to recognize that the men and women who lived in it functioned within a moral circumstance no less complex or difficult than our own, facing not history but life, wearing not costumes but clothes, achieving success or failure in as ambiguous and compromised a form as must we.

Consider, for example, the problem of race and slavery. Faulkner cannot sentimentalize or sidestep its moral consequences as Margaret Mitchell does, because, growing up as and when he did, he knew that people back in the antebellum period were men and women, too, and he could not create his art without exploring the implications of that fact in a society in which slavery and race were fundamental considerations. Human complexity and the necessity for moral judgment did not begin in the year 1865.

Dealing as Margaret Mitchell also did with the single most cataclysmic moral and social event in his region's history, William Faulkner saw history as a problem of moral knowledge, not of documentary authenticity. So he created a character who could be of his own time—just ten years older than himself—and he let this character be the center of consciousness, to whom the story is told by eyewitnesses and others and by whom it is sorted out, understood and, finally, judged. He recognized that the reason why the particular history was so much a part of his own consciousness was that emotionally, morally, in shame as well as pride, it was a problem of self-knowledge, and that in order to deal with it authentically it was essential to recognize it in terms of its impact upon himself as a twentieth-century southerner and Mississippian, as well as to recite what happened. He knew that in his mind and heart, as in the consciousness of any southerner of his generation possessed of imagination and compassion as well as pride and anger, the two were inseparable.

So he invented Quentin Compson, or utilized him (since he had already conceived him when he wrote *The Sound and the Fury* a half-dozen years earlier) and not only that, but he divided him into the two Quentins: "the Quentin Compson preparing for Harvard in the South, the deep South dead since 1865 and peopled with garrulous outraged baffled ghosts, listening, having to listen, to one of the ghosts which had refused to lie still even longer than most had, telling him about old ghost-times; and the Quentin Compson who was still too young to deserve yet to be a ghost, but nevertheless having to be one for all that, since he was born and bred in the deep South the same as she [Miss Rosa Coldfield] was—the two separate Quentins now talking to one another in the long silence of notpeople, in notlanguage."[20] Only through the two Quentins could the story of Thomas Sutpen be told, for it took both the detachment and the passionate involvement, the logic as well as the emotion, the moral conscience as well as the admiration and anger. It was Faulkner's purpose as historical novelist to reveal the past of his community, but he knew that understanding what happened in the past is a matter of interpretation, and that the interpretation, being necessarily performed in the present, had to exist in a moral as well as analytical relationship to a history so compelling as that which he proposed to use for his fiction. His genius led him to see that the best way to both chronicle and judge that history was to let it be discovered and interpreted by an observer, one who would be near enough to it to be involved emotionally, yet distant enough from it to view it in moral perspective. Had he merely selected the conventional point of view, as Margaret Mitchell and most historical novelists have done, the act of his judgment would have to be done anachronistically, from above. This would have forced him to view what for his own time was the most urgent moral issue involved in that past—the racial equation—in a way so differently from those of his historical characters that he would falsify the difficulties of their situation through undue emphasis and shallow oversimplification. Either that, or he would have to ignore the dimension of slavery and race altogether, as Margaret Mitchell did, and thus falsify what to him in his time was the essential moral problem of that past epoch. By letting Quentin Compson search out and evaluate the story, as a young southerner of college age in the year 1909 (or 1910), close enough to the events to hear about it from eyewitnesses and to experience the passions that were still involved four decades afterward, yet far enough removed to be able to see through the passions and not avert his eyes from the central dimension of race, he could tell the story as he wished it told. Writing the story himself a quarter-century after Quentin's involvement in it, he could portray Quentin and Quentin's imagination, as Quentin set out to reconstruct the story. Quentin could do the emphasizing and moralizing; he could show Quentin doing it. He could make his story that of the difficulty of reconstructing the past by showing Quentin trying to do it.

When Malcolm Cowley sent Faulkner the draft of a paragraph from the introduction he was preparing for *The Portable Faulkner* in 1944, he referred to Faulkner as one who "was writing a story, and one that affected him deeply, but he was also brooding over a social situation." Faulkner was quick to correct him: "I think Quentin, not Faulkner, is the correct yardstick here. I was writing the story, but he not I was brooding over a situation."[21] Precisely. By using Quentin as narrator, Faulkner was able to concentrate as artist on the characterization, to portray Quentin's emotional involvement, without the danger of any unmediated firsthand involvement on his own part inhibiting his ability to explore that "social situation." The result was a triumph of the art of historical fiction: an intensely felt rendition of an historical experience, passionately created yet free of either evasion or falsification. At the close, he could confirm Quentin's divided loyalties—"*I dont hate it. . . . I dont hate it*"—because he had permitted that ambivalence to be used, through the device of the two Quentins, as his method of structure and exploration.

To do this, however, he too had to pay a price. By telling a story about someone telling a story, not merely before and after the main story line as a frame device, but as a structural element throughout, there had to be a loss of surface immediacy. Thus no such lengthy and exciting episode as Margaret Mitchell's description of Scarlett O'Hara during the burning of Atlanta was possible; it could not have been sustained other than through direct, firsthand experience. Nor could he rely on the melodrama that made *Gone with the Wind* so widely popular. No major character could be left importantly unexamined; no character could be presented or considered apart from the attempt to analyze and explain the character's motives. There could be no such dashing, romantic lead as Rhett Butler, for his counterpart in *Absalom, Absalom!*, Charles Bon, had to be interpreted by Quentin (and his alter ego Shreve) as the victim of the social situation in order to get at the heart of the moral problem. Is Rhett Butler's change from a sardonic, cynical profiteer and rebel against his society's insensitivity into a sentimental seeker after social respectability and conformity really very convincing? The point is that in *Absalom, Absalom!* so potentially important a question as that could not be left unexplored, because the method of structural narration would immediately focus upon it. Quentin and Shreve could no more have ignored what lay behind Rhett's attitude toward his society than they could have ignored the question of why Charles Bon was drawn toward marrying Judith Sutpen. And if Rhett Butler had been subjected to that sort of psychological and moral exploration, what would that have done to the pathos at the close of *Gone with the Wind*: "My dear, I don't give a damn"[22]

It was just this inability to hold back from trying to understand and to judge that make Faulkner into a great novelist, for it also led him into the brilliant technical exploration that would permit him to get at what he wanted. Faulkner's so-called "experimental" technique was never an end in itself; it was always a means toward understanding. Sometimes this made for difficult reading; always it meant that the reader had to get involved in the telling as well as in what was being told. That was no way to write a best seller.

I don't think that it ever occurred to Margaret Mitchell that she couldn't recreate the past, so long as she was faithful enough to her documentation. The result is that she gave us a novel with a very modern heroine in lace and crinoline, whom she felt she had to punish for her emancipated attitudes by taking her lover away. But it is very powerful, for we too are ambivalent about doing what we have to do instead of what we have been taught we should do, and historically quite authentic, for the time and setting were one in which that decision was demanded in very dramatic and drastic form. The difficulty, which makes *Gone with the Wind* flawed in so many of its parts, is that the author was only intermittently aware of the choice that was being made. William Faulkner, on the other hand, recognized the ambivalence and made it into a technique for exploration of relation of the past to the present.

Both these novels were published in the South of the 1930s, a time when, as in the 1860s though less violently, old ways, old attitudes, old standards of conduct were being tested by economic necessity and found in need of adjustment. Another generation of Americans was learning for its time that it takes money to be a lady. Both Margaret Mitchell and William Faulkner were willing to explore the past in terms of what they knew. *Gone with the Wind* found immediate popular readership. *Absalom, Absalom!* did not; we had first to learn how to read it. For Faulkner knew what Margaret Mitchell could not quite face, and to explain why required a new way of telling a story. This was, that Melanie Wilkes, the traditionalist, the lady, and Scarlett O'Hara, the opportunist, the woman, were not really two persons, but, like the two Quentins, one and the same flawed human being.

Art and Artistry In Morgana,
Mississippi

On an afternoon in June in the small town of Morgana, Mississippi, not too long after the First World War, a teen-aged girl is in her room dyeing a scarf to wear on a hayride that evening, when she hears some notes of music being played on a piano:

She looks up from what she is doing and responds at once, "Virgie Rainey, danke schoen."

The girl's name is Cassie Morrison, and the tune she hears is the opening of "Für Elise," by Ludwig van Beethoven. Virgie Rainey, like her, was formerly a pupil of a German music teacher, Miss Lotte Elizabeth Eckhart, who had lived and given piano lessons in the McLain house next door. Virgie had been Miss Eckhart's star pupil, progressing from piece to more difficult piece. By the age of thirteen she had played Liszt's "Fantasia on Beethoven's Ruins of Athens," and gone on beyond that. The "Für Elise" was Virgie's theme song, her leitmotif perhaps, which she played on all occasions, even adapting it to the children's gymnastics at school. When Miss Eckhart listened as Virgie performed, she would respond with "danke schoen"; it was an expression of thanks, from teacher to pupil, or more than that, from master to apprentice, for having properly discharged her responsibility to the music she was playing. Virgie Rainey, Miss Eckhart insisted, would be heard from in the world some day. She had a gift: "She must go away from Morgana. From them all. From her studio. In the world, she must study and practice for the rest of her life."[1]

But now, on the day when Cassie hears the notes from "Für Elise," Virgie Rainey no longer studies music. She has a job playing the piano at the local movie house, while Miss Eckhart's present whereabouts are unknown; she is rumored to be living out at the county poor farm. Her days as music teacher are done, while her star pupil, no longer apprenticed to the Beethoven, "could do things with 'You've Got to See Mama Every Night' and 'Avalon'" (52).

Virgie Rainey, the German music teacher Miss Eckhart, Cassie Morrison and her brother Loch, and others of the citizenry of Morgana, Mississippi, are characters in Eudora Welty's *The Golden Apples*. In one sense almost nothing "happens" to any of these people; they merely grow up, grow older, leave town, come back, love and are loved, die, do the ordinary things that most humans do. But in another sense, Morgana, Mississippi, is the cockpit of the world.

The brilliant surfaces of Eudora Welty's fiction are such that, as in life, the meanings are always, if not hidden, then so thoroughly imaged in the texture of the fiction that they do not readily yield themselves up to thematic paraphrase. Add to that the fact that the people she normally writes about are persons whom one might encounter in the day-to-day routines of one's experience and not think twice about, and we have an art which, unlike that of that other great Mississippi author, William Faulkner, does not customarily exhibit the ferocity and angularity of the tragic mode. Yet the implications of the ultimate human condition are very much present; and just as both a Yeats and a Joyce could emerge from the cultural milieu of Dublin, so Eudora Welty's fiction is grounded as deeply in a southern time and place, and the necessities her characters confront are as starkly universal as those of the sole owner and proprietor of Yoknapatawpha County. "October rain on Mississippi fields," Virgie Rainey thinks at the conclusion of the story entitled "The

Wanderers": "The rain of fall, maybe on the whole South, for all she knew on the everywhere. She stared into its magnitude" (244). As indeed she might, for the human tragicomedy of which she has been part, however drenched in the particularities of a locale, has involved matters having to do with basic problems of life and art.

It is with a single, rather lengthy story in *The Golden Apples*, entitled "June Recital," that I want to concern myself—together with some references to another, "The Wanderers," which concludes the volume. These two stories deal with certain relationships that embody and exemplify the nature and role of the artist within a community. Miss Welty is writing about musicians and their music, but the implications go beyond that. Chronicling as she almost always does the ways of a richly delineated social community, she tells a story about a woman who comes into the community to teach music to its young people, and what thereafter happens. Among the seven related stories that make up *The Golden Apples*, covering altogether some forty years of elapsed time in the community, these two stories, it seems to me, and "June Recital" in particular, not only participate in the general concerns of the citizenry of Morgana, whether toward life or death, but implicitly touch upon what is involved in pursuing these concerns toward revealed meanings, which of course is what artists seek to do. "June Recital" is about certain people in Morgana; it is also about what the artist must be and must know.

Enough of abstractions and generalities. Miss Lotte Elizabeth Eckhart is a teacher. In Eudora Welty's fiction teachers are usually very important people. What teachers do is to see underlying meanings, often without personally profiting by it; they are present within the community in order to instruct its members in what is going on in the world. Their intellectual and emotional horizons do not end at the town limits; what they know is, as one of them puts it, that in human life in time "there was more than the ear could bear to hear or the eye to see" (50). The knowledge that they bring is not comforting; it is not even knowledge that can be acted upon; its virtue is that it can enable its possessors to understand who they really are. Possessed of that knowledge, citizens of Morgana, Mississippi, or anywhere else cannot perhaps do a great deal about their own destinies, but deprived of it they are at the emotional mercy of every vagrant manifestation of time and change. The difference between knowledge and ignorance is the difference between the human and the animal, thought and instinct, between self-realization and passive suffering. It is the difference, too, as a French novelist whose art is given echo in *The Golden Apples* might phrase it, between talent and vocation.

In the first book of Marcel Proust's *Remembrance of Things Past*, Charles Swann is very much taken with a motif from a sonata by a composer named Vinteuil. But instead of exploring its meanings, he identified it with his desire for a woman, and the little phrase from Vinteuil comes to symbolize for him his failure to do the artistic work he might have done, so that he lives and dies a dilettante. Later in Proust's novel the narrator, who has inherited Charles Swann's interest in the little phrase, hears it at a reception given by the Prince de Guermantes, and resolves to follow it through, to seek out its meaning for him in time—and the result is the novel in which it figures. For with its help the narrator now realized that his interest in society, his concern with people, which others had thought only snobbery and dilettantism, were indeed a vocation to create his art.

The notes from "Für Elise" which Cassie Morrison hears are described by Eudora Welty with just the term that Proust used: "the little phrase." When Marcel hears his little phrase in the last volume of *Remembrance of Things Past*, it goes along with certain other sensory impressions that jar his memory: an uneven pavement stone, the sound of silverware striking a plate. Similarly, when Cassie Morrison's brother Loch, who has been watching the house next door, hears the little phrase, he too thinks of his earlier years, and then—is it merely coincidence?—"a spoon went against a dish, three times."

If in *Remembrance of Things Past* what the narrator Marcel discovers at the close will enable him to write the book that we have been reading, no such consequence results from what happens in *The Golden Apples*. There are, for that matter, no successful artists in Morgana, Mississippi. There are only piano teachers—old Miss Eckhart—and pupils—Virgie Rainey and Cassie Morrison, the latter of whom eventually becomes a teacher. It would be difficult to imagine Eudora Welty writing about a practicing artist from the inside, for unlike Proust's, her art is not one of self-conscious autobiographical revelation. The distance between Paris and Morgana, Mississippi, is not merely one of an ocean and a thousand miles of land; it is one of a small town of seemingly "ordinary" people and a continental metropolis in which artistic and intellectual activity can enjoy a rich and accepted social existence out in public view.

All the same, *The Golden Apples* is about art and artists—not in the sense of persons actively creating works of art, or performing as concert artists do, but in its depiction of what certain characters come to learn. In an essay on time in fiction, Miss Welty says of Marcel Proust that he discovered "a way to make time give back all it has taken, through turning life by way of memory into art." Now this is what happens to some few of the people of Morgana. They come to be able to look at time—*their* time, themselves *in* time— in the way that Miss Welty insists that novelists do: "A novel's duration is, in some respect, exactly how long it takes the particular author of a particular novel to explore its emotional resources, and to give full power to learning their scope and meeting their demands, and finding out their truest procedure."[2]

If novelists, why not musicians? Miss Lotte Elizabeth Eckhart came to Mississippi from somewhere out in the world, rented quarters in the McLain house, and set out to teach the Beethoven to the children of Morgana. Upon the piano in her studio she places a plaster bust of Beethoven and her prize possession, a metronome, which otherwise she keeps in a wall safe. It is her badge of office, the sign of her profession. What she must teach her pupil is the beat that will space out the notes of the melody into proper sequence and juxtaposition. The metronome instills the consciousness of time— but not of clock or calendar time. Rather, the time measured by the metronome is the rhythm of duration itself, biological rather than social, steady and processional rather than transitory and personal. The student who would play the Beethoven must learn to order the notes by an absolute rather than a subjective rhythm—which paradoxically means that what is played can be possessed and replayed, repeated as desired, given independent existence of its own.

Virgie Rainey, the daughter of a poor family, quickly becomes Miss Eckhart's prize pupil, accomplishing as if by instinct what Cassie Morrison must learn only arduously and by constant practice. Each June Virgie's artistry is the culmination of the recital that Miss Eckhart's pupils give to conclude the term. Stern taskmaster that Miss Eckhart is, driving her pupils onward by peremptory command and threat, she nonetheless cannot disguise her pleasure in Virgie Rainey's accomplishments. Dearest thanks! she would say after each rendition. When the Raineys can no longer afford to pay for Virgie's piano lessons, Miss Eckhart continues to teach her.

But Virgie is a wild, rebellious child. There is a battle of wills, and Virgie's is stronger finally than her teacher's, for she instinctively senses the one advantage she has, which is that Miss Eckhart wishes to pass on the Beethoven to her pupil, the one pupil there in the little Mississippi town who she feels has the talent to receive it, much more desperately than Virgie thinks she wants to receive the Beethoven. As Cassie Morrison comes to realize about Miss Eckhart, "There was a weak place in her, vulnerable, and Virgie Rainey found it and showed it to people."

There comes a day when Miss Eckhart sets the prized metronome upon the piano in front of Virgie, whereupon the pupil announces that "she would not play another note with that thing in her face" (40). From that time on, Virgie Rainey comes to assert her will more and more; in small ways she tyrannizes over the German music teacher. And when she reaches her fourteenth birthday, she declines to study piano any longer, and takes a job playing at the movie house. For various reasons Miss Eckhart loses her other pupils, and after a time is no longer seen about town any more.

Yet there is more to the matter than that (just as there is more to *The Golden Apples* than the story of Virgie Rainey and Miss Eckhart). For in one very real sense it cannot be said that in setting aside Miss Eckhart's metronome, the symbol of the music teacher's vocation, Virgie has successfully rejected the Beethoven that has been offered to her so urgently. In the study of music there comes a time when the pupil no longer requires the mechanical aid of a metronome to fix the tempo of the composition. The sense of rhythm becomes innate, the beat is mastered; henceforth the pupil can play music without the help of an external reminder; it becomes part of the pupil's knowledge of time. Thus in declining to allow her teacher to set the metronome any longer before her as she plays, Virgie Rainey is also signaling that she no longer needs her teacher's metronome to play the Beethoven; the rhythm of music, which had until then been in Miss Eckhart's custody, is now her own as well. In rebelling, Virgie also accepts; in bowing to her pupil's ultimatum Miss Eckhart has not perhaps yielded after all. "At Virgie's words, Miss Eckhart quickly—it almost seemed that was what she'd wanted to hear—stopped the hand and slammed the little door, bang. The metronome was never set before Virgie again" (40).

If without knowing it, Virgie Rainey does accept the Beethoven from Miss Eckhart, however, it is not only with bad grace but under protest, and with every intention of following her own desires and not the vocation of music that the teacher exemplifies. And as Cassie Morrison realizes, there is much in Virgie's situation that conspires against any chance she might have, almost in spite of herself, to develop the artistic talent that she possesses. Not only are her parents poor, but Virgie is made to feel the stigma of their situation. As is Eudora Welty's way, any such relationship is revealed only obliquely, in little remarks and asides, since it is on such terms that such things are always manifested in a community. But there are hints, allusions which are there to be grasped, and they culminate in the realization, on Cassie's part, that "perhaps nobody wanted Virgie Rainey to be anything in Morgana any more than they wanted Miss Eckhart to be." At the annual recitals the audience of townsfolk always applauds more loudly for Cassie than for Virgie, and for little Jinny Love Stark, the spoiled daughter of the town's social matron, more than either. Crucially, it is Cassie, not Virgie, who receives the Presbyterian Church's music scholarship to go to college: "The only reason for that which she put into words, to be self-effacing, was that the Raineys were Methodists; and yet she did not, basically, understand a slight" (56). But Miss Eckhart does; she sends for Virgie and gives her a present, "a little butterfly pin made of cut-out silver, like silver lace, to wear on her shoulder; the safety-catch wasn't any good" (56–57).

Another author might have left the transaction there; Eudora

Welty knows that formulations of caste and class will not sufficiently account for the relationship between Virgie Rainey and the Morgana community. What is involved is something at once more personal and more profound. It lies in the link between Virgie and Miss Eckhart; more particularly, in what Miss Eckhart represents in Morgana, and what Virgie, perhaps without wanting to at all, also represents.

For the explanation of that, we must look at another summer day, which Cassie Morrison remembers upon hearing the notes from "Für Elise" in the June air, when a sudden storm blew up one morning and forced Virgie Rainey, Cassie, and little Jinny Love Stark to remain in Miss Eckhart's studio after their lessons were done. Miss Eckhart selects a piece of music, sits down at the piano, and for the only time that Cassie has ever seen her do so except when taking the second part in duets, she performs. As the little girls watch, the German music teacher "played as if it were Beethoven":

> The thunder rolled and Miss Eckhart frowned and bent forward or she leaned back to play; at moments her solid body swayed from side to side like a tree trunk.
> The piece was so hard that she made mistakes and repeated to correct them, so long and stirring that it soon seemed longer than the day itself had been, and in playing it Miss Eckhart assumed an entirely different face. Her skin flattened and drew across her cheeks, her lips changed. The face could have belonged to someone else—not even to a woman, necessarily. It was the face a mountain could have, or what might be seen behind the veil of a waterfall. There in the rainy light it was a sightless face, one for music only—though the fingers kept slipping and making mistakes they had to correct. And if the sonata had an origin in a place on earth, it was the place where Virgie, even, had never been and was not likely ever to go. (49)

The three little girls are very uncomfortable; "This was some brilliant thing, too splendid for Miss Eckhart." Cassie Morrison realizes that the composition Miss Eckhart is playing must be something she had learned long ago, when young, had almost forgotten, but it had taken "only a summer rain to start it again." The experience is too intense, too personal, "too much for Cassie Morrison. It lay in the very heart of the stormy morning—there was something almost too violent about a storm in the morning. She stood back in the room with her whole body averted as if to ward off blows from Miss Eckhart's strong left hand, her eyes on the faintly winking circle of the safe in the hall" (50).

At that moment Cassie thinks of something that had happened to Miss Eckhart. She had gone out walking by herself at night, and been assaulted by a Negro. Afterwards people in town were disappointed that she did not move away: "Then they wouldn't always have to remember that a terrible thing once happened to her. But Miss Eckhart stayed as though she considered one thing not so much more terrifying than another" (50). What the town cannot forgive in Miss Eckhart, Cassie realizes, is her disenthrallment—her implicit acceptance of the presence, within the rhythms of human life, of extraordinary things occurring, not to be encompassed and thereby gentled and made manageable within the rituals and the sympathies of the community: "things divined and endured, spectacular moments, hideous things like the black nigger jumping out of the hedge at nine o'clock." What Morgana has been unable to do, in part because Miss Eckhart could not help it to do, is to "place" her, make her part of the accepted goings on, the patterns and cadences of town social life. It was not merely that she was German and therefore different; that could have been accommodated. "Missie Spights said that if Miss Eckhart had allowed herself to be called by her first name, then she would have been like other ladies. Or if Miss Eckhart had belonged to a church that had ever been heard of, and the ladies would have had something to invite her to belong to . . . Or if she had been married to anybody at all, just the awfullest man—like Miss Snowdie MacLain, that everybody could feel sorry for" (58).

The music teacher, however, not only does not know how to make herself a full-fledged participant within the community; she does not want to, and why she does not is what Cassie, in retrospect, realizes as she remembers that stormy morning when Miss Eckhart played the piano for them. For the rhythms, the passions that are part of the composition Miss Eckhart is playing are not those of Morgana; they are those of primal nature, absolute, and uncaring. No wonder that as the music teacher played her face changed, became sexless, a "sightless face, one for music only"; her adherence is all for the music, which in the artistic finality of its rhythm demands absolute fidelity. The act of playing it, as basic and as regular and unforgiving as life, death, procreation, the movement of the heavenly bodies, demands a dedication that, once having been pledged, cannot be easily subordinated to the allegiances of the social community.

Listening to the music, the three little girls, including even Virgie, "looked at one another, the three quite suddenly on some equal footing. They were all wondering—thinking—perhaps of escape" (50). Jinny Love, who for all her few years is preeminently the spokesman for the community, has already gone over to the piano and begun turning the music, as if by doing so she might thereby convert the solitary engagement of performer and music into a social relationship. "Miss Eckhart did not even see her—her arm struck the child, making a run" (49). (She will attempt to do the same in another story, when Cassie's brother Loch, the lifeguard at "Moon Lake," kneels astride a drowned orphan girl attempting to administer artificial respiration; on that occasion Jinny Love takes a towel and tries to use it to fan the boy as he works away at restoring life.)

Cassie for her part thinks of what happened with Miss Eckhart and the rapist. What Virgie is thinking, we do not know. But we can guess what it means. For what the German music teacher's total commitment to the piece she is playing must signify to Virgie Rainey, however without her conscious articulation, is what Virgie is resisting, and will continue to resist for years to come: an absolute, unreserved response to necessity, to the controlled expression of the violence of passion, desire, heroism, human love and hate: the vocation and discipline of an artist that will enable her to give form and meaning to the rhythm of life itself. This is what Miss Eckhart has meant for her and will continue to mean; "Performing, Miss Eckhart was unrelenting. Even when the worst of the piece was over, her fingers like foam on rocks pulled at the spent-out part with unstilled persistence, insolence, violence" (51). It is what Virgie, the wild, uninhibited, free spirit that Cassie Morrison admires so much, dreads, will spend twenty years attempting to avoid. And yet, again without knowing it, it is only because she can instinctively apprehend and feel that passion, recognize that rhythm, that it threatens her, and she wishes to deny it.

Thus on the afternoon in June when Cassie Morrison, busy dyeing a scarf in her room, hears the notes of the Beethoven and responds at once with Miss Eckhart's words, "Virgie Rainey, danke schoen," she thinks of some lines from a poem:

> Though I am old with wandering
> Through hollow lands and hilly lands,
> I will find out where she has gone

The poem is Yeats's "The Song of the Wandering Aengus." Not until late that night, however, after the events of the afternoon and the hayride, does she remember the whole of the poem, and repeat the key line: "Because a fire was in my head." It requires what happens that afternoon to make her see-the meaning that the poem embodies.

While Cassie has been dyeing her scarf and thinking of the hayride to come, her brother Loch, bedridden upstairs with malaria, has been intently observing the house next door. Nobody lives there any more except for Mr. Boonie Holifield, the night watchman at the cotton gin. But as Loch looks on, a girl and a boy, the latter in a sailor's uniform, enter the house through the back door. Loch has observed them do so before. Their destination is a room upstairs, where Loch can see them through a window, and where they play games, as he thinks, on a mattress.

Presently an old woman comes down the street—Loch decides she is the sailor's mother—and enters the front door of the house. As Loch watches, the old woman begins to decorate the downstairs parlor with strips of old newspaper, hanging them about the parlor. "The old woman was decorating the piano until it rayed out like a Christmas tree or a Maypole" (27). She runs strips down from the chandelier to the piano and the four corners of the room. She leaves the house, goes across to another yard and picks a bloom from a magnolia tree, places it on the piano. Then she begins stuffing paper into cracks in the windows, and places an old floor mat and a quilt over the front windows. Loch realizes that she intends to burn down the house. Fascinated, he crawls out of the window into a tree, moves along a far-extending limb to where he can watch better. The old woman now places a strange object, shaped like an obelisk, up on the piano, and sets it to ticking away.

At this point Cassie, who has heard the notes of the "Für Elise"—Virgie had apparently played them, before she and the sailor went upstairs—and has been thinking about Virgie and Miss Eckhart, goes to the window and sees Loch hanging from the tree. Standing at the window watching and thinking about Virgie and Miss Eckhart, she strums her favorite song, "By the light, light, light, light, light of the silvery moon," on her ukelele: "She could never go for herself, never creep out on the shimmering bridge of the tree, or reach the dark magnet there that drew you inside, kept drawing you in. She could not see herself do an unknown thing. She was not Loch, she was not Virgie Rainey; she was not her mother. She was Cassie in her room, seeing the knowledge and torment beyond her reach, standing at her window singing—in a voice soft, rather full today, and halfway thinking it was pretty" (68).

As Loch watches, the old woman prepares to build a fire in the piano. Just then two men, Mr. Fatty Bowles and Old Man Moody, come down the street, and walk up on the porch to wake up Mr. Boonie Holifield. They too see the old woman through the window, as she places a lighted candle in the piano: "Flames arrowed out so noiselessly. They ran down the streamers of paper, as double-quick as freshets from a loud gully-washer of rain. The room was crisscrossed with quick, dying yellow fire, there were pinwheels falling and fading from the ceiling" (70).

Things now happen very rapidly. The two men step into the parlor, begin beating out the fire, throw the metronome out of the window close to where Loch Morrison is watching, and after the fire is extinguished they take the old woman out onto the street. Loch drops to the ground and retrieves the metronome. Then Cassie runs outside, "barefooted down the front walk in her petticoat and in full awareness turned toward town, crying 'You can't take her! Miss Eckhart!'" (78).

Now Virgie Rainey and the sailor emerge from the house. Some of the ladies who have been playing cards down the street come along the sidewalk. As Cassie and Loch watch, Virgie Rainey moves past them and towards the two men and the old woman. "'She'll stop for Miss Eckhart,' breathed Cassie" (79). But she does not: "Virgie went by. There was a meeting of glances between the teacher and her old pupil, that Cassie knew. She could not be sure that Miss Eckhart's eyes closed once in recall—they had looked so wide-open at everything alike. The meeting amounted only to Virgie Rainey's passing by, in plain fact. She clicked by Miss Eckhart and she clicked straight through the middle of the Rook party, without a word or the pause of a moment" (79–80).

That evening after supper Loch Morrison, the bold, the enterprising, thinks about the strange little object he has retrieved. "'Reckon it's going to blow up in the night?'" he asks the maid Louella. "All by itself, of its own accord, it might let fly its little door and start up. He thought he heard it now. Or was it his father's watch in the next room, already laid on the dresser for the night?" When Loch dreams that night "he dreamed close to the surface, and his dreams were filled with a color and a fury that the daytime that summer never held" (84).

It is Cassie, however, who understands what has happened in Morgana that afternoon. Back in her moonlit bed after the hayride, she thinks of Miss Eckhart and Virgie as they encounter each other on the sidewalk. "What she was certain of was the distance those two had gone, as if all along they had been making a trip (which the sailor was only starting). It had changed them. They were deliberately terrible. They looked at each other and neither wished to speak. They did not even horrify each other. No one could touch them now, either" (84–85).

People like the music teacher and her prize pupil live only surlily in the tidy everyday world, for they also inhabit a different kind of world, one that, like the rhythm of the metronome and the beat of the music, does not attune itself to the comings and goings of people in Morgana and places like Morgana—to the comforts, excuses and diversions of society—but to a more desperate and naked kind of existence that confronts more ultimate longings and starker truths. "*Danke schoen*. . . . That much was out in the open. Gratitude—like rescue—was simply no more. It was not only past; it was outworn and cast away. Both Miss Eckhart and Virgie Rainey were human beings terribly at large, roaming on the face of the earth. And there were others of them—human beings, roaming, like lost beasts" (85).

Places like Morgana—human communities—exist to ward off and mask, through ritual and social complexity, an awareness of the finally unanswerable and inexplicable nature of existence in time and eternity. They are founded on the agreement—it is an unacknowledged compact between its members—not to admit to the existence of chaos and violence that cannot be controlled, explained, scaled down to manageable proportion. Life must, in Morgana's scheme of things, work out, exhibit order, be sufficient to human needs. And anyone who cannot enter into such a compact, cannot play the game by the agreed-upon rules, is a threat to the security and place of all the others. It is the instinctive awareness on the part of the townsfolk of Morgana that neither Miss Eckhart nor Virgie Rainey is willing to accept life on such terms that creates the hostility and brings about their ostracism.

Why it is that Virgie and her teacher are unable to conform to the needs and demands of the town is what Cassie divines that night. It is implicit in the words of the poem several of whose lines she had thought of that afternoon when she heard the notes of "Für Elise."

> I went out to the hazel wood,
> Because a fire was in my head,
> And cut and peeled a hazel wand,
> And hooked a berry to a thread

So the poem begins—she remembers it in its entirety now—with its depiction of the person who "because a fire was in my head" cannot accept life on its surface terms. The little silver trout taken on the baited hook becomes

> a glimmering girl
> With apple blossom in her hair
> Who called me by my name and ran
> And faded through the brightening air.

It is the quest for the glimmering girl, a happiness that is more than of the world, that drives persons like Virgie Rainey and Miss Eckhart. Like the Aengus in Yeats's poem, the Master of Love of Celtic mythology who in the country of the young will forever pursue the girl holding the golden apple, human beings like Virgie and her teacher, "terribly at large, roaming on the face of the earth," can never accede to what is ordinary and attainable:

> Though I am old with wandering
> Through hollow lands and hilly lands,
> I will find out where she has gone,
> And kiss her lips and take her hands;
> And walk among long dappled grass,
> And pluck till time and times are done
> The silver apples of the moon,
> The golden apples of the sun.[3]

Now it would be all too easy to see such people as Virgie and Miss Eckhart as romantic heroines, Byronic in their splendid isolation and superior to the rank and file of their community in their greater perception of the truth, and therefore to view them simply as martyrs to mediocrity, whose triumph is of the spirit. But Eudora Welty's art is more involved than that. For in acting as they do—in heeding, let us say, only the rhythms of the Beethoven, rather than what Cassie Morrison's mother calls music that "dips" (41)—they neither change nor avoid those same limitations or mortality that the townsfolk would pretend do not exist. Miss Eckhart's effort to teach the Beethoven to Virgie Rainey, after all, ends in failure. Virgie Rainey will not be "heard from in the world some day"; the teacher's ineffectual attempt to burn down the house that had been her studio is the measure of her disappointment. As for Virgie, her furious rebellion, as we learn in the last story of *The Golden Apples*, will leave her, at the age of forty, seated in the rain under a tree, perceiving for the first time the implications of what she has thus far been and done. Can one, therefore, say that the inclination to heed a different drummer, so to speak, produces superior spiritual happiness, or at any rate consolation, than what the citizens of Morgana discover? All of them, seekers or not, know frustration, failure, death.

At the end, after Virgie's mother has died and she prepares to leave town, Cassie Morrison calls to her, " 'You'll go away like Loch. . . . A life of your own, away—I'm so glad for people like you and Loch,

I am really.'" (240). But if she does, it will not be to perform the Beethoven. The gift that was her talent has not been used, and she no longer even plays the piano. What Virgie *has* won through to is knowledge—of herself, of her relationship to Miss Eckhart, who, she realizes at the end, she had not hated but almost loved, and who had "offered, offered, offered—and when Virgie was young, in the strange wisdom of youth that is accepting of more than is given, she had accepted *the* Beethoven, as with the dragon's blood" (243). Certainly she has not in any way avoided the consequences of being human, as indeed she would not have done even had she accepted the Beethoven from Miss Eckhart early enough to learn to use her own talent. It is rather that because she has learned to see herself as she is, she will not be surprised, not be at the mercy of unsuspected emotions and desires. She will cease to be what Cassie Morrison saw as "terribly at large, roaming on the face of the earth"—because she will have accepted her own relationship to her experience.

We may recall what Miss Welty said that the novelist must do: learn the scope and meet the demands of his characters, find out their truest procedure. This is the kind of self-knowledge to which Virgie Rainey comes in her life. Virgie will not go belatedly to the musical career she once might have had. But she has attained something of the vision of the artist, or perhaps more properly, has learned to accept the existence of that vision within her.

If there *is* an artist among Miss Lotte Elizabeth Eckhart's pupils in Morgana—that is to say, one who not only possesses the talent but accepts its consequences in the form of a vocation—it has always seemed to me that it is not Virgie Rainey, but the pupil who *did* receive the Beethoven from Miss Eckhart: Cassie Morrison. Not that Miss Eckhart had thought her worthy of such a gift; only Virgie enjoyed that place in Miss Eckhart's regard. It was only through hard work that Cassie would each year at the recital perform the composition that Virgie had played so effortlessly the year before. But it is Cassie who, however it would have astonished her teacher, has taken up Miss Eckhart's allegiance, and will continue her mission of bringing the rhythm of the metronome to the children of Morgana. Preparing to go off to study music at college, she knows that "now stretching ahead of her, as far as she could see, were those yellow Schirmer books: all the rest of her life" (56).

It is Cassie who divines the meaning of what the piano teacher and Virgie Rainey were doing. If, as she thought that day at the window, she could not see herself ever do an unknown thing, and if the knowledge and torment were beyond her reach, nevertheless it is also true that she understands what they are, and is not therefore at their mercy. Cassie already knows what Virgie will spend years finding out:

> Yet things divined and endured, spectacular moments, hideous things like the black nigger jumping out of the hedge at nine o'clock, all seemed to Cassie to be by their own nature rising—and so alike—and crossing the sky and setting, the way the planets did. Or they were more like whole constellations, turning at their very centers maybe, like Perseus and Orion and Cassiopeia in her Chair and the Big Bear and Little Bear, maybe often upside down, but terribly recognizable. It was not just the sun and moon that traveled. In the deepening of the night, the rising sky lifted like a cover when Louella let it soar as she made the bed.
>
> All kinds of things would rise and set in your own life, you could begin now to watch for them, roll back your head and feel their rays come down and reach your open eyes. (51)

For if art requires talent, it demands also the dedication to the exercise of that talent. In Proust's words, in art excuses count for nothing.[4] And as Miss Welty herself has written, "The art of making is the art that has meaning, and I think beauty is likely to be something that has for a time lain under good, patient hands."[5] The romantic vision of untrammeled natural genius had and has its adherents, but I doubt that it is Eudora Welty's. And it seems to me that a character like Cassie Morrison—who perseveres in her craft not only because she treasures it but because it never occurs to her to do anything except persevere, and who possesses the vision that understands what lies in and under the surfaces of her experience without at the same time being so driven and distracted by that knowledge that she cannot live in a place—comes closer to the kind of artist that Eudora Welty is for us than either Virgie or, for that matter, even Miss Eckhart.

There is a great deal about moonlight and the night sky in *The Golden Apples*. The constellations wheel as Miss Eckhart plays the Beethoven. "By the light of the silvery moon," Cassie sings as she stands at the window. And at the end, as Cassie lies in her bed after the hayride thinking about all that has happened, she thinks of the poem by Yeats, remembers it perfectly. In the poem the end of the quest for unattainable beauty, it will be recalled, is "The silver apples of the moon,/The golden apples of the sun."

The light of sun is the fire of primal energy itself, the source of all life and motion. The light of the moon is a reflected light: not primal energy but art, the mirror of life. It is scarcely accidental, therefore, that as Cassie lies asleep, she "sat up in bed once and said aloud, *'Because a fire was in my head.'* Then she fell back unresisting. She did not see except in dreams that a face looked in; that it was the grave, unappeased, and radiant face, once more and always, the face that was in the poem" (85). So there is a fire in her head, too, as she sleeps. The light of the moon is one that can illuminate people like Virgie Rainey and Miss Eckhart, and Loch and the MacLain twins and old King and all the other inhabitants of Morgana, reveal them in the mystery of their place and time in the sun. "'You'll go away like Loch,'" Cassie Morrison tells Virgie Rainey. "'A life of your own, away . . . '" Cassie does not go away, other than to study music at college; she stays on in Morgana, teaching the Beethoven. That stormy morning when Miss Eckhart played the music for the three pupils, Cassie had thought of escape, but she had not fled. Instead, she had stayed on until she understood what it meant. As Virgie later concludes of Miss Eckhart, Cassie too "had absorbed the hero and the victim and then, stoutly, could sit down to the piano with all Beethoven ahead of her" (243). The old German teacher had, after all, found her apprentice.

What was the composition she played for the children that morning "as if it were Beethoven"? When Jinny Love Stark attempted to turn the pages of the music, Miss Eckhart paid no heed. As Cassie and Virgie both saw later, the music she had placed on the piano "wasn't the right music at all, for it was some bound-together songs of Hugo Wolf" (51).

"'What were you playing, though?'" Miss Snowdie MacLain asks. "'I couldn't say,' Miss Eckhart said, rising. 'I have forgotten'" (51).

Surely it could only have been Beethoven's Piano Sonata No. 14 in C-sharp Minor, known popularly as the "Moonlight Sonata."

Thomas Wolfe and the Place
He Came From

Thomas Wolfe and the South was the subject of the first essay on southern literature I published, almost a quarter-century ago. In that essay I went about demonstrating, or attempting to demonstrate, that Wolfe was indubitably a southern writer, as if that were of itself a kind of badge of literary honor; and to prove it I drew up a list of characteristics customarily ascribed to southern writers and tried to show how each applied to Wolfe's writing. These included such things as the fondness for rhetoric, the sense of place, the storytelling quality and the sense of the family that is supposed to go along with it, the consciousness of the past and of time, the sense of evil, and so forth. I came to dislike that essay very much, and the next time I had occasion to revise and augment the set of essays on contemporary southern literature in which it appeared, I scrapped it and got my friend and Chapel Hill colleague C. Hugh Holman to write one instead. He did so, and more to my satisfaction. My early essay, however, remains available; every so often somebody discovers it, and I am always embarrassed to see it quoted. I have not wavered at all in my conviction that Wolfe is a southern writer, but I don't think that lining up a set of the official characteristics of southern literature and then trying to show that Wolfe fits them and so is eligible for the prized blue ribbon—or should I say blue-and-gray ribbon—is very helpful in understanding either Wolfe or southern literature. It is something like trying to prove that a great batter like Ted Williams was a good baseball player because he knew how to play line drives off the left field wall in Fenway Park.

Wolfe isn't a southern writer because he sometimes wrote like William Faulkner or Robert Penn Warren, but because most of the time he wrote like Thomas Wolfe. And if a writer as good as Wolfe was at his best doesn't fit the official list of characteristics of southern writing, then what should be suspect is not Wolfe but the list. What I tried to do, I am afraid, both in that earlier essay and in part in the book I published on Wolfe several years later, was to make Wolfe into an honorary member of the Nashville Agrarians, which strikes me now as a pretty gratuitous enterprise. Wolfe did what he had to do, and they did what they had to do, and what is nice is that we have both.

On the other hand, it is instructive to recall why it seemed a good idea to try to show, back in 1953, that Thomas Wolfe was beyond question a southern writer. This was the time when the Southern Literary Renascence that began after the First World War was just beginning to be identified as an important phenomenon in American literary history—until then it had been thought of primarily as a fortuitous assortment of good books. The book for which my essay was written was the first full-fledged examination of the overall achievement of modern southern literature. William Faulkner, after years of toiling in something resembling critical obscurity, was only just beginning to be recognized as perhaps the premier writer of fiction of our century, and the excitement of this discovery was widespread. On the other hand, the southern poet-critics—Ransom, Tate, Warren, Brooks—were at the height of their authority, and what they said was so about literature meant a great deal (and still does to me).

We had recently been through a depression, a new deal, and a world war. Each of these phenomena had involved a great deal of ideological paraphernalia, and as is always the way, literature had been placed in their service. In the 1930s it was the Marxist, proletarian novel. In the 1940s it was the novel of involvement. We had gone through a long period of trying to make out that books such as *The Grapes of Wrath, U.S.A., For Whom the Bell Tolls, A Bell for Adano, Studs Lonigan, Strange Fruit,* and so on were the principal achievements of modern American literature.

We were a little tired of it; we wanted to learn how to read fiction and poetry again *as* fiction and poetry, for their formal literary excellence, and not as ideological documents. So the novelists such as Faulkner and Warren and Porter and other southerners, and the poets such as Tate, Ransom, and Warren, who had never lost sight of that fact and had generally refused to take part as novelists and poets in the various popular causes, were now being discovered or rediscovered with delight. These were, as a scholar-friend of mine once wrote, the southern years, and the traditional southern literary virtues of formal excellence and moral relevance, having been revitalized and given great imaginative energy as the literary South had moved into the modern world, now seemed very attractive indeed. There was also the additional advantage that the literary marketplace in New York had run out of ideological gimmicks, now that literary proletarianism and literary patriotism had run their course, so it couldn't put up much of a fight against literature as literature, however unsalable and superficially unexciting mere literary excellence might be. So until the civil rights movement got going in the late 1950s and New York had a good excuse for dealing with literature (some of it very good literature indeed) as ideology once again, the rich formal achievement of the best southern literature was permitted to be read and admired, as generally it wasn't before and hasn't been since.

For these reasons and others, then, the period of the late 1940s and early 1950s was a time when merely being a good southern writer seemed to be a gesture in the direction of literary distinction, and there was widespread and deserved appreciation of the best southern writing of our time.

The trouble was, however, that with any such consensus of taste, no matter how good, there always goes along a kind of orthodoxy. Virtues are soon codified; the approaches and techniques that are, for good writers, the creative means for the act of discovery that is literature are made into the ends themselves. Because some southern authors (*e.g.*, Faulkner and Tate) went at the art of literature in certain creative ways, and because those ways had clearly worked and filled certain genuine artistic needs, it followed that that was the southern way to do it, and any writer who didn't do it that way was inferior and not a true southern literary man. Thus, because

Wolfe didn't write fiction the way Faulkner wrote fiction, Wolfe was neither as important nor as "southern" a novelist as Faulkner.

Now I happen to believe that Wolfe *isn't* as important a writer as Faulkner, but the reason he isn't is not that he didn't write his books the way that Faulkner wrote his; it's because Faulkner wrote a different kind of novel better than Wolfe wrote his kind. And conversely, if Wolfe *is* an important novelist, as I certainly believe he is, the reasons why he is might well have nothing to do with resembling Faulkner.

Perhaps that seems obvious—certainly it is trite enough to be obvious—but it isn't the way literary movements and schools and groups tend to approach things. We tend to erect our characteristic methods, techniques, and attitudes into orthodoxies. We make the highly creative techniques of some writers into legalisms that impede our own imaginative response to other writers. One writer's method is another's impoverishment; one writer's need is another's inhibition.

Well and good. But what if one is so struck with the imaginative achievement of one group of writers and finds so much that is good and stimulating in the way they approach their craft and at the same time one is also powerfully drawn to another and different kind of writer, whom those writers and many critics generally don't like (and also don't always understand)? What does one do? I expect that one attempts to do what I think I tried to do with Thomas Wolfe: to take the insights and apparatus and attitudes that fit the one group and try to demonstrate—both to oneself and to others whom one likes and admires—that the writer in question has been misread and really isn't so different and is a good writer *because* at bottom he is really doing the same things that the others are. Thus Thomas Wolfe is an important southern writer, not because of Thomas Wolfe's own unique version of the human experience in southern guise, but because he resembles other important southern writers. Which is a pretty silly business.

Now the American South is a large and complex region, with some vastly different subregions within it, and the literature it has produced partakes of these divisions—Hugh Holman has identified these as the Tidewater, the Piedmont, and the Deep South. He has selected Ellen Glasgow as exemplar of the Tidewater sensibility in literature, Wolfe for the Piedmont, and Faulkner for the Deep South. But if you are not careful, you tend to think of the South exclusively in terms of one of these subregions and to say that the writing characteristic of the particular subregion is southern literature and anything else isn't southern literature.

It is also true that the sense of community was so strong throughout the South, and still in many ways remains so, that to say one is a southerner is not merely a description but an act of community identification. "In Dixie Land I'll take my stand." To be a southerner has meant to *belong* to a club, as it were, or perhaps a fraternity, a cult, a society, with some social prestige attached to the membership. In William Faulkner's novel *Absalom, Absalom!*, when Quentin Compson is told by a Canadian that he can't understand why southerners feel the way they do, Quentin tells him, "You cant understand it. You would have to be born there." I have seen that remark excoriated by some critics as snobbish, undemocratic, pretentious—but none of the critics who object to it is a southerner. Well, there *is* a certain amount of cliquishness attached to it; to an extent it is not just Quentin explaining, but his creator bragging a bit. Whether he had any right to feel privileged or whether anyone has such a right, because of being a southerner, is another matter; the fact is that many have felt that way, and still do, and that among them have been William Faulkner and also Thomas Wolfe.

Yet in certain ways Wolfe didn't appear to belong to the club. For part of this self-conscious identification as a southerner had, perhaps even still has, a certain amount of social overtone, as well as literary and critical assumptions, and in a kind of complex but not clearly defined way there was a relationship between the two. Most of the important southern writers of the 1920s, 1930s, and 1940s were of the gentry, or perhaps the upper middle class would be a better way of describing it; in any event, "of good family" as the expression went (which as I think Ellen Glasgow once pointed out was to say something very different from they were "of good people"—i.e., of the rural working or lower middle class, the so-called "yeomanry"). The southern writers weren't aristocrats, mind you, and none grew up in stately Tidewater mansions. But the "Big House" and the southern gentlemen were involved in the southern ideal, and almost every one of the twentieth-century southern writers has at one point in his or her work (often at frequent points) presented, with more than a little approval, characters who look down disdainfully upon the "trash" and the "riff-raff" without "family"—i.e., without approved social connections.

But Thomas Wolfe made a *point* of his working-class lineage. He wrote an autobiographical novel about growing up in a boardinghouse. He was actively hostile to and critical of southern aristocratic pretense, and he liked to boast that his background was working class, yeomanry. Now it would have been all right if he had simply accepted the fact; but to boast of it, and furthermore to suggest, as he sometimes did, that because of his origins *he* was honest and open and democratic and genuine, while those who weren't from similar origins were snobbish and defensive and aristocratic and full of pretense, was another matter entirely.

This was not merely a matter of subject matter or of authorial biography. It also, and more importantly perhaps, involved ideas about literary technique and attitude. The literary virtues of the best southern writing—formal elegance, a reverence for tradition, restraint, self-sufficiency—were, in an important way I believe, those customarily ascribed to the aristocracy. And the two tended to get all involved with each other, in a fashion that was not logical perhaps but was nonetheless pervasive.

Let me offer two quotations from the critical writings of Allen Tate (the man whom, I might add, I happen to admire most among all twentieth-century authors). In one, dated 1931, Tate was writing about poetry: "A mind without moral philosophy is incapable of understanding poetry. For poetry, of all the arts, demands a serenity of view and a settled temper of the mind, and most of all the power to detach one's own needs from the experience set forth in the poem. A moral sense so organized sets limits to human nature, and is content to observe them." In the other, dated 1936, Tate was writing about the Old South: "Antebellum man, insofar as he achieved a unity between his moral nature and his livelihood, was a traditional man. He dominated the means of life; he was not dominated by it. I think that the distinguishing feature of a traditional society is simply that. In order to make a livelihood men do not have to put aside their moral natures." The terms in the two passages are almost interchangeable; the same sense of restraint, of classical wholeness, of unified personality that characterizes the gentleman of the Old South is used to characterize the writing of poetry. Tate, to be sure, wasn't confusing the two realms, but many people did.

Such terms clearly didn't fit the work of Thomas Wolfe. His was no serenity of view, and his temper of mind was not settled but highly volatile and excitable. The idea of a harmonious unity of personality, dominating every facet of its experience, acting unconsciously and classically out of a completely traditional and accepted set of responses to experience, was the last way one might think to describe how Wolfe went about either living his life or writing his books. He was highly and voraciously romantic; he wanted to storm the gates of Heaven, and never mind the consequences. Restraint? Why, he poured the language on at all times, held back not at all. And as for detaching his own needs from the experience set forth in his books, it is obvious that no more literally autobiographical and nakedly personal a writer than Thomas Wolfe ever lived.

What I am suggesting is that those literary characteristics which were most valued by most of the southern writers of the 1920s and 1930s, and which in many ways exemplify the best features of much of their art, were also seen as socially characteristic of an aristocratic ideal—and there was the implication, though nobody ever came right out and said it, that the creator of Eugene Gant, though born in a state of the former Confederacy, was from the wrong side of the tracks and wrote like it. Mind you, the best of the other southern writers didn't think of it that way at all, as far as I know; but a good many lesser authorities who wrote about southern letters suggested as much.

I recall, for example, approaching an American literature scholar of some reputation, who liked very much to think of himself as a southern gentleman, and asking him to direct a dissertation I wanted to write on Thomas Wolfe as a southern writer. His response was that he didn't think of Wolfe as being a southern writer; he thought that in spirit Wolfe belonged among the midwestern writers. So I had to look elsewhere (and finally found a Frenchman who was willing to help me). Ostensibly the man was making a literary distinction—*i.e.*, that Wolfe's work could be best understood when viewed alongside such writers as Dreiser, Lewis, Anderson, Sandburg, and so forth, rather than alongside Faulkner and Warren and the other southerners. But he was also expressing, conscious of it or not, a social judgment; he was telling me that as a writer Wolfe was not a gentleman.

For like many other readers, this scholar had formed his notion of what a southern author should be from the local color and genteel literature of the late nineteenth and early twentieth centuries, and when the newer writers came along, once the shock of their being different was blunted, he had somehow managed to fit them into the same social milieu. The perspective from which the literature was ostensibly to be viewed and supposedly had been written was that of the gentleman. Since Thomas Wolfe wasn't a southern gentleman and had few of the virtues, either literary or social, customarily ascribed to southern gentlemen, it was quite clear that Wolfe wasn't a southern writer!

Consider another illustration of the same kind of bias, this time from, of all persons, Herbert Marshall McLuhan. (Few people recall that back in the old days, before Marshall McLuhan discovered mediums and messages, he was a mere literary critic.) Here are several sentences from his essay on "The Southern Quality": "The impersonal formal code which permits a formal expression of inward emotion makes it pointless for people to interpret one another constantly, as they do in most 'realistic' novels. There is thus in the Southern novel a vacuum where we might expect introspection. (It is quite pronounced even in *Huck Finn*.) The stress falls entirely on slight human gestures, external events which are obliquely slanted to flash light or shade on character."

The image—and McLuhan was quite aware of it—is of the gentleman, reserved, formal, punctilious, who is never so vulgar as to attempt to penetrate beyond the formal, arm's-length social ambience. McLuhan then goes on to point out that Thomas Wolfe partook of this impulse, too, but in his case the result was to leave him "locked up in his own passionate solitude." Wolfe, he continues, "has all the passion without any of the formal means of con-straint and communication which make it tolerable. He was a Southerner by attitude but not by tradition."

The implied social judgment is obvious. Wolfe was not a gentle-man, so didn't know the inherited rules of gentlemanly conduct, but since he was a southerner by birth, he couldn't help but have absorbed the proper attitude from his betters! Now what bosh and balderdash, as they say. The idea of the southern novel not permit-ting characters to interpret each other leaves out such episodes as Thomas Sutpen talking to General Compson and Miss Rosa Cold-field talking to Quentin Compson and Quentin Compson talking to Shreve McCannon in Faulkner's *Absalom, Absalom!* It leaves out Lacy Buchan's whole method of narration in Tate's *The Fathers.* It leaves out Jack Burden on the subject of Willie Stark in *All The King's Men.* It leaves out Eudora Welty's *The Optimist's Daughter.* It leaves out—but a better way to get at the appropriateness of that particular pronouncement might be to say what it includes. It in-cludes, so far as I can tell, Stark Young and Thomas Nelson Page, and not a great deal else.

Why such a pronouncement from a critic with as much intelli-gence as Marshall McLuhan? It was simply that McLuhan confused the subject matter of some southern fiction with its techniques—captivated with what Allen Tate, John Ransom, and others have written, often admiringly, *about* the southern gentleman, he moved insensibly to assuming that Tate, for example, wrote *as* a southern gentleman, which is precisely what Tate often went to demonstrate was quite impossible to do if one was a modern writer with any-thing important to say. That, Tate said, was why Poe had once been more or less driven out of Richmond, and why the good writers of his own generation had extreme difficulty in making a living while resident in the South. But such is the thematic pervasiveness of the gentlemanly ideal that it also hooked Marshall McLuhan into mak-ing numerous absurd statements, such as: "Even the characters of Erskine Caldwell are free at least from self-pity." And that state-ment is made about *Jeeter Lester*!

But I digress. What I have been attempting to do is to show what some of the problems are in discussing the question of Thomas

Wolfe and the South. We all have our Souths, to which in varying degree we are drawn. We also have the example of some very powerful and very persuasive authors and critics who had definite ideas of what the South was and should be, and who can have a very formative and even controlling influence upon our own ways of thinking about the South and its writers, and some of their ideas are very much intertwined with their social attitudes. Yet no matter how much we may admire and value such insights, we must finally judge for ourselves in matters that concern us.

Very well, what of Thomas Wolfe and the South? *Is* Wolfe a southern writer, or merely a writer born in the South but not of it, so far as his imagination and way of writing go?

I want now to quote a fairly well-known passage from *Look Homeward, Angel*, describing Eugene Gant in his eleventh or twelfth year.

> His feeling for the South was not so much historic as it was of the core and desire of dark romanticism—that unlimited and inexplicable drunkenness, the magnetism of some men's blood that takes them into the heart of the heat, and beyond that, into the polar and emerald cold of the South as swiftly as it took the heart of the incomparable romanticist who wrote *The Rime of the Ancient Mariner*, beyond which there is nothing. And this desire of his was unquestionably enhanced by all he had read and visioned, by the romantic halo that his school history cast over the section, by the whole fantastic distortion of that period where people were said to live in "mansions," and slavery was a benevolent institution, conducted to a constant banjo-strumming, the strewn largesses of the colonel and the shuffle-dance of his happy dependents, where all women were pure, gentle, and beautiful, all men chivalrous and brave, and the Rebel horde a company of swaggering, death-mocking cavaliers. Years later, when he could no longer think of the barren spiritual wilderness, the hostile and murderous intrenchment against all new life—when their cheap mythology, their legend of the charm of their manner, the aristocratic culture of their lives, the quaint sweetness of their drawl, made him writhe—when he could think of no return to their life and its swarming superstition without weariness and horror, so great was his fear of the legend, his fear of their antagonism, that he still pretended the most fanatic devotion to them, excusing his Northern residence on grounds of necessity rather than desire.
>
> Finally, it occurred to him that these people had given him nothing, that neither their love nor their hatred could injure him, that he owed

them nothing, and he determined that he would say so, and repay their insolence with a curse. And he did.

This passage has been cited to illustrate Wolfe's lack of relationship to the South. It is certainly a passage of repudiation. It rejects southern history, southern aristocratic pretense, southern manners, southern speech, southern womanhood, southern clannishness, southern notions of chivalry, southern culture; it describes southern life as a "barren spiritual wilderness," and it asserts that Eugene Gant eventually learned to recognize his superiority to what he had been taught to revere as southern, so that he had vowed to "repay their insolence with a curse," which, of course, was not only the passage itself but *Look Homeward, Angel* as a whole. The passage thus makes the direct autobiographical association between Thomas Wolfe's protagonist and the author himself, and is clearly intended to so do.

Now there is a passage somewhat reminiscent of that in William Faulkner's *Absalom, Absalom!* After Quentin Compson and Shreve McCannon have unraveled the long story of Thomas Sutpen and his descendants, Shreve asks Quentin why he hates the South, and Quentin replies "at once, immediately" that he doesn't hate it, repeating the statement a half-dozen times or so. Beyond doubt we are meant to see that Quentin does hate the South, and also loves it, and that love-hate relationship *is* the South for him—*is* Quentin.

But in Eugene Gant's instance there is no equivocation. He does hate it, all of it, and he wants to make it perfectly clear. He hates it because of what it did to him, and because of the hold it had for so long kept on him, and now he has told it off for good, repaid its "insolence with a curse."

Well, *is* that what he did? Not if *Look Homeward, Angel* is any indication. Along with considerable satire and savaging, there is also tremendous affection and admiration, passages of great delight with the people and places he knew in Asheville and elsewhere, passionate affirmations of its beauty, episode after episode infused with the creative joy of recollected memory, recreated experience. If one were to take all of the passages in the Wolfe fiction which attack the South and put them against all the passages which portray it, and his relation to it, in generally admiring fashion, I think they would just about balance out. In other words, there is every bit as much a love-hate relationship involved with Eugene Gant and Thomas Wolfe as with Quentin Compson and William Faulkner.

Wolfe in the passage quoted castigates the distortion of the southern plantation myth, the phony glamour of the legend of the Confederacy. He also wrote the story entitled "Chickamauga," however, and those descriptions of Lee's army en route to Gettysburg; and more importantly, he took his own particular family's history, the Westalls and Pattons who settled in the mountains of North Carolina, and the history of his father's people as well, and he did what almost every southern author of his generation did: portrayed his protagonists as the inheritors of a specific and tangible history, deeply marked and shaped by the past, and very much the creatures of the forces that placed them where they were and at the time in which they found themselves living.

Not only does the author of that passage concern himself with history and take it seriously enough to want to rectify it, but there is an important sense in which that passage *is* southern history. For what it exemplifies is the process of dislodgment, of the breaking up of the old closely knit southern premodern community before the forces of change. Wolfe describes Eugene Gant as having been born into and still very much molded by the older community, with its own history and mythology and its clearly defined social stratifications. He points out that even after he left it, he was for a long while so influenced by its pieties and its imaginative hold upon him that he pretended to a continuing allegiance. Then he says that finally he realized he was free, no longer bound and obligated, and his response was "to repay their insolence with a curse." Obviously he isn't nearly as free as he imagines, for if he were, there would be no need for so impassioned a denunciation. Wolfe is really in the position, as that paragraph amply demonstrates, of the two Quentin Compsons in *Absalom, Absalom!*—the Quentin who would live in the twentieth century and the Quentin who because he was of his time and place was still bound to the old ghost times, as Faulkner puts it. And just as Miss Rosa Coldfield suggested that Quentin might someday want to do, Wolfe has written a book about it. Surely this is precisely the cultural situation of the twentieth-century southern writer as elucidated by Allen Tate and many others: "With the war of 1914–1918, the South reentered the world—but gave a backward glance as it stepped over the border; that backward glance gave us the Southern renascence, a literature conscious of the past in the present."

But there is something more basically southern involved in the passage, even. To see it fully, we must put the episode in context. It occurs as Wolfe is describing Eliza Gant's yearly winter journeys into the South, to such places as Florida and Arkansas, for reasons of health and business. Wolfe tells how Eliza went South because of her innate suspicion of northerners—a feeling, he says, involving "fear, distrust, alienation"—and how Eugene was always taken along, "into the South, the South that burned like Dark Helen in Eugene's blood." He then proceeds to inform us of the "core and desire of dark romanticism—that unlimited and inexplicable drunkenness, the magnetism of some men's blood" that characterizes his feeling for the South.

Does this feeling evaporate when he grows older and learns to regard its mythology and its society as cheap, tawdry, oppressive? I would say that it does not, and not merely because of the evidence of so much of his work, but also because of the quality of the passage of explanation and repudiation itself. For clearly Wolfe is not describing merely a geographical section, or a set of objective environmental factors. When he depicts the South as "burning" like "Dark Helen" in his protagonist's blood, he is talking about a state of consciousness, a passionate emotional response, an entity of the spirit not to be discussed merely as quantity or as economic or sociological data. He portrays it in feminine terms, and though the South may not be "the proud Lady with the heart of fire" described in John Ransom's poem, she is a prideful woman even so; and if he has ultimately fallen out of love with her as he says, she still makes his blood run hot and he feels it necessary to tell her off in quite passionate terms. "And he did." To me, that dimension alone is enough to counter any arguments about the alleged absence of a "southern" relationship in Wolfe's work.

I recall something that Robert Penn Warren wrote in connection with Faulkner. "It is clear that Faulkner, though he gives a scrupu-

lously faithful report of the real world, is 'mythic' . . . he is drama-
tizing clashes of value in a root way." Wolfe's South—more importantly, Wolfe's relationship to it—may involve a great deal of
realistic description, but the affair goes beyond reportage or realistic
experience, because it is powerfully caught up in feeling and emotion and in values of truth and goodness. When Auden wrote of
Yeats that "mad Ireland hurt you into poetry," he was saying something that could as readily be declared of Wolfe and, for that matter,
of all his southern contemporaries. And like that of his contemporaries, Wolfe's response was not only to a set of specific acts and
topical problems; it was to a moral entity, one that had to be dealt
with accordingly. Not only was there no room for neutrality, but the
involvement involved the constant and often agonizing need to define his own moral identity in terms of the relationship to the time
and place. Wolfe saw places as suffused with moral qualities, and he
saw his South, above all other regions, in terms of place. "And suddenly Eugene was back in space and color and in Time," he writes
in describing his own return to North Carolina, "the weather of his
youth was round him, he was home again." This is not only a description of his feelings about reality; it is an accurate judgment of
his fiction, which most often is surest, most firm, most vivid and
least empty and forced, when it is grounded in "the South that
burned like Dark Helen" in Eugene Gant's blood. It is exemplary of
what Eudora Welty has written, that "it seems plain that the art
that speaks most clearly, explicitly, directly, and passionately from
its place of origin will remain the longest understood. It is through
place that we put out roots, wherever birth, chance, fate, or our
traveling selves set us down." And that place, for Wolfe, was his
South—North Carolina, not merely as locale but as passionate
realm of moral decision.

It is such imaginative dimensions as these and not the little descriptive motifs that I once used to "prove" a point that, presented
in that way, was not worth proving, that constitute Wolfe's southern
sensibility. Of course he has the addiction to rhetoric, and he uses
time thematically, and he has the famous regional storytelling
sense, and he is concerned with evil, and he has much to say about
death, and he has the passion for detail and not much skill at ab-

straction. But these are only the trappings of his art, and do not of themselves help account for its distinctiveness; they would apply equally well to the fiction of, say, Edna Ferber or the late Harry Stillwell Edwards. It is the passionate moral involvement in a time and place that lies beneath these, and gives them character and form, that constitutes Thomas Wolfe's relationship with the South.

We confront the fact, however, that there does exist an important element in Wolfe's fiction which is notably different from almost every other southern author of Wolfe's day. The passage from Eugene Gant and the South certainly exemplifies it. In that passage, Wolfe is not simply telling about a character named Eugene Gant and how his feelings toward the South changed; he *is* Eugene Gant, or more properly Eugene is Thomas Wolfe, and he wants the reader to know it. In that passage he comes very close to telling us that Eugene wrote the book we are reading, and what was at least part of his motivation for so doing. This is "autobiographical fiction"— which is a way of saying that not only does the material come pretty closely and directly out of the author's experience, but that we are compelled to read it that way, and, if it is done well, cannot otherwise properly appreciate the story.

This is a kind of storytelling that we do not often find in southern fiction. Faulkner, for example, uses a great deal of his own personal experience in his fiction, but nobody reads, say, "The Bear" with the feeling that the author is asking us to watch him in the woods as a boy. It isn't told that way. Faulkner the writer usually keeps out of his fiction, in the sense of requiring us to keep in mind at all times a personal relationship between what is being described and the biographical author writing the description.

Wolfe, by contrast, wants us to do just that, and he tells his story so that we will do so. There is thus little or no "objectivity," and the deliberate and intense assertion of the writer's personality, with a view toward making us think and feel emotion about him and what he has done and thought, is very uncharacteristic of other southern authors. It is this, I think, that more than any other aspect of Wolfe's art accounts for the dislike that many good southern critics have felt toward him. Robert Penn Warren (who later became quite friendly with Wolfe) declared of *Of Time and the River* that it "il-

lustrates once more the limitations, perhaps the necessary limitations, of an attempt to exploit directly and naively the personal experience and the self-defined personality in art." And he ended by
pointing out that Shakespeare "merely wrote *Hamlet*; he was *not*
Hamlet."

I rather doubt that the Warren who wrote the poetry he has been
writing for the past two decades would have put the matter quite in
that fashion if he were reviewing Wolfe's novel today. But the point
is well taken, and I think it is an objective way of recording a reaction that was—perhaps not for Warren so much as for some of his
contemporaries—not merely literary but personal. They didn't *like*
Wolfe's personality; they were less than charmed by his continual
assertions of uniqueness and sensibility, and thought him more
than a little boorish and egotistical. The professional writer, they
felt (and with considerable justification), didn't place himself on exhibition as a person, but let his art speak for him. Furthermore, that
person on exhibition was hugely and passionately romantic and fascinated by the intensity of his own emotional responses. As Warren
wrote, "The hero [of *Of Time and the River*] is really that nameless
fury that drives Eugene. The book is an effort to name that fury, and
perhaps by naming it, to tame it. But the fury goes unnamed and
untamed." Warren and his contemporaries had no objection to the
presence of fury in fiction. But they felt emphatically that the fury
should take the form of fiction, not the author's feelings about himself and his personal experience.

I once attempted to account for the presence of this subjective,
autobiographical assertion of personality in the Wolfe novels by noting the difference between Wolfe's background and early life and
that of almost all his southern contemporaries. He came from a
family that, as he portrays them, had little sympathy with intellectual interests and a tradition of literary sensibilities. The result was
that he was led to turn his deepest feelings inward, to erect a barrier
between the outside world and himself, and to develop a stern de-
fensiveness about his literary and intellectual interests. With no
public outlet for his feelings, the result was pent-up emotions and
a fierce self-preoccupation that ultimately erupted in an intense fictional assertion of his own uniqueness and of the justification for it.

If I may quote myself, "When the qualities of mind that made Thomas Wolfe into a novelist instead of a stone mason or a real-estate salesman did come fully into light, there was not surprisingly an explosive force to their emergence, a furious emotional subjectivity that could be disciplined only with great difficulty and always imperfectly."

I still believe there is considerable logic to that, so far as it goes, but upon reflection it seems too simple and too literal. The nature of artistic creativity, and the forms that it takes, are too complex and intricate to be ascribed to any such easy social formulation. I suspect that if there is an explanation of why Wolfe's artistic sensibilities sought the kind of expression they did, it would involve as much depth psychology as social studies, but the few attempts that have been made along that line have seemed less than impressive to me. Genius, Bernard DeVoto declared of Thomas Wolfe, is not enough, which may be true, but without it there would be no such interest as now exists in the novels and the man who wrote them, and because the genius was present, there are limits to logical explanation.

So perhaps it is best simply to accept, with considerable gratitude, that the man wrote as he did, and to note that there is little warrant for contending that the particular form that Wolfe's art took, with its passionate and direct assertion of personality, is somehow alien to his southern background. For while it is quite true that his southern literary contemporaries do not exhibit it, but on the contrary share with each other a marked formal objectivity, it is equally true that in other fields of activity there has been plenty of personal assertion on the southern scene. No one has ever suggested, for example, that Ellen Glasgow and James Branch Cabell were backward in writing quite personally and openly about themselves in their nonfictional writing, yet there is hardly much in the way of working-class experience in the background of those two Virginia patricians. Or consider more recent works such as James Agee's *Let Us Now Praise Famous Men*, or Willie Morris' *North Towards Home*, or such nineteenth-century productions as Mrs. Chesnut's *Diary*, first edited for publication by that lady herself, or the spate of memoirs of the Civil War period, some of them quite choleric, that were published during the late years of the last century and the early years of this. My point is not that they are comparable to Wolfe's writings, and still less that they are all equally works of art, but only that they are evidence that it has been by no means without precedent for a southerner to write directly and assertively about his own experience. Where Wolfe differs is that he did it in the form of autobiographical fiction—an important difference, but hardly a justification for considering him and his work as somehow not an outgrowth of southern experience.

I think it is wise, in considering the problem of Thomas Wolfe, and the South, to adopt Hugh Holman's insight: that Wolfe's subject is "the American self," that "this pattern of development is grounded in the South, but it is grounded in a South which is steadily expanding outward," that Wolfe's "fiction was determined by the Piedmont middle-class world which he knew," and that "when he moved from it, he moved outward to embrace the nation and to attempt to realize the promise of America." This is an old southern custom, you know: it began at least as early as Thomas Jefferson, and among its distinguished literary practitioners have been Mark Twain and the author of *Look Homeward, Angel.* So all in all, we would probably do well to take Thomas Wolfe as he comes; and the place he came from is Asheville, North Carolina.

In Search of the Country of Art
Thomas Wolfe's *Of Time and the River*

Thomas Wolfe's long second novel has never been mistaken for a harmoniously shaped, unitary work of fiction. Sprawling, episodic, uneven, often greatly overwritten, *Of Time and the River* contains, as is often said, some of Wolfe's best and some of his worst writing.

With the notion that it is indeed an up-and-down affair, sometimes very much overburdened, I have no quarrel. What I would contend is that, whatever its artistic sins, it is not merely the impressionistic anthology of a volatile artistic sensibility, an unshaped narrative achieving such coherence as it possesses only through the force of the author's personality. It is concerned with something of notably more specificity than a young artist's *wanderjahre* on two continents; nor is that something merely the protagonist's discovery of his love for America, as is so frequently asserted. What it involves is a young American writer's flight from a very detailed and palpable social milieu—his involvement in a middle-class southern community—and his subsequent effort to discover a better place in which to live and write, and it culminates not in the finding of such a Good Place, but of a perspective from which, as an artist, he can write about his experience.

In other words, *Of Time and the River* is the story of its protagonist's search for a way into his art. As such it details the process whereby as man and writer he first rejects his community, then finally learns the terms on which he can accept its meaning. It is my contention that this is worked out in considerably more definite and concrete terms than are usually recognized. I want to focus upon some details, especially in the opening section, that generally go unremarked, and to try to interpret what they signify.

We know that in *Look Homeward, Angel* Eugene Gant, born into a middle-class family in the city of Altamont in the mountains of Old Catawba, grows up, attends college at Pulpit Hill, then prepares to leave for a literary career in the northeastern United States. When *Of Time and the River* opens he is waiting with some members of his family at the railroad station for the train that will take him to Boston, where he will study playwriting at Harvard. His sister and mother gossip about others who await the train, and occasionally someone comes over to say hello. One such is George Pentland, the son of Will Pentland, Eugene's uncle. As we know from *Look Homeward, Angel*, Will Pentland has become very wealthy, and his son George detaches himself from "a group of young men and women who wore the sporting look and costume of 'the country club crowd'" to walk over and talk with the Gants. Eugene's mother has already made a remark about how George's mother considered the Pentland family "common." George Pentland tells Eugene that "'you'll be gettin' so educated an' high-brow here before long that you won't be able to talk to the rest of us at all.'" And the narrator tells us that "his speech had become almost deliberately illiterate, as if trying to emphasize the superior virtue of the rough, hearty, home-grown fellow in comparison with the bookish scholar."[1]

Next another young man turns up. We are told that he is wearing "a fine brown coat" and that he sports a Delta Kappa Epsilon fraternity key. This is Robert Weaver, the son of a judge. Eugene's mother declares that "'He's all right. . . . He's got good manners. . . . He looks and acts like a gentleman. . . . You can see he's had a good bringing up. . . . I like him!'" (19). His sister advises him to "'stick to people like that. . . . He looks like a nice boy and—' with an impressed look over toward Robert's friends, she concluded, 'he goes with a nice crowd. . . . You stick to that kind of people. I'm all for him'" (20).

The train arrives and the trip gets under way. That evening Eugene enters the smoker of the pullman car, where a group of Alta-mont businessmen are talking. One of them, the publisher of the local newspaper, recognizes Eugene. "'You're one of those Gant boys, ain't you?'" he asks. There is talk of Eugene's brothers. What is Steve doing? someone asks. Is he in business? "For a moment the boy was going to say, 'No, he runs a pool room and lives over it with his wife and children,' but feeling ashamed to say this, he said, 'I think he runs some kind of cigar store out there'" (44).

Then they talk about Luke Gant, and someone tells a story about Luke's youthful persistence as a magazine salesman in the streets of Altamont. After that there is talk of Eugene's brother Ben, who died several years earlier. The newspaper publisher recalls him ad-miringly as a former employee. Eugene remembers an occasion when Ben presented him with a gold watch, to keep time with: "'And I hope to God you keep it better than the rest of us! Better than Mama or the old man—better than me! God help you if you don't.'"

One of the men, a politician, then mentions Eugene's father, and specifically an occasion when W. O. Gant was supervising the un-loading of some blocks of marble and granite and some tombstones for his stonecutting shop. What impressed him, he says, was how well the elder Gant was dressed. "'He always wore his good clothes when he worked—I'd never seen a man who did hard labor with his hands who dressed that way. . . . Of course, he had his coat off, and his cuffs rolled back, and he was wearing one of those big striped aprons that go the whole way up over the shoulders—but you could see his clothes was good,' said Mr. Candler. 'Looked like black broadcloth that had been made by a tailor, and wearing a *boiled* shirt, mind you, and one of those wing collars with a black silk neck-tie—and not afraid to work, either'" (57).

A little later Robert Weaver shows up, along with two others, one of them a man named John Hugh William McPherson Marriott, who is "the younger son of an ancient family of the English nobility and just a year or two before he had married the great heiress, Virginia Willets." We are informed that the Altamont businessmen and oth-ers in the smoker are very much in awe of Marriott, for the Willets are immensely wealthy and live at a 90,000-acre estate near town, in "a huge stone structure modelled on one of the great châteaux of France," inside which few of the local folk had ever been invited. "To be a part of that life, to be admitted there, to know the people who belonged to it would have been the highest success, the greatest triumph that most of the people in the town could imagine. They could not admit it, but it was the truth" (61).

After everyone else except Eugene, Robert Weaver, and another youth, has left the smoker, Robert, we are told once again, "thrust one hand quickly and impatiently into the trousers' pocket of his well-cut clothes in such a way that his Delta Kappa Epsilon key was for a moment visible" (64). He begins teasing Eugene. "Do you know what they're saying about you at home. . . . Do you know what these people think of you?" (64). Eugene becomes quite upset, especially when told that one local woman has been praying for him because of the way he has supposedly been "going to the devil" since entering the state university. The three of them begin drinking, and they get very drunk. Later on, Eugene insists upon telling Robert something. I quote several portions of his conversation. "'You made a remark t'night I didn' like—Prayin' for me, are they, Robert? . . . Prayin' for me, are you?—Pray for yourself, y'bloody little Deke!'" (73).

It turns out, however, that what Eugene, his inhibitions removed by whiskey, really wants to chastise Robert Weaver for is not that remark, but something that had happened some years previously, when both had been students at a private school. Weaver, it seems, had been in the company of a number of other young people, and had remarked, upon encountering Eugene, "'Here's Mr. Gant the tomb-stone cutter's son.'" Weaver claims not to remember any such incident, but Eugene says, "'Yes, you do, you cheap Deke son-of-a-bitch—Too good to talk to us on the street when you were sucking around after Bruce Martin or Steve Patton or Jack Marriott—but a life-long brother—oh! couldn't see enough of us, could you, when you were alone?'"

He informs Robert Weaver that "my people were better people than your crowd ever hoped to be—we've been here longer and we're better people—and as for the tomb-stone cutter's son, my father was the best damned stonecutter that ever lived—he's dying of cancer and all the doctors in the world can't kill him—he's a better man than any little ex-police court magistrate who calls himself a judge will ever be—and that goes for you too—you—" (74).

The presence, and I think the significance, of the episode with Robert Weaver in Eugene's voyage northward to Harvard has not been properly noticed. The train trip from Altamont to the Northeast has generally been viewed, appropriately for the most part, as that of the outward-bound artist in quest of his destiny. Wolfe certainly saw it that way, as indicated by the narrator's remarks about its being the first occasion on which Eugene experienced an access of so-called Fury. He speculates on how the fury must have been present earlier in his life, but until then it had not been apprehended: "He never knew if fury had lain dormant all those years, had worked secret, silent, like a madness in his blood. But later it would seem to him that fury had first filled his life, exploded, conquered, and possessed him, that he first felt it, saw it, knew the dark illimitable madness of its power, one night years later on a train across Virginia" (30).

By *Fury* is obviously meant the impassioned, emotion-filled apprehension of his experience, which finds its literary expression in the kind of rhetorical evocation that characterizes the narrative method of much of *Of Time and the River*. The technique throughout is for the youthful Eugene to feel the "fury" and for the approving narrator to interpret how he felt. That the narrator, the authorial personality who tells us Eugene's story, is the somewhat older, remembering Eugene, is obvious.

Leaving Altamont for the Northeast, therefore, is the act which had first brought out into open consciousness his intense hunger for experience, for emotional fulfillment: and with this the intensity of the creative urge that ultimately led him to articulate and give form and meaning to its apprehension. In this sense the episode is similar to Stephen Dedalus' realization, while strolling along the shore, that instead of becoming a Jesuit father, he wishes to be a priest of the imagination of man and thus eventually write *A Portrait of the Artist as a Young Man*; or to the speaker's response to the bird in Whitman's "Out of the Cradle Endlessly Rocking":

> Never more the cries of unsatisfied love be absent from me,
> Never again leave me to be the peaceful child I was before
>   what there in the night,

By the sea under the yellow and sagging moon,
The messenger there arous'd, the fire, the sweet hell within,
The unknown want, the destiny of me.

What seems clear is that the apprehension and enunciation of the impulse toward artistic fulfillment, and the celebration of such fulfillment, are directly linked with the Robert Weaver episode and what it represents. For they happen almost simultaneously, in alternating and interwoven sequence. The drunkenness that enables Eugene Gant to express his long-cherished grudge against Robert Weaver is also what triggers the access of "Fury," as he calls it. In both instances, we must assume, the impulse had been present for some time; the whiskey merely released it into open consciousness and uninhibited assertion.

Thus if we place the outburst against Robert Weaver within the context of social detail of which it is the culmination, it seems obvious that the urge for artistic fulfillment is directly tied in with the prospect of liberation from the social snobbery and sense of caste and class, and his own position vis-á-vis them, within his home community. Eugene—the Eugene of that time, and the remembering narrator—resents the social hierarchy of Altamont. He resents being thought of merely as one of the Gant boys. He does not want to live in a community in which he is labeled as a stonecutter's son, even if that stonecutter does wear collar, tie, and protective apron when working with his hands. He resents the fact that his mother operates a boardinghouse—in *Look Homeward, Angel* she embarrassed him when she came to visit him at college by seeking to drum up trade among his friends. He resents the fact that Robert Weaver, unlike him, is a member of what Andrew Turnbull referred to as "the Asheville clique which qualified automatically for the old-line fraternities . . . the snobs who stared superciliously from the porches of fraternity row."[2] He resents his sister's penchant for social climbing. Later in the novel, when Gant is dying, Helen is made to gravitate instinctively toward the more socially distinguished of the townsfolk who come to pay their respects, and to tell herself that her father was not a working man but a businessman, a property owner. But then she realizes that W. O. Gant was indeed one who worked with his hands, and that his true friends were other working men who were also there, stonecutters, jewelers, plasterers, plumbers, building contractors, "men who had all their lives done stern labor with their hands, and who were really the men who had known the stone-cutter best, [and who] stood apart from the group of prominent and wealthy men who were talking so earnestly to Eliza" (248).

It seems to me that, particularly in the opening episodes of *Of Time and the River*, an unusually strong emphasis is being placed upon Eugene's awareness of considerations of caste and class; thus the admonition he remembers Ben having given him upon presentation of the watch, to make better use of his time than the others in the family have done, would appear to be a way of saying that Eugene must not allow himself to be entrapped within the materialism and petty social striving of the town. His furious wish to pursue an artistic career, therefore, is a way of fleeing from confinement within the values of that community.

The prospect of escape, of being an artist and achieving fame, fortune, and status upon his own, is tremendously exciting. Now that he is departing from Altamont he can begin by telling off Robert Weaver, just as later, in his writing, he can also begin paying off old scores with the community. (In *Look Homeward, Angel* we are told that "finally, it occurred to him that these people had given him nothing, that neither their love nor their hatred could injure him, that he owed them nothing, and he determined that he would say so, and repay their insolence with a curse. And he did."[3]

Yet if this is so, it would seem an anomaly that some of the best writing in *Of Time and the River*, as well as almost the entirety of *Look Homeward, Angel*, is set in and among those people, and however caustic the portraiture becomes at times, it is by no means without much affection for and joy in that town from which Eugene is so desperately escaping. For we must remember that not only are both *Look Homeward, Angel* and *Of Time and the River* inescapably autobiographical in form, involving the narrator's recall of the protagonist's life as a basic dimension of the telling, but also that in a real sense the second novel is a book about learning how to write the first. Clearly the Eugene who is riding the train north from Altamont is in no condition to begin writing anything resembling

Look Homeward, Angel. He is looking for fulfillment as an artist, all right; but he is also fleeing from involvement in a social situation that is so strident in its claims that the only thing he wants to do with it, the only response he wants to make, is to tell it off and put it behind him. Something will have to happen before he can begin to deal with it for the purposes of literary art. And what happens is the story related in *Of Time and the River.*

The drama workshop at Harvard is Eugene's first experience with Fashionable Culture—with life and work in a group supposedly dedicated to artistic activity. He is free at last of the provincial world of philistinism and social caste. But he finds his fellow *litterateurs* precious, mannered, effeminate. He feels ill at ease among the sophisticates of the drama at Harvard. He is unfamiliar with their ways of talking about literature and the arts. He considers them overrefined, ignorant of real life.

He does, however, form one close friendship, with Frank Starwick, who though of plebian origins like his own has adapted very well to the Harvard style of Culture. Starwick's sophistication, his offhand manner, his fashionable enthusiasms and even affectations are acceptable to Eugene, not because he would emulate them, but because they seem to go along with a considerable admiration for his own genius. Though living and flourishing among the aesthetes and pretenders, Starwick supposedly can recognize the genuine article when he sees it. Thus Eugene can entertain the hope that once he succeeds as a playwright he too will be honored, admired, valued in a world of devotees of art. He will find the Good Place, where he can know true literary and social fulfillment.

That place, however will not be Cambridge, with its ultrarefinement, its artificiality, its pseudoartistic fashionableness. Nor does he find the nonartistic inhabitants of Cambridge and Boston, the working-class Irish of a northern industrial city, any more compatible than the devotees of Culture. They are brutal, barren, ugly. He compares the Boston Irish with the Irish he had known back in Altamont; the Boston variety has "none of the richness, wildness, extravagance, and humor of such people as Mike Fogarty, Tom Donovan, or the MacReadys—the Irish he had known at home" (160).

Eugene's next stop, in order to earn his living by teaching while living close to the place where plays are produced and books published, is the city of American cities, New York. Here at the night school classes of the School for Utility Cultures he encounters another kind of people: urban Jews. Unlike the Boston Irish they are not sterile or brutal; they are filled with passion, and like him many of them are eager for literature, culture. But their ways are not his own; as a southern Protestant from the provinces he finds them alien and ugly. His xenophobia, his hatred and fear of the foreign, the strange, the different, comes to the forefront. Moreover, the Jews are very much at home in the city, whereas the massive impersonality of the metropolis, his sense of insignificance among its huge buildings and swarms of urban dwellers, brings him only frustration and futility. The Shining City of his youthful dreams of glory and fulfillment has become a place of spiritual and physical imprisonment, a charnel house: "Already he had come to see the poisonous images of death and hatred at work in the lives of a million people—he saw with what corrupt and venomous joy they seized on every story of man's dishonor, defeat, or sorrow, with what vicious jibe and jeer they greeted any evidence of mercy, honesty, or love" (421–22). The compacted impersonality, ugliness, and unfamiliarity of the city, as he now experiences it, is profoundly disturbing. Wherever the Good Place is, it is not New York City as he now knows it while working as an instructor in the School for Utility Cultures.

In the midst of his sojourn in the metropolis there comes an interlude in which he moves briefly from one social extreme to the other. He leaves the city for a visit to the Hudson River estate of his friend Joel Pierce's family. It is as if he had been abruptly transported to the fabulous Willets estate back in Altamont. He has never before known the life of the ultra-rich. The magnificence of the place, the extensive and costly library, the pantry stocked with the finest foods in lavish profusion, astonish him. From his bedroom he looks out upon the landscape by night, "a landscape such as one might see in dreams," and he is overwhelmed: "It seemed that all his life he had dreamed of one day finding such a life as this, and now that he had found it, it seemed to him that all he had dreamed was but a poor and shabby counterfeit of this reality—all he had imaged as a boy in his unceasing visions of the shining city, and of the glamorous men and women, the fortunate, good and happy life that he would find there, seemed nothing but a shadowy and dim prefigurement of the radiant miracle of this actuality" (539). That night he reads the play he has been writing to Joel Pierce and his sister, who listen intently and admiringly. Ultimately Joel invites him to stay in the gatekeeper's lodge of the estate and do his writing: "'It's no use to anyone the way it stands, and we'd all be delighted if you'd come and live in it'" (583).

At once Eugene declines the invitation. For despite his admiration for his friend and his enthrallment with the beauty of the setting and the comfort of their home and surroundings, he would be out of place there. He has the sense of a basic futility and triviality among those who are so rich that they need not work for a living, which, together with his awareness of the social injustice involved in the privilege attendant upon great wealth, makes him feel that a life among the very rich would not be sufficiently *real* for him: "It was a bitter pill to know that what had seemed so grand, so strong, so right and so inevitable at the moment of discovery was now lost to him—that some blind chemistry of man's common earth, and of his father's clay, and of genial nature, had taken from him what he seemed to possess, and that he could never make this enchanted life his own again, or ever believe in its reality" (571).

Moreover, despite his friends' admiration for his play, he knows that in such a place of enormous wealth and privilege, the talents of an artist, even a successful one, would count for comparatively little. Only wealth and family would confer status among the Hudson River aristocracy; such interest in art as he has seen there is that of the dilettante, the collector. The immense library of the house is crowded with fine books, in costly leather bindings and paper "white and soft and velvet to the touch"; but in that great house, amid "that proud power of wealth and the impregnable security of its position," books count for little: "All of the great poets of the earth were there, unread, unopened, and forgotten, and were somehow, terribly, the mute small symbols of a rich man's power" (588–89). So he gets aboard the New York City-bound train, listens to the banality of the chattering Jews and the foul anger of a drunken Irishman, and he returns to his hotel room in the metropolis.

Thus far we have seen the protagonist depart from the community in which he was born and grew up, wishing desperately to put behind him everything it seemed to symbolize in the way of materialism, caste and class, limitation. Intent upon becoming a writer he has gone first to Harvard and then to New York City. He has rejected the affectation and pose of the Fashionable Culture of the university, and found urban life as a teacher in the metropolis ugly and alien. His visit to a palatial estate on the river has convinced him of his inability and unwillingness to fulfill himself as man and artist among the very rich. So now he travels across the ocean to Europe.

First he visits England, where the poets and dramatists he has studied and loved once walked the earth; at Oxford "was the whole structure of an enchanted life—a life hauntingly familiar and just the way he had always known it would be" (611). But it too proves unreal, alien to him, "another door Eugene could not enter" (613). He lives in an English home, but cannot enter the lives of those who live there. He visits a group of Americans who are Rhodes scholars, and who profess to be rapturously at home at the English university—all except one man, a Jew from the Northeast, who much to Eugene's approval declares bluntly that *he* isn't at home at Oxford, that none of the others has been, and that " 'you can stay here for three years and none of [the English] . . . will ever give a tumble to you! You can eat your heart out for all they care, and when you leave here you'll know no more about them than when you came. . . . W'at t' hell do you get out of it that's so wonderful?' " (636).

So the Old Home, as the New England writers used to call it, the country of poets and literature, will not serve as the Good Place, and Eugene goes on to Paris. There is a period spent wandering about looking at pictures and places, sampling the coasts of Bohemia, and thinking about Literature and being a Literary Man. The report is in the form of journal entries—excerpts from a Diary of the Artist as a Young American, as it were—and is full of a painful self-consciousness.

A diary is the least coherent of literary forms; its only order and progression are chronological. James Joyce, in *A Portrait of the Art-*

ist as a Young Man, has Stephen Dedalus keep a diary, and gives it the effect of randomness while actually developing his story page by page. Eugene Gant's diary *is* random. Yet the randomness does serve a formal purpose, I think. Eugene Gant, the apprentice artist, has traveled all the way from the boardinghouse in Altamont to the City of Light, the place where Artists hold forth, where one can live in Montparnasse, the Latin Quarter, visit the Louvre, sip drinks at sidewalk cafés, go strolling along the Seine. The diary displays him trying to comport himself like a Man of Letters, have creative and critical opinions, compose literary anecdotes, meditate upon the nature of Art and Time, absorb the artistic atmosphere. His performance reeks of contrivance and artificiality. He is very much out of place, and absolutely without direction.

Then he encounters Frank Starwick, who is in Paris with two American women, and all changes. Eugene is very happy now, not only because he is among friends, but also because his companions know how to play the role of Americans in Paris: "The whole world became an enormous oyster ready to be opened, Paris an enormous treasure hoard of unceasing pleasure and delight" (692). But soon this too passes. Starwick, the brilliant man of sensibility and culture, of "rare and solitary distinction" (681), turns out to be a homosexual. Eugene for his part falls in love with one of the women, who will have none of him; both women are infatuated with Starwick. There are quarrels, ugly scenes, until finally Eugene, enraged at Starwick's petulant behavior and his selfishness, hurls him against a building. The next day there is an attempt at reconciliation, and in perhaps the most overwritten and embarrassing episode in the novel, Eugene bids his former friend farewell.

"You were my one true friend—the one I always turned to, believed in with unquestioning devotion. You were the only real friend that I ever had. Now something else has happened. You have taken from me something that I wanted, you have taken it without knowing that you took it, and it will always be like this. You were my brother and my friend—"

"And now?" said Starwick quietly.

"You are my mortal enemy. Good-bye." (783)

Robert Penn Warren declares that "the dialogue, the very rhythms of the sentences, and the scene itself, scream the unreality"; Starwick, he says, "is at the same time a social symbol and a symbol for a purely private confusion of which the roots are never clear."[4] John Peale Bishop comments that "what we have been told about Starwick from his first appearance in the book is that, despite a certain affection and oddness of manner, he is, as Eugene is not, a person capable of loving and being loved. What is suddenly revealed in Paris is that for him, too, love is a thing the world has forbidden. In Starwick's face Eugene sees his own fate."[5] The narrator's own explanation of Eugene's difficulties with Starwick, in the novel itself, is that "the feeling that Starwick would always beat him, always take from him the thing he wanted most, that by no means could he ever match the other youth in any way, was now overpowering in its horror" (780).

To these hypotheses I would add a fourth, which is that, as is pointed out several times, Starwick, like Eugene, has made his escape from an undistinguished middle-class provincial social situation, and has exemplified for Eugene the young man of taste and ambition who has won through to a cultural and social distinction that can replace those provided by wealth or social standing. To have him revealed as a homosexual and a shameless sponger off his friends seems to tell Eugene that—just as the middle-class citizenry of Altamont would assume—the only way to earn the friendship and admiration of those who are successful in the world of Culture that Starwick represents is at the cost of one's masculinity and personal integrity. Only a feminine sensibility like Starwick's, in other words, can exemplify the attitude toward the value and importance of artistic experience that Eugene finds so admirable; one cannot be a middle-class American male and a genuine artist at the same time. As George Pentland had warned, " 'You'll be gettin' so educated an' high-brow here before long that you won't be able to talk to the rest of us at all.' " *That* is what Eugene fears; it is what Starwick's emergence as a homosexual seems to confirm which is why he rages. (One might add that if this hypothesis is valid, then it only places Eugene Gant and his creator in the same social and cultural situation as Faulkner and Hemingway, in both of whom very much the same equation was at work.)

Why is Starwick Eugene's "mortal enemy"? The answer is that if Eugene Gant is ever to become the writer he intends to be, it will have to be by rejecting everything that Starwick seems to represent: which is to say, an art that seeks to escape from the terms, conditions, subject matter, and meanings of general American experience through avoiding them. For Starwick exemplifies, in Eugene's mind, the Man of Culture—a preference for George Moore's *Confessions of a Young Man* rather than the *Saturday Evening Post* and Booth Tarkington—and Starwick's homosexuality symbolizes what Eugene fears that Fashionable Culture, and a secure place within it, means: an art, and an existence as an artist, devoid of passion, vitality, reality. Thus when Eugene asserts his horror at the apparent fact that "by no means could he ever match the other youth in any way," what he means is that the approach to life that Starwick represents is what the literary world to which Eugene also aspires honors and rewards. The fact that the two women with whom he and Starwick have been touring France love Starwick and are not attracted to Eugene symbolizes for Eugene what he most dreads: that Starwick's aestheticism, his preciousness, his lack of masculine passion are what are expected of an artist. And the knowledge that he could never, either as writer or as member of fashionable literary society, fulfill that requirement, or want to, is what prompts him to hurl his erstwhile friend against the building and resume his wandering.

From what had become the nightmare of Paris Eugene departs for the French provinces. At Orléans he encounters an absurd little countess, who had traveled to America during the recently ended First World War to promote the war effort. To Eugene's astonishment she not only knows that Altamont exists; she has visited there, and her acquaintances include persons known to Eugene. She passes Eugene off as a correspondent for the New York *Times* in order to gain an invitation to the great château of the Marquis de Mornaye. "'Think what it means to me,'" she begs Eugene when he balks at the deception. "I am so poor, so miserable—for years I have waited for an opportunity to see this woman—it means so much to me, so little to you'" (847).

At the château the marquise showers Eugene with attention, feeds him a sumptuous meal, and proposes that he write—for a percentage of the profits—an article for the *Times* that will raise a large sum of money for a veteran's hospital. She also reveals herself as a monarchist, an implacable foe of democracy: "'Zere vill never be a France until ze kink is restored to his rightful office and zese creeminals and traitors 'ave been sent to ze guillotine vere zey belonk" (840). Mornaye too has a fine library, with fine bindings and costly editions, but the marquise does not read, and she has no more use for the modern French authors than for the political leaders of the Third Republic.

It is a comic episode—but in terms of what has happened thus far in *Of Time and the River* it is considerably more than random comedy. For the visit to Mornaye is also a parody of the visit to the Pierce estate on the Hudson River, even down to the splendid table fare and the magnificent but unread library. More than that, the château at Mornaye is precisely the kind of place upon which the Willets estate outside Altamont is modeled, and the little countess' burning desire to gain admission to it is on a par with that of the citizens of Altamont to be admitted to the Willets estate. And if Eugene Gant is at Mornaye on false pretenses, he had felt equally out of place at the Pierce estate, and would presumably feel so at the Willets' mansion as well.

In short, the episode at Mornaye is a vivid demonstration for Eugene of the absurdity of just those notions of caste and class that had helped make his situation at home seem so unpalatable. Here in a foreign province he encounters the real aristocracy, of which the Willets and the Pierces can only be pale copies; Mornaye is no imitation château made possible by great wealth earned in industrial America, but the genuine thing, the seat of centuries of aristocratic privilege. And what Eugene finds is the same materialism, social injustice, literary insensitivity, and snobbery that had impelled him northward from Altamont.

It is the final, comic perspective on what he has experienced. On the one hand, Eugene has learned to discount the falsely materialistic values of wealth and social status within his society. On the other he has discovered the incompatibility of his integrity as an artist with the life of a Fashionable Culture that eschews or sidesteps everyday American life; Paris has shown him that. In effect

Eugene Gant's European apprenticeship is now all but complete; in England, in Paris with Starwick, and now at Orléans and Mornaye he has learned to identify what he does not want or need, either as man or as artist.

The cycle of withdrawal and return has almost runs its course. Now "he had come at last to a place of quietness and pause; and suddenly he was like a desperate man who has come in from the furious street of life to seek sanctuary and repose in the numb stillness of a tomb" (857). In the old city of Tours he is filled with thoughts of home; he knows "the impossible, hopeless, incurable and unutterable homesickness of the American, who is maddened by a longing for return, and does not know to what he can return" (857–58). What he now sees and hears in the French provinces, following all he has experienced in Europe and in America, can provide him with the key to the door, the access to the texture of the life he had known at home.

In good Proustian fashion he now receives a series of signs. He hears a church bell ringing, and is reminded of the bell that rang for classes at college in Pulpit Hill. Inhabitants of the town walk by the café where he is seated, "and suddenly he was a child, and it was noon, and he was waiting in his father's house to hear the slam of the iron gate, the great body stride up the high porch steps, knowing his father had come home again" (897). An automobile speeds through the town square; he thinks of the gay blades of Altamont, boasting of their sexual prowess as they lounge outside a drugstore: "Then, for a moment there was a brooding silence in the square again, and presently there began the most lonely, lost and unforgettable of all sounds on earth—the solid, liquid, leather-shuffle of footsteps going home one way, as men had done when they came home to lunch at noon twenty years ago, in the green-gold and summer magic of full June, before he had seen his father's land, and when the kingdoms of this earth and the enchanted city still blazed there in the legendary magic of his boyhood vision" (898). It is only then that he begins to write his book.

If the "fury" passage in the train sequence at the outset of *Of Time and the River* is in effect the assumption of the artistic vocation, then this sequence, near the close, announces the discovery, there in the town of Dijon in southern France, of the true substance of what that art must be. It will be his memory: *his* America, the experience of *his* childhood in Old Catawba. That older time is gone now, and, he says, "drowned beneath the brutal flood-tide, the fierce stupefaction" (898) of modern industrial urban society. What remains is "a suddenly living and intolerable memory, instant and familiar as all this life around him, of a life that he had lost, and that could never die" (898).

In other words, he will write about the stuff of his childhood: Altamont, his family, his early years. But it should be noted that what is "drowned" beneath the "flood-tide" and "brutal stupefaction" of modern America is not the town itself, or even the ways of the town; rather, it is *his* experience of it. He is the one who has gone out into the urban life of the Northeast; what has been lost is what that life had been for him as a child. Thus what he recalls and will be writing about is not merely that early experience as such, but also and crucially the experience of growing up and therefore away from it. His book will be structured by the passage of time, and imbued with the dimension of change. His art will be its recovery; he will find his fulfillment as an artist through the recapture, in language, of what he has known and been.

At last he has escaped from the domination of that experience *as life*—as that which had compelled him as a child and as a young adult to respond to it in certain compulsive ways, act out a certain role, attempt to deny important aspects of his own identity. He can begin to recreate it on his own terms, which is to say, to discover its meaning as art. But it will not be the art of nostalgia, for the perspective from which he can now view his early experience is through, and *as*, change. To recreate it will be to show it as structured by time, and his experience of time.

To be a writer, then, is not to search for escape from the life he has known into a Good Place where Being an Artist is possible for the protagonist. What happens at the close of *Of Time and the River*, with the protagonist alone and beginning to write, in the southern provinces of a foreign land in so many ways reminiscent of his origins and yet inescapably alien, is that he realizes that he will find his true milieu and ambiance as a writer not in playing a role as Sensitive Artist in an appropriate social setting, but in re-creation of his own middle-class experience, the life he has known, in language. He has learned that the pretense of trying to find the Good Place was "always to seek the magic skies, the golden clime, the wise and lovely people who would transform him. . . .always to seek in the enchanted distances, in the dreamy perspectives of a fool's delusions, the power and certitude he could not draw out of himself." It was within himself that his art was to be found. " 'The place to write' was Brooklyn, Boston, Hammersmith, or Kansas—anywhere on earth, so long as the heart, the power, the faith, the desperation, the bitter and unendurable necessity, and the naked courage were there inside him all the time" (835).

So, just as Stephen Dedalus can think himself into being an Artist but must learn how to view his relationship to his own human ex-periences in order to become a writer, so Eugene Gant is ready now to go back home to America. As he boards the ship that will take him there, he sees for the first time a woman, who, he tells us, is to become his lover, and that "from that moment on he never was again to lose her utterly, never to wholly re-possess unto himself the lonely, wild integrity of youth which had been his" (911).

This is what "happens" in *Of Time and the River*. I have sought to show that, rather than being merely an overwritten rhetorical evocation of the alienated American artist who discovers his love for his homeland while in a foreign country, it has a quite specific and articulated social context, and develops a very definite pattern involving the discovery of a perspective from which to view his ex-perience so that he can use it as a writer rather than merely be-ing used by it as a man. In Aristotelian terms, this is its "plot," its structure.

But there is more to *Of Time and the River* than this. As noted, it is related to us by a remembering author, who not only describes what Eugene Gant is doing and thinking, but often addresses him-self directly to the reader. And here we get into trouble. For a great deal of what that older narrator has to say about the meaning of Eugene Gant's experience is less than entirely convincing as an interpretation of that experience. Indeed, many of the most over-written, least credible sections of *Of Time and the River* are not those in which Eugene's experience is being described, but those in which that remembering narrator is directly speaking to us. The truth is that the authority with which the story is told to us is, if anything, diminished by that narrator's direct utterance, and is strongest when he is recreating the social texture rather than pronouncing the imaginative meaning of Eugene's actual experience. We feel quite often that the narrator is attempting to force upon the remembered experience a significance in excess of what it actually embodies. And in the worst-written episode in the novel, that involving Eugene's break with Starwick, the perspectives merge so that the youthful Eugene and the somewhat older remembering narrator are as one: action and interpretation, dialogue and rhetoric are fused into histrionics. All distance between the naïve youth and the supposedly more mature narrator disappears.

Consider, then, what we have. On the one hand *Of Time and the River* is a novel that describes, in detail and often with considerable wisdom, Eugene Gant's discovery of the perspective for creating his art. To write the literature he wants to write, he must divest himself of the social and cultural compulsions of his middle-class American background, without also losing his passionate commitment to the texture and meaning of his own experience. We observe the stages of this process of discovery, which will permit the recapture of the past as an aesthetic act. On the other hand, it is a novel in which the narrator's relation to his autobiographical protagonist is all too often without proper artistic distance, so that it develops into hyperbolic self-celebration and self-justification. How can these conflicting dimensions—the move toward artistic maturity, the assertive denial of it—exist within the same work?

For coexist they do, and without destroying the work containing them. The explanation I would propose is that in this story about a young man searching for a way to tell his own story, the intensity of his attempt at self-definition and self-discovery is such that we will accept him, warts and all, even when he seems absurdly and histrionically confused about what his own experience means. For the best sections of this novel are so very good, so beautifully and honestly rendered, that very early on we become convinced of the basic integrity of this young man's talent, and thereafter, no matter how vexed at his clumsiness and recurrent failure at self-under-standing we may become, we do not doubt either the sincerity of his quest or the rightful importance that he places upon learning how to use what he knows. When he fails it is because he is unable to give the young Eugene Gant's experience the significance that as remembering author he feels it should have, and not because he is pretending to a significance and importance that he does not him-self really believe is there.

In the hands of a more disciplined writer, Eugene Gant's discovery of the true perspective for his vocation as an American writer might have been related with considerably less fustian and loose rhapso-dizing. But a more disciplined, more restrained writer might never have told this story in the first place. A less egocentric and romantic author would have trained upon the Sturm und Drang of the youth-ful Eugene a mocking irony that would doubtless have made it im-possible for us to view Eugene Gant's particular quest in other than satiric terms. And that, no matter how literarily more acceptable, would be to falsify it. For it seems to me that Thomas Wolfe, more so than any other American writer I have read, was engaged totally and wholeheartedly in writing *about* the intensity with which an incipient young author such as himself apprehended his experience. And it was not only his authorial stance; it was his actual subject matter. It may well be, as Robert Penn Warren said, that his per-formance demonstrates "the limitation, perhaps the necessary lim-itations, of an attempt to exploit directly and naively the personal experience and the self-defined personality in art."[6] But has anyone else ever tried just that with anything like the degree of Wolfe's success?

It seems to me of more than merely descriptive interest that Eu-gene Gant is a young American from the provinces. For in terms of what happens in the novel he is engaged in doing what many American authors have done, but no others have written about in just that way. He is not only moving toward a point at which he can attain an aesthetic perspective upon his experience, but engaged in the discovery of a cultural and social perspective for an American writer who would understand his place within American life; and this is his *theme*. To aid him in this attempt he has available to his imagination no such richly delineated religious tradition as was James Joyce's by right of birth, no lucidly defined intellectual and literary heritage such as the young Marcel Proust found around him, against which to measure the intensity and authority of his imagination. He had to do it all for himself.

Needless to say, this has been a problem for the American author from the early nineteenth century onward. Melville's invocation to the muse in *Moby-Dick*—"if then to meanest mariners, and renegates and castaways, I shall hereafter ascribe high qualities, though dark; weave round them tragic graves"—is a statement of the issue, as is Hawthorne's preface to *The House of the Seven Gables*, and James's discourse upon Hawthorne and upon the "complex fate" of the American. The lines that open "Song of Myself,"

> I celebrate myself, and sing myself,
> And what I shall assume you shall assume,
> For every atom belonging to me as good belongs to you,

are a succinct enunciation of where the transaction must take place. Mark Twain, for whom the problem was a lifelong artistic preoccupation, humorously suggests its implications in *Huckleberry Finn* when the Duke and the Dauphin put together their Shakespearean monologue. John Crowe Ransom confronts it in his remarks in "Philomela" upon the literary nightingale:

> Not to these shores she came! this other Thrace,
> Environs barbarous to the royal Attic;
> How could her delicate dirge run democratic,
> Delivered in a cloudless boundless public place
> To an inordinate race?

And so on. But with Thomas Wolfe, precisely because of the egocentric intensity of his talent, the problem becomes an overt theme, the shaping experience of plot and characterization. What is remarkable may not be that much of it is overwritten and full of imprecision and exaggeration, but that so much of it *is* apprehended. That Wolfe could, however awkwardly and unevenly, invest Eugene Gant's experience with so much form and passion is really quite astonishing.[7] By all the truths of aesthetic distancing and necessary authorial detachment, no one, working with Wolfe's assumptions and attitudes, should have been able to make literary sense of such experience; yet Wolfe does it again and again. And it is that success, however flawed, that gives an authority to the autobiographical protagonist's search that finally validates it, when all the remembering narrator's efforts to do so through emotive rhetorical assertion cannot do so.

There is a problem of fictional form here that the terms one normally uses seem unable to encompass. This is, that the contrast between the powerfully rendered account of the young Eugene Gant's experience, and the attempts of the narrator intermittently to force inappropriate or excessive meanings upon that experience, seems to set up a kind of autobiographical tension within the fiction, an artistic crisis, the resolution of which makes the best episodes in *Of Time and the River* extraordinarily authentic and helps validate the overall shaping as well. Maybe this is what Wright Morris meant when he remarked that "if one desires what one cannot have, if one must do what one cannot do, the agony in the garden is one of self-induced impotence. It is Wolfe's tragic distinction to have suffered his agony for us all."[8] Yet it must also be obvious that the romantic agony was, however imperfectly, made into art, since otherwise it would not be available to us as readers. It succeeds as language, as fiction; which is why one would not willingly part with *Of Time and the River*.

Allen Tate, 1899–1979

Allen Tate was born in Winchester, Clark County, Kentucky, on November 19, 1899. He died early on the morning of February 9, 1979, in Nashville, Tennessee, where he had moved several years earlier, and where more than half a century earlier he had been a student at Vanderbilt University. The journey of seventy-nine years, from Winchester to Nashville, and back finally to Nashville again, involved stops in New York City; Clarksville and Sewanee, Tennessee; Greensboro, North Carolina; Princeton, New Jersey; and Minneapolis, Minnesota. It encompassed a vocation as poet, critic, essayist, novelist, editor, teacher. He was, and he considered himself to be, a Man of Letters in the Modern World. It was a vocation that he did not dishonor: it involved a literary dignity that was never compromised.

To depict and assess the place of Allen Tate in the literary life of his day is a difficult task. In inviting me to write the obituary for the magazine that Tate himself edited for two distinguished years, the present editor of the *Sewanee Review* has bestowed both a notable privilege and a thorny assignment. Though never an intimate friend, I knew Tate for more than a quarter-century, and I admired him tremendously. When I wrote something that he liked, as occasionally I was able to do, his praise meant more to me than anyone else's. Toward the end we became estranged—an experience in which I was by no means alone. One result was that when last spring I published a critical book entitled *The Wary Fugitives: Four Poets and the South*, in which he was the central figure, he sent me a note in which he declared that I had unduly restricted his work and his identity to the South—this despite his having read in manuscript every word that I had written. A week later came another note: he had now read the entire book, he said, and he wished to withdraw his earlier criticism. I did not answer either communication; what was there to say?

He was human, sometimes very much so indeed. He cared, toward the end perhaps overly so, about his renown. The author of the "Ode to the Confederate Dead," "Tension in Poetry," and *The Fathers* need scarcely have concerned himself about an ultimate place in literary history. The matter was more complex than that, however. For during the height of his career as Man of Letters (not as poet; that came a little earlier), in the 1940s and 1950s, Allen Tate was a major and formidable presence on the American literary scene. His word could get books of poetry published, procure fellowships, set up literary awards and secure financial grants, arrange reviews, and assure academic appointments. There was no more influential presence in the province of poetry. Allen was quite able and willing to exercise such power, almost always for the best of ends. He liked to arrange things. To young poets and critics he could be generosity incarnate; to older friends he was the one who could be counted upon to help when aid was needed. And—I want to stress this—the enormous leverage he could and often did exert was never, to my knowledge, employed on behalf of Allen Tate himself. I do not wish to say that it was selfless, for he liked to be known as one who could help; but neither was it selfish. Very little of the largesse he was able to help distribute ever rubbed off on him; he died a relatively poor man. Had he wanted to, he could have done very well for himself; but then he would not have been Allen Tate.

No one can seriously contend that Allen's role in the literary firmament of his day was ultimately other than salubrious and beneficial. He detested sham and despised mediocrity, and whatever he wrote and did was designed to reward merit and encourage genuine talent. He was a partisan for craftsmanship; he was a *force* for *good*.

I go into such matters because when the history of letters in our time—not just what was being written, but how and under what circumstances it got published and received—is told and assessed, Allen's tremendously formative and useful role is likely to be slighted and even misunderstood. What gets recorded about such doings often takes the form of resentment on the part of those who feel improperly appreciated, or who are jealous of power however generously exercised. When in the early 1960s a new literary generation arose, and new fashions in writing poetry and criticizing it came into vogue—when, one might say, the Age of Eliot and Tate gave way to the Age of Pound and Bly—Allen Tate, and what he represented and did, tended to become the target of ambitious would-be literary regicides; he seemed to embody what they learned to call the Poetry Establishment. I know that Allen resented it, that he felt frustration in the waning of his role, and so clung, too anxiously perhaps but understandably, to what emblems and trappings of his earlier authority still remained. Now it is over; may those who succeed to his hegemony be able to say, when in their turn they are eased out, that they accomplished half as much good, and recognized and aided one-fourth as many of the meritorious and deserving, as Allen did.

It is highly ironic, if perhaps inevitable, that Allen came in his later years to symbolize, for some of the newer literary generation, a conservative "Establishment" (to use again a word that he despised). For Allen Tate was no literary conservative; he was a radical literary revolutionary. In the 1930s, in protest against the literary Marxists, he used the word *reactionary* to describe his stance. I don't care for the term, in that both politically and socially it connotes entrenched privilege and repressive bigotry; and these were alien to everything he was in the republic of letters. In any event he came onto the literary scene in the mid-1920s as practitioner and partisan of modernity in verse, the intellectually rigorous and emotionally genuine in contemporary poetry; his enemy was loose logic, shifty moralizing, evasive expediency, diffuse sentimentality in poetry and in writing about poetry. Very early he discovered T. S. Eliot, and thereafter his admiration for Eliot and his work remained intense. There is no discounting the influence of Eliot's poetry and criticism on Allen's work; but he made them his own. Though Allen imitated, he was not an imitative poet; what he admired he took into his own substance.

His other master, as he liked to say, was John Crowe Ransom, his teacher at Vanderbilt and fellow Fugitive poet and Agrarian polemicist. All his life he was fascinated by the personality of John Ransom. They became close friends, and yet it is fair to say, I think, that it was an intense literary and professional rather than personal friendship. For Ransom, with all his humor and kindness, was an elusive and reticent figure who kept his inmost feelings and ambitions hidden, while Allen Tate was anything but these. In the early 1920s there was for a brief time a quarrel. Allen has depicted himself as the callow impetuous youth who was solely responsible; doubtless he was those things to an extent, but I believe that the older poet was by no means innocent either. In any event it was soon patched up. A literary friendship and critical collaboration resulted that over the course of the next several decades was enormously formative and creative. It continued almost until Ransom's death; one of the last literary essays that Ransom wrote was a reassessment of "Gerontion," intended for the Eliot memorial issue of this magazine that Allen edited.

Whereas John Ransom's creative years as a poet were principally those of the early 1920s, Allen did much of his best work in poetry later in that decade and in the early 1930s. As a fledgling poet he had published a great deal of verse in the *Fugitive* and elsewhere, of which he chose, rightly, to preserve little in book form. But with the "Horatian Epode to the Duchess of Malfi" (1922) he began to formulate his true style. The poems in *Mr. Pope and Other Poems* (1928), *Poems: 1928–1931* (1932), and *Selected Poems* (1937) constitute the major part of his best verse. There are also the four-part "Seasons of the Soul," written during the Second World War, and the three poems in terza rima that appeared in the early 1950s, which he announced at the time as parts of a long work but which he came to treat as if they were individual poems. The body of Allen's poetry, therefore, is slim—as slim as Eliot's and Ransom's. He published one novel, *The Fathers* (1938). A remarkable work, it was never widely popular; but like Allen's best poetry, it remains in print, and I think it is destined to last.

Why did one so greatly and variously gifted write and publish so little? What he said of his friend John Ransom was not, I think, true of him: that he set out deliberately to be a Minor Poet (I am not sure it held for Ransom, either). My observation is that as an imaginative writer Allen had a gift that was highly and intricately autobiographical. This may seem odd, in that his poetics placed a premium upon achieved anonymity, classical restraint, the primacy of craftsmanship over subject—the antithesis of the romantic subjective artist whose work is the fervent unmediated outpouring of his own sensibilities. "As a poet I have no experience," he once remarked. Yet—and perhaps the paradox is the key—almost all that Allen wrote is drawn either directly from his own situation or from that of his immediate forebears. He used to speak of himself as having conducted his education in public, and if by that statement he meant that his writings consisted of his openly enunciated response to his own experience, it is quite appropriate.

As poet and critic Allen had impeccable taste. His literary coat of arms might well have borne the motto *nil admirari*—to be astonished at and by nothing. So fastidious was his literary sensibility that he could not tolerate blemish or imperfection, and this habit of mind no doubt served to lessen, or at any rate to restrict, his response to much work that was flawed but powerful. But whatever he admired was well worth the admiring, and he was almost never wrong in his enthusiasms. I believe that this fastidiousness was what inhibited him from publishing or even continuing to work for very long on anything of his own that did not seem absolutely right to him. His sensibility and his taste were whole and unified; had it been otherwise, he might have written more. Again, though, he would not have been Allen Tate. What he did write is not merely distinguished: it is unique in its distinction.

Allen's almost lifelong involvement with the South must bulk large in any estimate of his life and art. His mother was a Virginian by birth, related to the northern Virginia squirearchy but come upon greatly reduced circumstance. His father was a Kentuckian whose antecedents were of the plain folk. His own childhood, from the account in his brief but stunning memoir of his early years, was largely unhappy. His parents became estranged; he was moved about from place to place—"We might as well have been living, and I been born, in a tavern at a cross-roads," he declared. His mother was overly protective, but he was physically frail and the object of considerable bullying. He was precociously well read, and when he arrived at Vanderbilt he came into his own, evolving swiftly into poet, campus *bon vivant*, fraternity man, man about town. He recognized his vocation early; he was to be a writer, an intellectual. Overnight, almost, he transformed himself into the professional man of letters.

Allen lacked the solid grounding in a stable family and community experience that the other Fugitives inherited. Decades later John Ransom wrote revealingly of Allen's tenure at Vanderbilt in terms of its impermanence: "Allen had a mission in Tennessee which he was ten years discharging, during his intermittent residence with us." Upon graduation he headed for New York City, was married, earned a precarious livelihood as critic and reviewer, and set about building a career and a reputation. In 1928 he went to Europe, and when in 1930 he returned, it was not to New York City but to Clarksville, Tennessee. In the late 1920s he had become involved in the South and in Agrarianism, and when he came back he was making an ideological as well as a geographical commitment. He was, indeed, looking for his home.

Years after the Agrarian venture, in 1950, as a recent convert to Roman Catholicism, Allen wrote: "As I look back upon my own verse, written over more than twenty-five years, I see plainly that its main theme is man suffering from unbelief; and I cannot suppose that this man is some other than myself." At about the same time he wrote as follows about his involvement in Agrarianism: "What I had in mind twenty years ago, not too distinctly, I think I see more clearly now; that is, the possibility of the humane life presupposed, with us, a prior order, the order of a unified Christendom." I cite both these comments because I believe that Allen's years of intense imaginative engagement in matters southern represented, for him, the assertion, intellectually and emotionally, of a desire to be part of a human community with roots in the past and a present-day involvement in institutions and beliefs, and that the movement away from Agrarianism and toward Catholicism constituted not a break with but an extension and continuity of belief and impulse. He felt earlier that he had been robbed of such involvement by American history; his protagonist in *The Fathers*, Lacy Buchan, who I believe would have represented a great-uncle of the author, spoke for him: "Is it not something to tell, when a score of people whom I knew and loved, either out of violence in themselves or the times, or out of some misery or shame, scattered into the new life of the modern age where they cannot even find themselves?" How to regain that lost consciousness of identity in time and place? In his essay in *I'll Take My Stand* he asserted that to regain his tradition the modern southerner must proceed by violence—by a self-conscious act of the will. Such was the fulcrum of his involvement in Agrarianism; certainly he never believed in it as a practical mode of action. We could say that Agrarianism did not, finally, work out for him in his new life, and that instead he moved on into the church. But to put the matter in these terms is to miss the point that what, as poet and novelist, Allen Tate was in search of was a theme, not an answer, and that for ten years and more he achieved it—and that thereafter, though he sought to extend its implications, he never saw any need to abandon it.

Of Allen's Catholicism I am not qualified to judge. His friend Robert Heilman declared once that Allen was "the most protestant of Catholics"—and I think I understand the psychological point being made. I do know this: that Allen Tate never mistook theology, however intensely felt, for literature. His instinctive response to the problem of theology and literature was identical to that of Agrarianism and literature: it was that contained in Yeats's injunction: "Irish poets, learn your trade,/Sing whatever is well made." I think that Allen's conversion to Roman Catholicism was desperate, wholly sincere, and intense—and that it also was an act of violence. (Others will disagree with both my conclusion and my premises.)

As a literary critic Allen, like many other poets, was active and assertive. "I never knew what I thought about anything until I had written about it," he once wrote. "To write an essay was to find out what I thought; for I did not know at the beginning how or where it would end." Clearly this is not quite true: there is too much consistency in Allen's critical judgment to be accounted for by any such haphazard procedure. It would be more accurate, perhaps, to say that he wrote his criticism to identify and formulate what he felt— that, like Wordsworth, Coleridge, and his master Eliot, he wrote about literature, and sometimes edited it for publication, in order to instruct his audience in how to read the literature which he admired and championed, including his own. My own belief is that he possessed the most brilliantly conceptual mind of his generation of poet-critics, and that, had he elected to do so, he could have produced a body of critical work such as no other critic in the English language, not even Johnson, Coleridge, or Brooks, ever evolved. He did not choose to do so, and for some of the same reasons that I proposed earlier about his poetry and fiction. I know that in the particular field of critical scholarship with which I am most familiar, that involving southern literature, he produced, casually and in passing, insights and observations that lesser intellects (including my own) have since laboriously developed into books.

We shall not be able to replace Allen Tate. We have the poetry, the novel, the essays; but as he declared of another poet,

> he who dribbled couplets like a snake
> Coiled to a lithe precision in the sun
> Is missing.

In the sixty years during which Allen played his role on the literary scene, those whom he affected, almost inevitably for the better, found him indispensable. I shall name only a few: Ransom, Davidson, Warren, Brooks, Lytle, Lowell, Rahv, Read, Blackmur, Berryman, Crane, Cowley, Nemerov, Mizener, Bishop, Dickey, Shapiro, Wilson, Tolson, Van Doren, Wright, Hecht, Spears, Fergusson. And numerous other writers. I can speak for one, of a considerably lesser order. For thirty years he was the man to whom I looked most for approval, and whom, as writer, I chose as model. God knows he had his faults, but he was worthy of one's esteem. His children will be able to hold their heads higher because he was their father. He was for me, simply (and with much complexity), a hero, the bravest man I ever knew. "Around a crooked tree / A moral climbs whose name should be a wreath."

Flannery O'Connor's Company of Southerners
Or, "The Artificial Nigger"
Read as Fiction Rather Than Theology

A hallmark of Flannery O'Connor's fine art of fiction is the observation of the Georgia plain folk. She knew how they talk and how they think. She could pick up the incongruities that make for comedy and reproduce them, down to the most delicate perception of voice and gesture. That, at least as much as her theological insight, is what made her an important writer.

Such at any rate is my bias. It is not, I am afraid, a particularly popular one among so many admirers of Flannery's work. There has grown up in recent years a kind of cult, made up principally of well-bred young acolytes who regret the fall of Richmond in 1865 and the Fall of Man some years earlier than that, and Flannery's fiction has been used principally as a weapon for belaboring the heathen—the heathen including most of us who must traffic with the post-Reformation world. It is against this tendency in Flannery O'Connor criticism that the present paper is directed.

In "The Artificial Nigger" Mr. Head and his grandson Nelson, having become lost and separated in Atlanta, receive directions to the train station, and on the way they come upon a cement lawn statue of a Negro:

> The two of them stood there with their necks forward at about the same angle and their shoulders curved in almost exactly the same way and their hands trembling identically in their pockets. Mr. Head looked like an ancient child and Nelson like a miniature old man. They stood

gazing at the artificial Negro as if they were faced with some great mystery, some monument to another's victory that brought them together in their common defeat. They could both feel it dissolving their differences like an action of mercy. Mr. Head had never known before what mercy was like because he had been too good to deserve any, but he felt he knew now. He looked at Nelson and understood that he must say something to the child to show that he was still wise and in the look the boy returned he saw a hungry need for that assurance. Nelson's eyes seemed to implore him to explain once and for all the mystery of existence.

Mr. Head opened his lips to make a lofty statement and heard himself say, "They ain't got enough real ones here. They got to have an artificial one."

The incongruity lies in the distance between the significance of the emotion and the expressive form it takes. Mr. Head's response to the situation is trite and immediate. What he has seen is so awe-inspiring that he does not know how to express what he feels. His recourse is to sarcasm, a desperate, defensive attempt at bravado. He masters the situation, but just barely. Here Flannery draws upon one of the oldest devices of southern humor: the contrast of the literary language of culture and the vernacular language of uneducated speech. It goes all the way back to William Byrd II and the *Secret History of the Dividing Line*.

No one could have written such a passage without a great love for the kind of people she is writing about. Equally, no one could have written such a passage without a notable distance from the way such people think and feel and talk. It is a passage of great sophistication, and like the old southwestern humor, it was designed to be read not by the "good country people" being described but by a sophisticated audience.

I mention all this not only because Flannery O'Connor's humor too often goes unremarked, but also because it seems to me that the bulk of critical commentary on her work is almost uniquely shaped so as to ignore the *literary* excellence of so much of the fiction. O'Connor criticism is usually not an expression of literary taste but of theological allegiance. It concentrates upon the religious authenticity of her fiction. It is thematic, not formal criticism. As such it sidesteps or obscures so much that is central to her literary art. Properly speaking, it is not really interested in the author's literary imagination at all. It is next to useless in helping the reader to understand the human texture of this intensely southern author's work. So far as a great deal of the critical commentary on Flannery O'Connor's fiction is concerned, one might as well be dealing with *Pilgrim's Progress* or the book of *Jeremiah*.

In so saying, of course, I enter onto contested terrain. The dispute is at least as old as Plato and Aristotle, whose delineations of the basic critical stances are still pretty much authoritative. And the issue is further confused by the fact that when Flannery herself wrote about the art of fiction as she saw and practiced it, it was most often in terms of its religious dimension. A statement such as "I have found, in short, from reading my own writing, that my subject in fiction is the action of grace in territory largely held by the devil"—such a statement is theological and not literary. Or more accurately, such a statement isolates from the complex entity of fiction a single aspect of the work of art, its thematic concern, and appears to assert that in writing her fiction Flannery was exclusively concerned with its religious significance.

The fact is, however, that that is not what the statement really says at all, and in other remarks she has made about her high art—remarks that I am sorry to say seem to be less heeded by many of her admirers than her strictly theological pronouncements—she has been at pains to indicate that to write good fiction is to concern oneself with people in time and place, not with religious revelation as such. Literally, what Flannery was asserting was that when, having written her fiction, she then looked back at what she had created, she was able to recognize the religious dimensions implicit in the work. She called this her "subject"—and it would have been more accurate, I think, if she had chosen another word, such as "theme." For in a story such as "The Artificial Nigger," for example, her "subject" is an old man and his grandson who catch an early morning train to Atlanta, walk about the city and get lost, and what transpires before and after they get back on the train and return to their home in the Georgia countryside. Elsewhere she has asserted that "it is the free act, the acceptance of grace particularly, that I always have my eye on as the thing which will make my story work," and that in the story in question "it is what the artificial nigger does to reunite Mr. Head and Nelson." Such things, she says, "*represent* the working of grace for the characters" (italics mine). The difficulty with so much that is written about Flannery O'Connor's work is that it blithely ignores the word *represent* there, and leaps forward to deal exclusively with the problem of the "the working of grace for the characters," just as if there was absolutely no representation of reality, no fictional artistry involved—as if all the critic need do is to discover and identify the religious significance imbedded in the text. I quote from one such commentary, describing the meaning of the discovery of the statue of the Negro for Mr. Head and his grandson: "Suiting Mr. Head's character, the explanation is given in terms of his fear and scorn of Negroes and of city people who live with them. But at a deeper level, of which he is certainly not conscious, it also scorns those who make idols of man's own broken nature, and increase man's suffering." What has happened there? Simply that a great vaulting leap has been executed, in which we have left the firm ground of two Georgia country folk staring at a lawn ornament and have attained the cloudy and speculative realm of religious homiletics. The literal, everyday social context of Mr. Head's response is only there accidentally, because it "suits" his character. The "deeper level" is where the critic's intention properly belongs. Mr. Head, in short, is no more than a symbol, and even that is a bit too concrete—to make a pun—for what the critic seems to see him as being; a transparent figure of allegory would be more like it. Mr. Head and his grandson are no longer human beings who in their implications *represent* two fallen human beings reunited before the awareness of a mystery; the concrete lawn ornament no longer *represents* the working of grace. They are made to become their theological signification; the lawn ornament is itself the emblem of grace, which is asking too much of a lawn ornament in Atlanta, Georgia. In so doing, what is abandoned is the fictional terrain, the Georgia scene, the two countrymen, the concrete lawn statue of a Negro eating a watermelon in the suburbs of Atlanta. It is no longer a short story but the parable of a religious experience that we are reading. And the usefulness of a religious parable, needless to say, is not to be judged by its faithfulness to human complexity as such, but by its efficacy in bringing the believer into the presence of God: in short, its theological efficacy.

It is instructive to keep in mind Jean-Paul Sartre's critique of one of François Mauriac's less successful novels: "M. Mauriac has . . . chosen divine omniscience and omnipotence. But novels are written *by* men and *for* men. In the eyes of God, Who cuts through appearances and goes beyond them, there is no art, for art thrives on appearances. God is not an artist. Neither is M. Mauriac." As to which is the better artist I happen to prefer François Mauriac to Jean-Paul Sartre, and Flannery O'Connor at her best to either, but in this particular argument M. Sartre has got the advantage of M. Mauriac. And if we think that Flannery O'Connor violates Sartre's admonition in "The Artificial Nigger"—which if we are to judge by so much of the criticism of her work she most certainly does—we might look again at just exactly what it was that she said: "It is the free act, the acceptance of grace particularly, that I always have my eye on as *the thing which will make my story work*" (again, italics mine). Note the priority there: the act of grace, the representation of a religious experience, is to be used to make the short story, the work of fiction, function as art. The premises of criticism such as that I have quoted would seem to assume the reverse: that Flannery was writing the fiction in order to show the act of grace working. That is what a theologian might do; it is not what an artist such as Flannery O'Connor sought to do in her best fiction. And it follows, I think, that if the artistic quality of the work of fiction is dependent upon the quality of the *representation* of the reality it depicts, not upon the reality itself, then the proper appreciation of Flannery O'Connor as a literary artist must lie in an appreciation of her representation—which is to say, her people, her depiction of the time and place she writes about, the thick and rich texture of her fiction.

What I propose to do is to speak out for Flannery O'Connor as a southern writer rather than as a theologian, to confront her as the master artist who has given us a powerfully concrete and tangible gallery of men and women and children with southern accents and whose life and thought are deeply grounded in the regional experience. I want to try to demonstrate that the southern milieu in which her art is set, rather than being a mere stage setting for theological concerns, which is the assumption of so much of the criticism of her work, is not only part and parcel of her fiction but significantly modifies and shapes the meaning, the theme, of her fiction. And by this I am not merely talking about southern fundamentalist Protestant Christianity, but southern secular society, human forms and political, social and moral interests.

I have deliberately chosen for my exegesis the story entitled "The Artificial Nigger" both because it is Flannery at her best, and also because—in my quarrel with Flannery's theological exegetes—it could be said to be "the terrain of the devil," or of the enemy at least, which is to say, a story which is consciously and effectively imbued with religious symbolism all the way—a Dantean descent into the Inferno, a tale of initiation complete with portals of Hell, prophecy and revelation, Adamic pride, miraculous light, and one in which the omniscient authorial voice itself asserts at the end a pronouncement upon the religious meaning of what happens in the story. I want to show that when Flannery said that "the two circumstances that have given character to my own writing have been those of being Southern and being Catholic," she was saying something other than that because she happened to know the South best, she used it as a stage setting for theological demonstrations.

The two characters whose experience "The Artificial Nigger" relates are countrymen. Mr. Head is sixty, while his grandson Nelson is about ten. They live in the deep woods, several miles from a railroad junction, somewhere in the Georgia hill country, so far from any town or city that Nelson's new clothes must be ordered by mail. The story begins early in the day that they are to make a trip to Atlanta. Mr. Head has been to the city twice before in his life; Nelson was born there, but since infancy has lived in the remote countryside, and it will be his first experience of the big city. So isolated is their existence that Nelson has never once seen a black man; there are none in their community, the last one, as Mr. Head says, having been run out some twelve years before.

In short, the story is to be the classic humorous situation of country-come-to-town, and these particular country folk are very innocent indeed of the ways of the big city. They are hayseeds, rubes, red-necks, crackers, as the ordinary clichés would have it—strictly speaking, they are not what is known as "poor white trash," in that they are in no way viewed as indolent, debased, debilitated, or victimized, but they are poor and white, and definitely in the lower economic and social echelons. It is obvious that Flannery viewed these people with affection. She liked them, and she respected them for their integrity—nothing could be further from her attitude than the kind of contemptuous bawdry with which Erskine Caldwell dealt with somewhat similar people. Flannery's plain folk have a dignity that is free of disdain on the author's part (she generally reserves that for people of education and prosperity). Like Faulkner's Bundrens, her poor folk are not animals; they have immortal souls, and their lack of learning is in no way portrayed as inhibiting their spiritual and moral worthiness. The Heads are indeed *good* country people. Though Flannery was very conscious of class and caste, she has absolutely no economic determinism or social militancy in her depiction of the workings of class. Flannery's depiction of her people is free of sentimentality; there is no overlooking the human limitations of these people merely because of their rural proletarian status. They are not at all like Steinbeck's Joads; "The Artificial Nigger" contains, for instance, some telling observations on the nature of lower-class southern racial prejudice. Equally, however, their lives are portrayed as neither bleak nor emotion-starved; there is nothing here of Ring Lardner's bitterness or Sinclair Lewis' satire. In her sense of their individuality, her zest for their talk, her delight in their manners and attitudes, her respect for their shrewdness, and her unwillingness to portray them as mere economic or social exemplars, Flannery's depiction of these poor white farmers is very much in the southern literary tradition, and of a piece with the fiction of such authors as Faulkner, Eudora Welty, Thomas Wolfe, and James Agee.

It is, however, even more specifically located than that. For Flannery O'Connor's rural whites are only among the latest, perhaps the best, exemplars of what has been one of the most long-lasting and powerful literary genres in southern literature: Middle Georgia humor. And here I must make an excursion into literary history. It has long been a truism in the study of southern history that the country of Middle Georgia is the font and foundation of southern humor. As Joel Chandler Harris once wrote, "By-the-by, if you will take a map of Georgia, pick out Putnam County, and then put your finger on the counties surrounding it—Morgan, Greene, Hancock, Baldwin, Jones, and Jasper—you will have under your thumb the seat of Southern humor. Major Jones' Courtship belongs to Morgan County. Colonel Richard Malcolm Johnston's characters to Hancock. Unc' Remus was in Putnam. Simon Suggs was a native of Jasper. Polly Peachblossom was from Baldwin. Jonce Hooper went to school in Monticello (Jasper), when a boy, and there saw Simon Suggs." The boundaries need be extended only a little farther and the roster includes Augustus Baldwin Longstreet, who was more or less the founder of the school of Georgia humor, as well as "Bill Arp, so-called," a virtuoso of the dialect commentary. As Henry W. Watterson wrote in 1882, "Why it is I know not, but certain it is that Georgia, which is made the scene of so much of the humor of the South, has furnished a very large proportion of the humorists themselves." William Malone Baskervill, writing in the 1890s, perhaps put it best, in words that, with due allowance for the stylistic conventions of an earlier day, might almost apply to Flannery O'Connor herself: "The Middle Georgians are a simple, healthy, homogeneous folk, resembling for the most part other Southerners of like rank and calling in their manners, customs, and general way of living. But they have developed a certain manly, vigorous, fearless independence of action, and an ever increasing propensity to take a humorous view of life. In their earlier writings it is a homely wit, in which broad humor and loud laughter predominate; but tears are lurking in the corners of the eyes, and general sentiment nestles in the heart." With the exception of Harris, the humor of Middle Georgia was notable for its depiction of rural whites, and these not men of great wealth and position, living on plantations, but small farmers, without great wealth, unsophisticated and folksy, unlettered and uncultured in the ways of the city but shrewd and witty. Negro characters are few and mostly of minor importance.

Did Flannery O'Connor know the Middle Georgia humorists? I cannot say. My guess is that she must have read Longstreet's *Geor-*

gia Scenes, and obviously she knew Joel Chandler Harris. Whether she was acquainted with William Tappan Thompson, Richard Malcolm Johnston, "Bill Arp," and others, I have no idea, and in any event it is not important. What is important is that her childhood and youth were spent in the same Middle Georgia milieu as theirs, among the same people, and her depiction of rural whites grows out of the same social climate, however modified by the decades. A story such as "The Artificial Nigger," for example, is based directly upon the humor of country-come-to-town which almost every one of the Middle Georgia writers employed at one time or another. It is part and parcel of the humor of the Old South. Here is Johnson Jones Hooper describing the father of Simon Suggs, a Hard-Shell Baptist preacher from Middle Georgia:

> The Reverend Mr. Suggs had once in his life gone to Augusta; an extent of travel which in those days was a little unusual. . . . There were two propositions which witnessed their own truth to the mind of Mr. Suggs— the one was, that a man who had never been at Augusta, could not know any thing about that city, or any place, or any thing else; the other, that one who *had* been there must of necessity, be not only well informed as to all things connected with the city itself, but perfectly *au fait* upon all subjects whatsoever.

It should be obvious that there we have pretty much the same situation as that in "The Artificial Nigger," in which poor Mr. Head, who had been to Atlanta, is irked because Nelson, who has not, insists that his grandfather's experience of the big city does not constitute a moral superiority. But there is a much more important resemblance, which is true not only of the Simon Suggs sketch but of almost all Middle Georgia humor, and this is that the comedy draws much of its mirth from a contrast in language, which is also a contrast in viewpoint and in culture, and, implicitly and ultimately, by extension, a contrast in moral vision. The narrator of Hooper's sketch, like that of the *Georgia Scenes* and of most of the humor in this genre, is *not* an uneducated, unsophisticated, untraveled rustic. Rather, he is a commentator of learning and sophistication recounting the doings of the plain folk, for the benefit of others like himself, and he tends to exaggerate his literary sophistication in order to play off the crudeness (and the *vigor*) of rustic speech against it.

Thus, following the remarks above, Hooper has the elder Suggs express his indignation in his own words:

> "*Bob Smith* says, does he? And who's *Bob Smith?* Much does *Bob Smith* know about Augusty! he's been thar, I reckon! Slipped off yerly some mornin', when nobody warn't noticin', and got back afore night! It's only a hundred and fifty mile. Oh, yes. *Bob Smith* knows *all* about it! I don't know nothin' about it! *I* a'n't never been to Augusty—*I* couldn't find the road thar, I reckon—ha! ha! Bob—*Sm-th!* The eternal stink! if he was only to see one o' them fine gentlemen in Augusty, with his fine broadcloth, and bell-crown hat, and shoe boots a-shinin' like silver, he'd take to the woods and kill himself a-runnin'."

The effect is comic incongruity, and the narrator of the traditional southern humor sketch intensifies this by using very ornate and extremely literary language to describe people, objects, and events that are quite mundane and in no way elevated. Thus Longstreet's description of the tail of a most decrepit horse in "The Horse Swap": "From the root it dropped into a graceful festoon; then rose in a handsome curve; then resumed its first direction; and then mounted suddenly upwards like a cypress knee to a perpendicular of about two and a half inches. The whole had a careless and bewitching inclination to the right." The contrast between the elevated diction and the prosaic fact, the horse's tail, is designed to incite risibility, and it succeeds.

Now consider the opening paragraphs of "The Artificial Nigger":

> Mr. Head awakened to discover that the room was full of moonlight. He sat up and stared at the floor boards—the color of silver—and then at the ticking on his pillow, which might have been brocade, and after a second, he saw half of the moon five feet away in the shaving mirror, paused as if it were waiting for his permission to enter. It rolled forward and cast a dignifying light on everything. The straight chair against the wall looked stiff and attentive as if it were awaiting an order and Mr. Head's trousers, hanging to the back of it, had an almost noble air, like the garment some great man had just flung to his servant; but the face on the moon was a grave one. It gazed across the room and out the window where it floated over the horse stall and appeared to contemplate itself with the look of a young man who sees his old age before him.
>
> Mr. Head could have said to it that age was a choice blessing and that only with years does a man enter into that calm understanding of life that makes him a suitable guide to the young. This, at least, had been his own experience.

What makes that opening work so well, it seems to me, is precisely the same kind of humorous linguistic incongruity. We are not quite sure how to take that moonlight—seriously, poetically, mystically—until we get to the trousers hanging on the back of the chair with "an almost noble air"—whereupon the comic exaggeration becomes unmistakable. Much the same kind of effect is achieved in the second paragraph, with its orotund solemnity, which is quickly undercut by the sarcasm of the second sentence.

It is, however, not merely a *comic* exaggeration of diction, though it is very definitely that. Flannery is having fun, just as Longstreet is with the tail of the old plug horse in "The Horse Swap," but she is not finally ridiculing either Mr. Head or his pants. A little later, for example, she declares of Mr. Head that "He might have been Vergil summoned in the middle of the night to go to Dante, or better, Raphael, awakened by a blast of God's light to fly to the side of Tobias." Again, comic incongruity—old Mr. Head as Vergil or Raphael. But in his own way, as the story develops, that is a description of the role he will play in the story. For Flannery takes Mr. Head, and Nelson, and all her variegated company of southern plain folk, with considerable seriousness. Indeed, she tends to prefer them to sophisticated, educated folk, and when she confronts the one with the other, it is the rustic who usually comes out best. Sometimes this is simply for instant comedy, as when Mr. Head, with Nelson on the train to Atlanta, is instructed by the waiter in the dining car: "'Passengers are not allowed in the kitchen!' he said in a haughty voice. 'Passengers are NOT allowed in the kitchen!' Mr. Head stopped where he was and turned. 'And there's good reason for that,' he shouted into the Negro's chest, 'because the cockroaches would run the passengers out!'" More often it goes beyond the obviously comic and involves matters of morality and even vision, notably in Flannery's Fundamentalist prophets such as Hazel Motes and the two Tarwaters, in which the primitive fervor of their spiritual hunger is portrayed as far more admirable than the smugness and rationality of the educated, complacent city folk who view them as rustic freaks. But here again, the same attitude is implicit in much secular Middle Georgia humor. Amused and even appalled though the urbane, genteel narrator of the traditional humorous sketches is at the crudeness and vulgarity of the backwoods plain folk, he is also rather impressed at their vigor and their ability to cope with the real world. Indeed, in some instances, the narrator's elegant language, literary diction, sophisticated syntax are often exaggerated by the author until they seem artificial, and become a device not for confronting the everyday world but for avoiding it and refusing to face it. For Middle Georgia literature, however it pokes fun at the naïvete and crudeness of the plain folk, seldom finally demeans the rural white at the expense of more cultivated or wealthy city people. The countryman may be discomfited, embarrassed, ridiculed, but the element of integrity is usually his and not the city dweller's. Pitted against another countryman, the Middle Georgian can be and often is knavish, crude, even cruel; the literature is not squeamish. But let it become a matter of country versus city, and the Middle Georgia writer, educated Whig gentleman though he may be, almost always comes down on the side of the plain folk.

Flannery O'Connor's bias in this respect is notorious; the relationship is usually portrayed in moral and religious terms—the uneducated believer in the Bible as contrasted with the educated urban modernist who lacks ultimate moral conviction. When she discusses the position of the Catholic novelist in the Protestant South, she makes it clear where her emotional loyalties lie, as when she remarks that the Catholic "will feel a great deal more kinship with backwoods prophets and shouting fundamentalists than he will with those politer elements for whom the supernatural is an embarrassment and for whom religion has become a department of sociology or culture or personality development." Whatever the theological compatibility or incompatibility, however, it must surely be obvious that historically, socially, even politically, the dichotomy she sets up in her fiction between rural and urban plain folk and urban sophisticate echoes a long-standing characteristic of the writing of her part of the South.

And Flannery does not usually stop with the theological comparison, either. There are other bases of contrast; in *The Violent Bear It Away*, for example, there is one point in which she even compares country food to city food. When Francis Marion Tarwater had been living in the country, "he and his great-uncle had eaten well. . . .

Never a morning he had not awakened to the smell of fatback frying." This is compared with the food that his city dwelling schoolteacher serves: "For breakfast, he poured a bowl of shavings out of a cardboard box; in the middle of the day he made sandwiches out of lightbread; and at night he took them to a restaurant, a different one every night run by a different color of foreigner so that he would learn, he said, how other nationalities ate. The boy did not care how other nationalities ate. He had always left the restaurants hungry, conscious of an intrusion in his works." Whatever the merits of rural and urban cuisines, it is obvious that the comparison is aimed at developing the artificiality of city ways and the healthy naturalness of the backwoods.

My point in all this is not that the religious concerns of Flannery O'Connor's fiction, with its dichotomy of passionate Fundamentalism and flaccid modern rationality, are either forced or less than central to her fiction. It is rather that I want to insist that the religious theme is quite compatible with a basic social and secular attitude toward the rural-urban confrontation, a suspicion of the sophisticated and intellectualized, a strongly held belief in the greater vitality and integrity of rural life and the people who live in rural places, that is characteristic of the southern literary imagination, with emotional roots that go far back into regional history, and that of itself is in no way dependent upon Flannery's Catholicism as such. The Agrarian symposium entitled *I'll Take My Stand: The South and the Agrarian Tradition*, not one of the twelve contributors to which was a Roman Catholic, shares almost precisely the same attitude toward urbanism, modernism, science, rationalism, and progress that Flannery O'Connor exhibits throughout her fiction. Thus the notion, which so many critics of Flannery O'Connor's fiction seem to hold, that it is the religious allegiance that gives her work its principal thrust, while the specifically southern regional material is little more than a setting in which religious concerns manifest themselves, is hardly valid.

Indeed, if anything it might appear to be the other way around: one might almost say that the religious concerns—the so-called drama of salvation—provided her with a thematic device for focussing a set of attitudes, secular rather than religious, toward the nature of man in human time and in society, that were deeply grounded in the life of her region, with tenacious historical underpinnings, and held in common with a galaxy of writers, few of whom shared her specific religious concerns. Or to return to the story entitled "The Artificial Nigger," we might state it this way: if the visit of Mr. Head and his grandson Nelson to Atlanta is Dantesque, if it seems to them a trip to the underworld, the author had only to add the religious dimension to an emotional experience that was already strongly shaped by her social and historical heritage.

I do not wish, however, to rest my analysis on an argument based upon such extrinsic considerations, no matter how valid. I should like, therefore, to try to show how, in "The Artificial Nigger," the significance of the final religious revelation, the "free act, the acceptance of grace . . . what the artificial nigger does to reunite Mr. Head and Nelson," to cite the author's own words again, is deeply dependent artistically upon the secular southern context.

We have already seen how, in the opening paragraphs of the story, Flannery deliberately, and for humorous purposes, describes Mr. Head and his trousers hanging on the chair in an exaggerated, elevated diction, in which the linguistic clash between the lofty formal rhetoric and the backwoods actuality achieves a comic incongruity. I have pointed out that such a procedure was a stock device of the old Middle Georgia humorists, and that the method being used is that of narration from outside and above, in which an educated, sophisticated storyteller writes about simple vernacular characters for the edification of readers who are not simple rustics but likewise persons of education and sophistication.

Throughout the story Flannery uses language to describe Mr. Head's and Nelson's excursion to Atlanta that is far more complex and literary than the characters themselves would ever use. She does not hesitate to invest their trip to Atlanta and their experience there with a meaning and significance that are very much in excess of any possible interpretation the two characters themselves would know how to articulate. When Mr. Head has denied his relationship to Nelson after his grandson knocks down a woman loaded with packages, for instance, she writes of Nelson that "his mind had frozen around his grandfather's treachery as if he were trying to preserve it intact to present to the final judgment. He walked without looking to one side or the other, but every now and then his mouth would twitch and this was when he felt, from some remote place inside himself, a black mysterious form reach up as if it would melt his frozen vision in one hot gasp." This is hardly what Nelson is literally thinking. When finally the terrified Mr. Head admits to a stranger that he is lost in the big city, and is given directions to the suburban railroad station, the two of them walk toward the station and see the concrete lawn ornament, the artificial Negro. Then comes the passage cited earlier. Once again the meaning of the statue is far in excess of anything that either Mr. Head or Nelson could articulate. The author, not the characters, pronounces that meaning. When Mr. Head tries to make an appropriate comment, all he can say is that "they ain't got enough real ones here. They got to have an artificial one." They go on to the station, get back on the train, and ride back to the junction nearest their home. As the train, having deposited them at the junction, moves off, Mr. Head looks around him at the familiar scenes, and there then follows a paragraph of interpretation:

> Mr. Head stood very still and felt the action of mercy touch him again but this time he knew that there were no words in the world that could name it. He understood that it grew out of agony, which is not denied to any man and which is given in strange ways to children. He understood it was all a man could carry into death to give his Maker and he suddenly burned with shame that he had so little of it to take with him. He stood appalled, judging himself with the thoroughness of God, while the action of mercy covered his pride like a flame and consumed it. He had never thought himself a great sinner but he saw now that his true depravity had been hidden from him lest it cause him despair. He realized that he was forgiven for sins from the beginning of time, when he had conceived in his own heart the sin of Adam, until the present, when he had denied poor Nelson. He saw that no sin was too monstrous for him to claim as his own, and since God loved in proportion as He forgave, he felt ready at that moment to enter Paradise.

This particular passage has proved an embarrassment to many of Flannery's admirers, for it has been criticized as being redundant, an authorial intrusion, and so forth. Why, the argument goes, is it necessary for the omniscient author to point all this out, in language that Mr. Head would not use? If the moment of the realization of grace does not speak for itself, then the story is flawed. To defend the passage's presence, or excuse its absence, critics have been led to some ingenuity. Thus David Eggenschweiler admits that "it does seem too articulate and too theologically precise for Mr. Head," and he justifies the passage only halfheartedly, saying that "she is merely formulating those insights better than Mr. Head could do and in contexts of which he has not shown any awareness before; she is yielding to the temptation to address the reader through her characters and to explain what he senses but could not so thoroughly explain."

This, I am afraid, is what too often happens when fiction is approached thematically, by critics who are interested only in the supposed "message" or Truth. No one seems to object to the passage as such; only to its redundance or inappropriateness. The fact is that the passage is not only appropriate but necessary, for not merely the final episode but *the entire story* has been told that way, from outside and above, by a narrator whose descriptive commentary not only goes far beyond Mr. Head's verbal and conceptual limitations but works with and against the actual mundane situation throughout, for purposes of comedy and pathos. What we have to realize in a story like this is that there is a deliberate and carefully constructed distance between narrator and character, which is embodied in the language but goes beyond that into viewpoint and attitude. This is the technique not only of Middle Georgia humor but of such other nontheological gems as Faulkner's "Spotted Horses" and the episode of Ike Snopes and the cow, in *The Hamlet*. The narrative voice, which is sophisticated, educated, virtuoso in function, is separated from the plain folk who are characters in the story, and the distance between them, which, to repeat, is embodied in language but also involves cultural, social, and even religious attitudes, produces the incongruity of comedy.

The narrator compares Mr. Head and Nelson to Vergil and Dante; the Georgia grandfather and grandson not only have never heard of either, but live, act, speak, and think in a cultural milieu that is comically inappropriate to the comparison. When Mr. Head shows Nelson the sewer opening and describes it to the boy, saying that "at any minute any man in the city might be sucked into the sewer and never heard from again," Nelson is frightened, and thinks of the sewer opening as the entrance to hell. We know that it is no such thing, and so does the narrator. The joke is shared by the narrator and reader, and is at the expense of the rustic characters.

But what Flannery does is to dramatize what Mr. Head and Nelson are thinking and feeling as they tour Atlanta and encounter what for them are strange and alien sights and people, until finally they are lost and desperate, so that what is at first a comic distance between narrator and character is bridged (not removed), so that we come to feel compassion for them and on one level at least to identify with them. Like the narrator, we as readers know very well that the sewer isn't going to suck Nelson into the pit of hell and that the hideous underworld of the city of Hades isn't going to take them into its clutches forever if they miss the train, but we have known what it is to be lost, bewildered, and frightened. More than that, we have known what it is to be alienated from those we love, and to have failed them when they needed us. So the distance is spanned, and what was at first amused superiority at the simpleminded yokels becomes compassion.

Yet to repeat, the distance is not removed; it is only bridged. We do not forget that they are lost in Atlanta, Georgia, and not Hell—the two places are not, after all, identical. And when following their rescue they walk toward the suburban station and come upon the artificial Negro, we remain very much aware that it is, comically, not "some great mystery, some monument to another's victory that brought them together in their common defeat," but a concrete lawn ornament that has seen better days and is in bad taste anyway. We recognize how *they* feel, and having come to know them we understand why; but nonetheless it remains a lawn ornament. Thus we feel both amusement (which is to say, incongruity) and compassion (which is the bridging of distance), and the reconciliation of the incongruity is the acknowledgment of love and the resolution of the story. Yet the distance remains. Do we not, after all, find it a bit amusing that Mr. Head now feels so certain that he is ready to enter Paradise?

The voice of the narrator, with its comic exaggeration and sophistication, and the actions and thoughts of the rustic characters have been in counterpoint throughout, and the counterpoint is the way we have been made to look at the story. Had the authorial commentary not been there from the start, the story would have been either grotesque or sentimental, depending upon how we looked at it, and perhaps both. But through comic irony and incongruity of language and object the author has provided integrity and authenticity, which is to say, believability. So it is not only permissible, but essential, that following the discovery of the artificial Negro and the reunion of grandfather and grandson, the authorial voice, which had first been used for comic distancing but had come gradually to function as a bridge between the reader and the characters, offers a final, summarizing commentary in which the human meaning and significance of what has happened are pronounced. The two modes of discourse—which have involved language and attitudes—must be finally confirmed harmoniously. If this were not done, the story would be incomplete.

Perhaps the best way to see this is to think of what the story would be *without* that final commentary. It would, I think, seem truncated, abrupt, even arbitrary; for that authorial voice, which has been present all the way along and a large part of our way of perceiving the story, would not itself have participated in the resolution.

The point, as I see it, is that we cannot separate the action of a story from the way it is told, nor can we isolate the usable religious meaning from the action and the language in which it is expressed. In just the same way, we cannot deal successfully with the fictional art of Flannery O'Connor if we view it as mere theological parable and demonstration, and fail to consider the flesh-and-blood experience of reality being represented so expertly and (in several senses) craftily in language.

My dissatisfaction with so much of the criticism that has been published about Flannery's work remains profound. I find it simplistic, reductive, thin. It largely fails to account for the complexity of the art of a very complex and gifted writer. Too frequently it yields to the temptation (which I fear Flannery herself occasionally abetted in some of her own remarks about her work) to moralize. After all, the work seems so temptingly "explicable," the religious and moral commentary so very near the surface, so readily extracted and usable—a prime target for eager young moralists.

But the simplicity is deceptive. The so-called religious dimension is not to be lifted out of its artistic relationship to the formal complexity of the fiction; indeed it is part of that complexity, adds to it, is even itself *fictional*. The notion, which so much that has been written about Flannery and her work assumes—that the author of these novels and stories was a detached, dispassionate Roman Catholic observer set down in an exotic and alien Middle Georgia wilderness and left to proclaim certain strange affinities with the native Protestants—is a dangerous one for criticism to adopt. *She* was a Middle Georgian, too, as well as a Catholic communicant, and more than that, she was a modern southern writer, and a great many other things besides. There is little that is easy or facile about either the artist or her art, and a great deal that is complex and enormously creative. It is true that she read Teilhard de Chardin and Maritain and Mauriac; she also read Ralph McGill and Joel Chandler Harris and Henry W. Grady. She wrote about primitive unlettered Fundamentalists; but she was herself a very sophisticated and widely read young woman who was not a Hard-Shell Baptist but a Roman Catholic communicant. The trouble with many of those who write about her fiction is that they oversimplify both it and her.

Some seventeen years ago I took part in a panel discussion at Wesleyan College over in Macon, along with Flannery and several other writers. We got to talking about the function and place of symbolism in fiction, and Flannery said something that I have always remembered. It was, "So many students approach a story as if it were a problem in algebra; find x and when they find x they can dismiss the rest of it." That is what I feel uncomfortable with about so much that has been written about her stories. Find x—find the act of grace, find the religious theme, and nothing else matters. It may be good exegetical theology; it makes for wretched literary criticism, for it ignores the richness and mystery in order to fasten upon the immediately usable. It reduces the gallery of characters with whom the O'Connor fiction is peopled, that magnificently motley company of southerners, to the level of one-dimensional figures in a latter-day morality play. What we need is criticism that will explore the complexity of the work, and not merely seek to use it to make theological observations.

Flannery O'Connor, you know, was a peacock fancier. She raised them, and she wrote an article about them. In it she made among other observations, the following remark, which I shall conclude by quoting, and leaving the application for you to work out: "Many people, I have found, are congenitally unable to appreciate the sight of a peacock. Once or twice I have been asked what the peacock is 'good for'—a question which gets no answer from me because it deserves none."

Carson McCullers: The Aesthetic of Pain

I think it is not without importance that the all-night restaurant in Carson McCullers' first novel, *The Heart Is a Lonely Hunter*, is called The New York Cafe. In the small-sized southern city in the late 1930s, when the story takes place, there is little doing at night and none of the people involved in the story are either very contented or very hopeful; the New York Cafe is the only place for them to go, and its forlorn hospitality is indicative of what is barren and joyless about the lives of those who go there. From Columbus, Georgia, to New York City is a long way.

Biff Brannon's restaurant is presumably called the New York Cafe because of the ironic contrast between what it is and what its name signifies. The name is an attempt at sophistication, at the glamour of the big city, at a greater than provincial importance; New York is the metropolis, where important things happen and ambitions come true and talent is rewarded and all is exciting, rich, romantic. Set in the backwaters of civilization (as Carson McCullers' imagination saw it, anyway), the pathetic name given the all-night restaurant mocks the romantic dream with its commonplace actuality. The habitués are there because they live in a small city in southwestern Georgia instead of New York, or even Atlanta. It is like the blue hotel in Stephen Crane's story of that name, set out on the Nebraska prairie and painted a surrealistic blue to signify the exaggerations of its pretension amid the lonely, terribly barren, and empty expanses of a late nineteenth-century West only recently changed from being uninhabited prairie and now only the dreary backwash of a crude provincial life. Just so, the inappropriateness of the name New York Cafe is meant by the author to convey a sense of cultural starvation, the provincial dreariness of the kind of city where the sidewalks, as they used to say, are rolled up each night at ten o'clock. As well call it the Café de Paris.

Is that what Columbus, Georgia, was like? I suppose it depends upon the viewpoint, and Carson McCullers' viewpoint at the time she was writing *The Heart Is a Lonely Hunter* was not exactly that of the Nashville Agrarians, or even of William Faulkner or Eudora Welty. Frankie Addams' view of Columbus and her own, she once remarked, were identical. From Virginia Carr's fascinating and I think horrifying biography, *The Lonely Hunter*, we know that during those years, the late 1930s, Carson and Reeves McCullers wanted above all to get to New York City. Carson had had a taste of it as an apprentice writer, and though living on short rations she had no doubt whatever that it was the place for her. There were to be found the writers and artists and teachers and publishers, the people who understood, as she thought, what was really worthwhile in life. New York was the place of art, of culture, of fulfillment, where the dreams of the lonely provincial could come true. She wrote *The Heart Is a Lonely Hunter* for numerous reasons, and an important one was so that it might make her famous and enable her to move to New York and escape the dreariness of the provinces forever. Which it did—though it cannot be said that ultimately she found what she was looking for there, either.

In this respect, as in several others, she is reminiscent of another southern author, Thomas Wolfe. In the novel published as *You Can't Go Home Again*, Wolfe explains how it was that the townsfolk of Libya Hill got involved in a frantic real estate boom in the 1920s, resulting in disgrace and disaster when the Depression came on.

> As he stood upon the hill and looked out on the scene that spread below him in the gathering darkness, with its pattern of lights to mark the streets and the creeping pin-pricks of the thronging traffic, he remembered the barren nighttime streets of the town he had known so well in his boyhood. Their dreary and unpeopled desolation had burned its acid

print upon his memory. Bare and deserted by ten o'clock at night, those streets had been an aching monotony, a weariness of hard lights and empty pavements, a frozen torpor broken only occasionally by the footfalls of some prowler—some desperate, famished, lonely man who hoped past hope and past belief for some haven of comfort, warmth, and love there in the wilderness, for the sudden opening of a magic door into some secret, rich, and more abundant life. There had been many such, but they had never found what they were searching for. They had been dying in the darkness—without a goal, a certain purpose, or a door.

And that, it seemed to George, was the way the thing had come. That was the way it had happened. Yes, it was there—on many a night long past and wearily accomplished, in ten thousand little towns and in ten million barren streets where all the passion, hope, and hunger of the famished men beat like a great pulse through the fields of darkness—it was there and nowhere else that all this madness had been brewed.

Like Carson Smith McCullers, Thomas Wolfe was raised in a small southern city, of lower middle class origins and status, and yearned to get away. Eugene Gant looked out northward and eastward over the mountains toward the shining city of his dreams; Frankie Addams and Mick Kelly, unlike their creator, are less precise about exactly where they wish to go, but they are sure they want to get out of their imprisoned circumstances. In neither McCullers nor Wolfe is the hold of the southern community upon characters very real. Neither is very much involved in the kind of historical tradition or community identification that writers such as Faulkner and Welty use for the stuff of their fiction.

A major difference between McCullers' South and Wolfe's is that there is no sense of Wolfe himself feeling trapped in it. He is going to leave. Carson McCullers' people are there to stay, and their yearning for something better and finer and more fulfilling has a kind of painful *angst* about it. Their yearning for the metropolis, as has often been said, is like that of Chekhov's provincial Russians for Moscow: for a place of impossible fulfillment that is too far off in time and space to represent anything more than a forlorn hope.

II

The Heart Is a Lonely Hunter burst upon the national literary scene in 1940; thirty-seven years later and it is still going strong. *Reflections in a Golden Eye* followed the year after; of all Mrs. McCullers' fiction it is probably the most bizarre, the least pleasant. It is a *tour de force*, a sustained exercise in pure pain, without respite or humor. In 1943 she published *The Ballad of the Sad Cafe*, one of the most intense short novels of the twentieth century, in many ways the essence of her art. In 1946 came *The Member of the Wedding*, the most enjoyable—if that is a word to be used with *any* of her work—of all her books, and also, so far as living in the everyday world that most of us must inhabit is involved, the most "normal." In those books, produced over a period of less than a decade and while the author was still in her twenties, we have a very impressive body of fiction indeed.

That was all. Nothing that she wrote in the remaining two decades of her life adds much to her achievement. *Clock Without Hands* was an artistic disaster; only her most devoted admirers could say much for it. Whatever it was she had in the way of a gift, she had lost it. When she died in 1967, I doubt that anyone felt that she was leaving good books unwritten.

We are dealing, therefore, with certain works of fiction written and published during a period of intense and often brilliant creativity, by a young writer, a *wunderkind* as it were, one who did not develop or extend her range afterward. I think it is important to remember that. Whatever the faces and tensions that were central to her life and art, and which ultimately destroyed both, they attained, during this period, an equilibrium that made her fiction possible.

A writer, too, whom I have found can exert a very powerful influence on young people, in particular other young writers. I have taught courses in creative writing for some years, and so do not undervalue the considerable influence she can have on a certain kind of young writer. All in all, it is a benign and valuable influence, for if the young writer is any good the more obvious imitative elements are soon thrown off, while what remains is the sense of the possibility of self-expression. What she has to teach the young writer is the realization, which seems obvious but is not, that the qualities of youthful artistic sensibility, of being "different" and unwilling or unable to conform to the expected patterns of conventional adolescence, are not merely uselessly burdensome and painful, but can be transformed into the insight and awareness of art. The impetus to self-fulfillment involved in that realization can be enormously creative.

Mrs. McCullers' fiction, in particular *The Member of the Wedding*, can speak to the adolescent reader in very intense fashion, for what it conveys is the frustration and pain of being more than a child and yet not an adult, with the agony of self-awareness and sense of isolation thereby involved. There is the shock of recognition—something of the same kind of reassurance through identification that books such as *Look Homeward, Angel* or *The Catcher in the Rye* have been known to provide. It is fashionable, of course, to outgrow such identification—and also inevitable, if the young writer is to develop his or her own talent—and what it means is that much of the criticism that has been written about Carson McCullers' work is either pedestrian or else unsympathetic, because the kind of perspective that makes the act of criticism meaningful is something that is possible only when the reader gets beyond the intense, uncritical emotional response that characterizes the youthful impact of a novel such as *The Member of the Wedding*.

Please understand: I am not saying that only persons without critical discernment can enjoy Carson McCullers' fiction; clearly that is not so at all. What I am contending, however, is that the way in which her work can speak to the young reader is not susceptible to very much critical analysis, because it comes at a stage at which the reader's response is based upon intense emotional assent and identification rather than a mere selective discrimination. When the reader subsequently comes to acquire that intellectual discrimination, he can no longer muster the emotional assent in the intense way that was possible when he first read Carson McCullers. Mrs. McCullers' fiction, in other words, taught him that his feelings were worthwhile and could be given artistic dignity, enabling him to recognize what he must have felt. But having learned that, the reader, if he is to develop his critical talents, goes on to other writers and becomes interested in exploring the quality and nature of his response to works of literature as well as exposing himself to the naïve intensity, and so needs to investigate that response in terms of fiction that yields more to careful discrimination.

In short, Carson McCullers is in certain important ways a writer for young readers, and one has to be young to receive what she offers. She speaks not to the intelligence so much as to the untutored emotions, and with such tremendous intensity that one must either accept it or reject it. There is almost no middle ground. She does not let you think about it, choosing this and suspending judgment on that as you go along; it is all of a piece, and if you like the experience of fiction to be intricate and subtle, she is probably not for you.

The McCullers fiction, I believe, has at its center a fundamental premise: which is that solitude—loneliness—is a human constant, and cannot possibly be alleviated for very long at a time. But there is no philosophical acceptance of that condition, and none of the joy in it that one finds in, say, Thomas Wolfe or even Hemingway. The solitude is inevitable, and it is always painful. Thus life is a matter of living in pain, and art is the portraying of anguish. Occasionally, a character of hers knows happiness, but never for very long. Thus in the *Ballad of the Sad Cafe* there is a time when Miss Amelia believes she has the love of Cousin Lymon, and so permits her cafe to be a place of joy, but it cannot last. Marvin Macy shows up; Cousin Lymon has been waiting for someone like him; Miss Amelia's happiness disintegrates; you might as well go listen to the chain gang, the narrator tell us.

Mrs. McCullers explains it by her remarks on love, which she says involves the lover and the beloved, who come from two different countries. There is no way that such love can be shared, for one of the two must love and the other be loved; no reciprocal relationship, whereby one both loves and is loved in turn, is possible.

Obviously love in this definition involves possession. The lover, she says, "is forever trying to strip bare his beloved. The lover craves every possible relation with the beloved, even if this experience can cause him only pain." For this reason, she points out, it is much more desirable, and most people wish, to be the lover rather than the beloved, since the "beloved fears and hates the lover" who is trying to possess him. It is something like Frost's "Fire and Ice": love can be destructive because it wishes to consume the beloved, or because in reaction it produces the glacial impenetrability of freezing disdain. But Frost was making a different moral entirely. He was speaking against love that involves only possessiveness, or self-protective hate that refuses to open itself to human warmth. Carson McCullers not only declares that it *must* be that way, but that the very nature of being loved, which is to say, wanted and needed by another, is intolerable.

Such of course is the scheme of *The Heart Is a Lonely Hunter.* "In the town there were two mutes, and they were always together." Singer is the lover, Antonopoulos the beloved. Antonopoulos accepts Singer because it is convenient and comfortable for him to do so, but then he loses his intelligence and also his need for what Singer can provide, since as a vegetable he requires nothing outside himself. So Singer is left, bereft, loveless. As long as he could retain the illusion that Antonopoulos had a place for him in his affections, he could cope; Antonopoulos' very inchoateness and lack of awareness were an advantage, since they permitted Singer to believe in the fiction that his love understood and returned.

Singer's self-deception in turn makes possible the self-deception of all the others—Biff, Dr. Copeland, Jake, Mick Kelly. So long as Singer will sit and listen to them speak their troubles, they can, for a time at least, function. Singer understands them only imperfectly; he depends upon lipreading. The fact that he cannot answer back, cannot carry on a dialogue, is what makes him so satisfactory, for in that way the others are enabled to believe that he understands, sympathizes, and accepts all that they say and feel. In this respect, Singer fills the role of the beloved; he allows himself to be loved, because he is insulated from the demands and the possessiveness of love by virtue of his deafness. If he were not deaf, and thus solitary in a world of talkers, he could never tolerate the others, of course, and this not because he is selfish or mean—he is neither—but because he is a human being. Thus Singer serves the others as the object of their love (which obviously is self-love), while Antonopoulos fills a similar role for him, and the self-deception works—until Antonopoulos dies, whereupon the occasion for Singer's love collapses and he shoots himself, and the others are left stranded. The artistry is in the pain—Mrs. McCullers has never let us participate in the deception; we have witnessed it at all points for the ruse that it is, and when the arrangements collapse we perceive only the inevitable outcome of what we have seen developing all along. Again, you might as well go listen to the chain gang—which is pretty much what as readers we have been engaged in doing.

III

The Heart Is a Lonely Hunter was and is a remarkable book—that a 23-year-old woman could write with so much mastery and so much perception about so diverse a range of characters was odd indeed. The talent that was able to observe the variety of experience that went into those characterizations was something close to genius. The capacity for observation, for perceiving and detailing the concerns of the various people, was stunning in its virtuosity. What I find most remarkable, reading the novel over again and in light of those that followed and also from what I have learned from Mrs. Carr's biography, is that a writer whose imagination is so subjective, whose art is so suffused with emotional coloration and is based upon the capacity to convey the endless sameness of human suffering, could at the same time see and record and catalogue so much, with such clear specificity and concrete objectivity of detail. For one whose view of the human condition is so thoroughly pessimistic to be able to combine that with the kind of knowledge of people and things outside of her that surely stems from a considerable fascination in observing the varieties of experience seems odd, to say the least.

The question that it poses is this: what is the relationship between the obvious fascination with which Mrs. McCullers viewed various kinds of human life and the terrible loneliness and anguish that she felt was hers and everyone's lot? By all logic one would think that the conviction of loneliness and separateness should involve a closing down of the blinds, so to speak, a withdrawal from what she would say is the impossible attempt ever to reach out to include others. Or conversely, that so rare a talent for observing and understanding and feeling compassion for others would produce something other than the anguished conviction of emptiness and solitude. One thinks of Eudora Welty, whose marvelous gift for observation and insight into many kinds of people goes along with a real joy in the life-giving mystery of human personality.

With Carson McCullers, it did not work that way, however, and perhaps one avenue toward understanding the apparent contradiction is to think about what Mrs. McCullers has Biff Brannon say about his fondness for freaks:

> What he had said to Alice was true—he did like freaks. He had a special friendly feeling for sick people and cripples. Whenever somebody with a harelip or T.B. came into the place he would set him up to beer. Or if the customer were a hunchback or a bad cripple, then it would be whiskey on the house. There was one fellow who had had his peter and his left leg blown off in a boiler explosion, and whenever he came to town there was a free pint waiting for him. And if Singer were a drinking kind of man he could get liquor at half price any time he wanted it.

Mrs. Carr begins her biography with an incident, which I assume was told her by Mrs. McCullers' childhood friend Helen Jackson, that demonstrates Carson McCullers' lifelong interest in the freak shows at the Chattahoochee Valley Fair. She remarks rightly that "deeply compassionate, the youngster was becoming increasingly aware that one's physical aberration was but an exaggerated symbol of what she considered everyman's 'caught' condition of spiritual isolation and sense of aloneness in spite of his intense desire and effort to relate to others." This is quite true. The physically grotesque is a way of exaggerating the everyday by making it all-important and inescapable. But perhaps there is more to it than that, even. I recall a remark of Flannery O'Connor's when asked why so many southern novelists tended to describe grotesques. The South, she said, was the last section of the country where you could still recognize a freak when you saw him. What Miss O'Connor was suggesting, I suppose, with her customary wit and hyperbole, was that the southern experience was still very much an affair of the complex patterns of community life, with the comings and goings of individuals taking place within a clearly recognized set of expectations and assumptions. In that kind of established social context, individual behavior ran along expected forms, so that there were certain agreed-upon limits and standards of human conduct. Anything truly deviant, genuinely aberrant, would therefore stand out, since there was something against which it could be measured and identified. I'm sure Flannery would have been the first to insist (after laughing at any such pompous interpretation of her remark) that it was no stifling conformity that was produced, but a kind of set of agreed-upon manners and formalities that made social experience convenient and tolerable, with a minimum of abrasiveness and considerable respect for privacy. She would also, I believe, insist that the implicit but firmly defined set of social forms went along with a set of similarly defined moral assumptions and values, so that moral freakishness—*i.e.*, deviation from what is agreed upon and expected—was also and equally recognizable.

This is the context, I think, within which so much of Flannery O'Connor's fiction operates, and Carson McCullers', too. The difference is in the use of the freakishness—*i.e.*, of the characters and the conduct that deviates from the accustomed and comfortable. Miss O'Connor uses her Hazel Moteses and Misfits and Francis Marion Tarwaters and the like to comment upon the moral and spiritual evasions and shortcomings of the supposedly "normal" community; they appear freakish because in their exaggeration they dramatize moral ultimates, and refuse to abide by the comfortable evasions of a too complacent, too secular society. Their apparent grotesqueness is actually spiritual consistency: the true freakishness is the secular materialism of the everyday, which Miss O'Connor felt was spiritually grotesque. Thus, in *Wise Blood*, when Hazel Motes takes to wrapping barbed wire about his chest to mortify himself for his sins, his landlady tells him that people have quit doing that a long time ago, whereupon Hazel replies that people haven't quit doing it so long as he is still doing it.

By contrast, Carson McCullers focusses upon her maimed, misfitting, wounded people not as a commentary upon the complacent "normality" of the community which would term them freakish, but as exemplars of the wretchedness of the human condition. It isn't that freaks are commentaries or criticisms on normality; they *are* normality. Their physical grotesquery merely makes visible and identifiable their isolation and anguish; "normal" people do not confront these on quite such immediate and inescapable terms, perhaps, but they are really no better off, no happier. Everybody that is human is on the chain gang; on some the stripes and chains are merely more readily visible.

IV

The particular vision of Carson McCullers, the capacity for recognizing and portraying the sympathetically identifying with pain and loneliness, could arise only out of a social situation in which the patterns and forms and expectations of conduct and attitude are very firmly and formidably present, so that the inability or failure to function within those patterns seems crucial. If everything is permitted and expected, then there is no need to feel pain or frustration because one's own behavior and inclinations are different from those of others. But if there is a strong set of expectations, and one is unable to fulfill them and yet be oneself, then one searches out for kindred sufferers, in order to feel less lonely through assurance of their pain as well. Thus the portrait gallery of Carson McCullers' "freaks"—*i.e.*, of those who must accept being set apart. And the conviction that this is the way the world goes, and no genuine human sharing is possible.

The appetite of Mrs. McCullers for viewing and identifying the details of human life, and the accuracy with which she was able to create so many sharply delineated people, then, was not exactly a joy in the richness and variety of experience, so much as a hunger for possession. It wasn't enough to see and identify; she had to demonstrate that, despite the varied surfaces and individually realized characterizations, they were really all alike, and what lay at the core of each was suffering and pain deriving from loneliness. One is reminded of a writer that Mrs. McCullers very much admired: Marcel Proust—significantly, a homosexual, as Mrs. McCullers was a lesbian. In that brilliant and profound panorama of men and women who appear in the seven volumes of the *Recherche du Temps Perdu*, each individual struggles to possess and to use others. Charles Swann, Gilberte, Saint Loup, the Baron Charlus, Morel, Bloch, the Duc and Duchesse de Guermantes, Albertine Simonet, above all, the narrator himself, who calls himself Marcel—at the core of each one is the unsatisfied desire to possess, to use, to pleasure oneself through or upon (never with) others, and it is all doomed, for life in human time is meaningless, since everything changes and nothing remains. Only the art that derives from personal, involuntary memory can achieve meaning; art is *not* life, but its subjective re-creation in the possessive imagination of the artist.

Something like this, I imagine, is what the writing of fiction was for Carson McCullers; art was a way of possessing. It was the creative act of taking what she saw and molding it, transforming it beyond identifiable shape into the form of art, so that it represented her kind of world. And I am tempted to say that, in the tension between the observed authority of the recalcitrant materials she drew upon and the powerful, possessive will to shape them to her desired meaning, the artistic equilibrium came that made her best work possible. Her first book, *The Heart Is a Lonely Hunter*, produced the most convincing and richest of all her characters, Dr. Benedict Maby Copeland, the black physician, and this is because, more so than with any of the others, there was a kind of palpable and inescapable social integrity in the material itself. With the other characters in the novel (and all have their individual integrities), the pain and loneliness were personal, subjective; with Dr. Copeland, there was added a specific and very formidable social deprivation. We may not quite believe in Jake Blount's outrage over the victimization of the proletariat—not that the victimization does not exist, but that Jake's outrage seems motivated less by social injustice than by his own thwarted desire for violence. The social consciousness seems to be something of an excuse for Jake to use for his own personal needs. Biff Brannon's loneliness is believable, but it seems insufficiently anchored. As for Mick Kelly, ancestor as she is of Frankie Addams, it is adolescence, not the eternal misery of the human condition, that gives her loneliness its authority, and when the author seeks to insure its permanence through family economics and misfortune, it seems somehow gratuitous, excessive; I can't really see her job in the five-and-ten as any kind of permanent entrapment. But Dr. Copeland is an educated, talented black man in the segregated society of southwest Georgia; any chagrin, mortification, rage he feels requires no dependence upon personal, subjective sensibility. Thus the kind of sensibility with which Mrs. McCullers invests him—the loneliness and anguish—blends so completely with the social outrage that the one gives body to the other. Each time I reread *The Heart Is a Lonely Hunter*, I am the more impressed with the characterization of Dr. Copeland. He is masterful, one of the reasons I share David Madden's feeling that the first novel is the best of all her full-length works.

I say this despite my admiration for so much of *The Member of the Wedding*. Frankie Addams is the most appealing of Mrs. McCullers' people; I like her better than Mick Kelley because she is less strident—less written, I think, to a thesis. She is what Mick Kelly would perhaps have been, had there been room for her to have a whole book of her own. In *The Heart Is a Lonely Hunter*, the "Mozart" motif always seemed a bit incongruous and sentimental to me, as if it were somewhat forced upon the characterization. Frankie Addams has the same sensibility without the extraneous element, as I see it, and her struggles with preadolescence are entirely convincing and wondrously done—up to a certain point. That point is reached when, two-thirds of the way through, Frankie's sensibility moves beyond that inherent in her situation and becomes something bizarre and genuinely distorted—when the piano tuner goes to work and Frankie and Berenice have some kind of surrealistic, mystic vision of pain and misery. After that point, I cease to believe fully in the meaning Mrs. McCullers is (as it now seems) forcing upon Frankie. That's not Frankie as we have known her, and she never recovers. The novel, in other words, goes beyond the pain of preadolescent awkwardness and becomes truly aberrant; it drops off the deep end into distortion for the sake of distortion. The death of John Henry, for example: he seems to be killed off gratuitously, in order to provide more misery. And in the epilogue, when Frankie enters full adolescence, becomes Frances, and is made into a "normal" teen-ager, it seems too arbitrary, too pat. That isn't Frankie, either.

It is interesting, and particularly in light of the revelations in Mrs. Carr's biography of Carson McCullers' adult sexual ambivalence, that her two important artist figures, Mick and Frankie, cannot go beyond the point of incipient sexual awakening and yet remain consistent with their characterizations. These young girls, both with masculine names, remain fixed in preadolescence; when they have to become women, as they must, they are, as characters, all but destroyed. Mick seduces Harry Minowitz; her initiation accomplished, she wants nothing whatever to do with him, and gladly lets him run away. Frankie, more innocent, smashes the vase over the head of the soldier, dreams of escaping into a world of snow and wintry calm, then becomes Frances and is Frankie no more. I think of those photographs in Mrs. Carr's biography, of Carson at Yaddo looking like a boyish preadolescent girl, and of what she did to poor Reeves McCullers.

V

The psychology of the artist is a complex matter, and I have no intention of trying to work it out as it involves Carson McCullers. I shall suggest only this. Those seven years, from the time she wrote *The Heart Is a Lonely Hunter* up through *The Member of the Wedding*, must have represented, in Mrs. McCullers' career, a period during which the confusion, chaos, and contradiction that characterized most of her adult life could be made into art because the issues that were involved still seemed capable of solution. She could, in other words, embody the contradictions in language; they could evolve into a counterpoint, which she as an artist could see as significant. The quarrel within herself was genuine, and she could make poetry out of it. But the time came when she capitulated, ceased as a writer to struggle against the confusion of her life by attempting to give it order and form through language, as she had been doing, and let the subjective, ultimately destructive element have full sway. This is the impression I get from Mrs. Carr's biography. The creative tension was relaxed. The personal suffering continued, but no longer could she approach it with the assumption that the suffering represented a deprivation, a frustrated yearning for a more beautiful and happier situation *outside* herself which was, at least theoretically, attainable in this world. Instead, the pain became itself the objective; there was nothing more to be discovered through and with it. Now she knew physical pain as never before; her life revolved around it. It seems clear that, in some strange but powerful way, the mental anguish becomes physical, and is henceforth made permanent and acceptable. In Marcel

Proust's explanation, "the life of the writer does not end" with the work of art he makes out of it, and "the same temperament which caused him to undergo certain sufferings which have been incorporated in his work will continue to exist after the work is completed. . . . Viewed as an omen of misfortune the work should be regarded solely as an unhappy love which is the forerunner of others and will end in the poet's life resembling his work, so that he will scarcely have any more need to write, such a faithful forecast of what is to come will he be able to find in what he has already written."

I was struck by the way in which, as evidenced in Mrs. Carr's biography, Proust's dictum was borne out in Mrs. McCullers' life. She herself noted, with more than a little satisfaction, that everything that happened to her characters either had been or would eventually be experienced by her in her own life. David Madden has stressed the intensity of this imaginative relationship between her art and her own life: "One might say that all her work is autobiographical in the sense that whatever she read and whatever she conjured up in her imagination *really happened* to her." This is something more, I believe, than what is usually signified by autobiography: *i.e.*, than Flaubert's famous remark that he was Emma Bovary. Instead of her characters representing aspects of Carson McCullers' sensibility, they seem to have *become* her sensibility. Not only was the gap between life and art erased; the fantasy, and the suffering it embodied, were allowed to become the reality. Whatever anchor to everyday life had existed before, in the form of her childhood identity, her early experience, the necessity of having to fit into and live in a world beyond and outside her emotional needs, ceased to hold. The pain, the suffering, the yearning, no longer a commentary upon experience, were now the experience itself. Were the crippling illnesses that increasingly ravaged her psychosomatic in origin? Her friends suspected as much; perhaps she too knew it, as Mrs. Carr notes. She was caught up in her pain, and did not struggle to escape it because the pain was, as she saw it, her art and her identity.

Again the profound insight of Marcel Proust into the nature of suffering and sexual abnormality is instructive: "When life walls us in, our intelligence cuts an opening, for, though there can be no remedy for an unrequited love, one can win release from suffering, even if only by drawing from it the lessons it has to teach. The intelligence does not recognize in life any closed situations without an outlet." But this, Carson McCullers was unable to do; she is each of her suffering characters, in turn, but the next, ultimate step, which enabled Proust to create his great apologia, she was ultimately unable to take. She could not draw from the pain and loneliness the truths that, in Proust's words, "take the place of sorrows," since "when the latter are transformed into ideas, they at once lose part of their noxious effect on the heart and from the very first moment the transformation itself radiates joy." For Carson McCullers this never happened. "She was never an intellectual," a onetime friend said of her; "she only felt." If so, she had reached a stage at which the perception of pain was not enough, if she was to go beyond the early fiction. But that was all she knew. There was, for her, no Recapture of Lost Time, but only *Clock Without Hands*.

Like certain other of her contemporaries, Carson McCullers, it seems to me, constructed her art out of the South, but not out of its history, its common myths, its public values and the failure to cherish them. What is southern in her books are the rhythms, the sense of brooding loneliness in a place saturated with time. Compare *The Heart Is a Lonely Hunter* or *The Member of the Wedding* with, say, *Winesburg, Ohio*, and the relationship with the region is obvious. Sherwood Anderson's grotesques are more simple; a few clear, masterful sentences and we get their essential quality. Carson McCullers must show her misfits, whether spiritual or physical, in an extended context; there is plenty of time for everything. The southern quality is unmistakable, in the unhurried fascination with surfaces, the preoccupation with the setting in which the characterization reveals itself. Character is not for McCullers, any more than for Eudora Welty or William Faulkner or Thomas Wolfe, an idea, but a state of awareness. To repeat, there is plenty of time. And when the violence comes, as it so often does, it erupts in a place and a context, and it jars, queerly or terribly or both, the established and accustomed patterns. Before and after, there is lots of waiting, lots of time to think about everything.

Robert Penn Warren, in his novel *Flood*, has a southerner explain to a friend from the North that the key to the southern experience is lonesomeness. "It is angry lonesomeness. Angry lonesomeness makes Southerners say the word *South* like an idiot Tibetan monk turning a broken-down prayer wheel on which he has forgotten to hang any prayers." No southerner, he continues, "believes that there is any South. He just believes that if he keeps on saying the word he will lose some of the angry lonesomeness." Warren was writing fiction, not an essay on the South, but if we discount the metaphysical hyperbole that is proper for the particular characterization, the remark makes sense. What is involved, I think, is the same contrast between the formidable community patterns and social context mentioned earlier and the solitude of the private individual confronting these. Southern literature is filled with depictions of characters who, set for one reason or other on the outside, contemplate the intense coming and going of a community life from a private distance. The Reverend Hightower, Jack Burden, Eugene Gant, most of Eudora Welty's people—this is an essential element in southern fiction, and in no other southern author's work is it more essential than in the fiction of Carson McCullers.

Surely this situation lies at the heart of her relationship with the South, and nowhere is it given more pathetic rendering than by her. This is what one takes away, most of all, from Carson McCullers' people in their time and place: the way that it feels to be lonely.

That is why her people do and say what they do. That is the source of the pain. That is why the New York Cafe keeps open all the time: "the only store on all the street with an open door and lights inside." And that is why her best work may survive.

Trouble on the Land: Southern Literature and the Great Depression

It is a painful thing sometimes to read history books that are written for children, and to realize the view of the past that is being given them. Recently I happened upon Volume 14 of the *American Heritage New Illustrated History of the United States*. It was subtitled *The Roosevelt Era*. The author of Volume 14 provided his young readers with a year-by-year chronicle for the 1930s. I quote from the section for the year 1935:

> During the year, Technicolor came to the movie screen, and the WPA Federal Arts Project came to the aid of hungry artists, many of whom had a built-in predilection for the "Ash Can School" of painting—stark slum scenes being a favorite subject. Plays expressed the same preoccupation with social messages in this period. . . . In the world of fiction, William Faulkner was gaining worldwide praise for his naturalistic novels portraying for the most part sordid slices of low-class life in the South. Within this realm, Erskine Caldwell had recently contributed *Tobacco Road*. The third book of James Farrell's *Studs Lonigan* triology appeared in 1935, looking at squalor further north, in Chicago. . . .

It saddens me to think that this is the picture that today's young readers will receive of William Faulkner, and of southern literature for the period. For the 1930s were the high point, the culmination, of the South's literary history, and relatively little of the books written by southern authors during the period had much to do with "sordid slices of low-class life."

152

From roughly the coming of the Great Depression up to the attack on Pearl Harbor, the southern literary renascence was at perihelion. A roll call is in order. Faulkner published *The Sound and the Fury, As I Lay Dying, Light in August, Absalom, Absalom!*, and *The Hamlet*. Thomas Wolfe published *Look Homeward, Angel, Of Time and the River*, and two posthumously edited novels. Robert Penn Warren published his first book of poems and his first novel. *Gone with the Wind* came, was read and then seen on film, and has endured. Caldwell published *Tobacco Road, God's Little Acre*, and other novels; until censorship standards were relaxed in the 1950s they were unsurpassed as popular pornography. Carson McCullers published *The Heart Is a Lonely Hunter*. Katherine Anne Porter published almost all of her best work. Allen Tate wrote most of his best poems and his novel, *The Fathers*. Eudora Welty's first book, *A Curtain of Green*, was published. James Agee published his first two books. Richard Wright wrote the stories in *Uncle Tom's Children*. In drama, Lillian Hellman did most of her best work. And so on.

From the standpoint of what is now almost a half-century's perspective, it does seem undeniable that a disproportionate share of the more impressive literature by Americans during the Depression years was written by southern authors. Yet not only is there only a moderate amount of "sordid slices of low-class life" included in that literature, but the truth is that most of it does not importantly concern itself with what many of our historians and critics still seem to believe was the major and almost the sole literary theme of the period: Social Consciousness, as manifested in exposés of capitalistic society, greed, sympathetic delineation of the downtrodden, depictions of class struggle, etc. There are, of course, exceptions; but mostly that sort of thing was not what seems to have kindled the literary imagination in the South of the 1930s.

Now I trust that nobody needs to be reminded that if this is so, it is certainly not because the southern states were in any way exempt from the consequences of the debacle of 1929 that in the Northeast sent most of the intellectuals off to the Finland Station. "It is my conviction," President Roosevelt declared in 1938, "that the South presents right now . . . the Nation's No. 1 economic problem." The Depression brought widespread joblessness and deprivation. The region had for many decades lagged behind the remainder of the country in all the relevant economic indices as it was, and the Depression hit with devastating effect. Banks failed, farm prices hit rock bottom, mortgages were foreclosed, tenants evicted, businesses folded, factories and mines shut down. Few if any of the social themes that the Depression made available to the American writer were barred to southerners. There were strikes, agitation, violence. Communists showed up to exhort the strikers, and the police treated them with the expected enthusiasm. There were Fascist movements here and there. Huey Long proposed to Share the Wealth. When President Roosevelt and the New Deal took hold to do something about the situation, the South voted for him overwhelmingly, and continued to do so for as long as he lived. The Great Depression and the ensuing recovery were very much a part of the southern way of life.

Writing about the impact of the crash upon American writers, Malcolm Cowley has declared that "thousands were convinced that hundreds of thousands were half-persuaded that no simple operation would save us; there had to be the complete renovation of society that Karl Marx had prophesied in 1848. Unemployment would be ended, war and fascism would vanish from the earth, but only after the revolution. Russia had pointed out the path that the rest of the world must follow into the future." Clearly Cowley was not thinking about the southern writers when he summed up the literary scene in such terms. Neither was Alfred Kazin when he wrote that "more than the age of the ideologue, of the literary revolutionary and the proletarian novelist, roles usually created within the Communist movement, the Thirties in literature were the age of the plebes—of writers from the working class, the lower class, the immigrant class, from Western farms and hills—those whose struggle was to survive." None of the southern writers of the period was a plebe except for Richard Wright, who was a black plebe. With but one or two exceptions, all the better writers had university educations. Though they had financial problems, personal survival was not one of them.

In the South, therefore, we have a region hard hit by the catastrophic crash, with severe ramifications felt throughout rural and urban southern society. The decade in which the crash occurred was that in which the literature being written by southern authors was reaching the very height of its artistic achievement. Almost none of that literature was so-called escapist literature: it dealt with human beings in struggle and travail. Yet even though we know that what was happening economically, socially, and politically within the region, the nation, and the world was of considerable concern to the men and women who were writing the literature, relatively little that they wrote was *about* the Depression and its impact. Moreover, what was written about it was for the most part only moderately successful at delineating that particular experience.

There would seem to be something of a conundrum involved here, and so what I want to do is to examine it. I want to deal with three southern authors of stature who did try to write about the Depression, in order to get at what it may have been that prevented them from succeeding in what they set out to do. My hope is that in so doing, it may be possible to throw a little light, however wavering, on the nature of the southern literary imagination, through what it was *not* as well as what it was.

My concern is not with the avowedly proletarian novelists among the southerners, who sought to write fiction in accordance with the approved party formulas. There were in point of fact a few of them. Olive Tilford Dargan, until the Crash a local-color poet of the Carolina and Tennessee mountains, assumed the pen name of Fielding Burke and wrote several protest novels. Also there were Mary Page and Grace Lumpkin, and doubtless others of whom I know not. The fullness of time, however, has not ratified their literary importance. As novelists they are forgotten. It may be that if ever the Revolution does arrive, the work of these writers may be revived. For now we must turn elsewhere.

Erskine Caldwell asserted, in fiction and nonfiction both, his political and social militancy during the decade.* He did write about

---

* Critics such as Kazin and Cowley who identified Caldwell as being of plebian origins are quite mistaken, by the way. Though as a young man he spent some time among the proletariat, he came from an educated family with a record of leadership in the Presbyterian church. Both his father and mother were college graduates, and the elder Caldwell was a well-known minister of the ultraconservative Associate Reformed Presbyterian Church.

an actual textile strike in *God's Little Acre*, and in *Tobacco Road* he produced a work of formidable reputation, though it may be that the Broadway play adaptation was equally responsible for its long vogue. The Caldwell novels, which sold in the millions in paperback editions, did not, however, enjoy their vogue on the merits of their political assertion. They made their popular mark because they were bawdy and suggestive, even though they avoid four-letter words of the wrong sort and the sex act is never described clinically. If in recent years they have lost their popularity on the drugstore paperback rack, it is because now that the standards for pruriency have been dispensed with, few would purchase *Tobacco Road* when *Emmanuelle* or *Fear of Flying* is available. I wouldn't even buy it myself.

Assuredly there is considerably more than pornographic suggestibility to *Tobacco Road*. For one thing, it is *funny*. So are *God's Little Acre* and *Journeyman*. Jeeter Lester, Dude Lester, Sister Bessie, Ellie May are sterling exemplars of a southern literary tradition that goes all the way back at least to William Byrd II's *Dividing Line* histories of 1728. The tradition is of low-life high jinks; as in all such buffoonery the art consists of depicting human beings as animals. It is a Georgia freak show that Caldwell offers us, and like all theatrical ventures it is successful in direct proportion to the extent that the strangeness can be dramatized.

Caldwell's contemporary William Faulkner was not above providing similar entertainment for us. I don't suppose there is anything in Caldwell's low comedy that offers more raunchy subject matter than Ike Snopes's romance with the cow in *The Hamlet*. As I. O. Snopes puts it, "A man cant have his good name drug in the alleys. The Snopes name has done held its head up too long in this country to have no such reproaches against it like stock-diddling." The difference is that Faulkner's lowborn rustics are complex human beings. However grotesque in form the expression of their humanity may seem, they are not often turned into beasts. Faulkner's lyric apostrophe to Ike Snopes's romance with the heifer, with its rhapsodic depiction of the idiot courting his inamorata, is amusing because Faulkner comically ennobles the liaison. He celebrates Ike's tryst in language that would be appropriate for the courtship of Romeo and Juliet, and though the contrast between what is happening and the language used to describe it is comically ridiculous, it works the other way around, too. The idiot and his cow are, in their own fashion, neither more nor less in their love than Shakespeare's star-crossed lovers.

Erskine Caldwell offers little such comic dignity to his Tobacco Road folk. When Sister Bessie asserts of her yen for the 16-year-old Dude Lester that "the Lord was speaking to me. . . . He was telling me I ought to marry a new husband," the comedy resides in her sorry effort to justify her biological compulsion by biblical reference. The language of scripture is used to cloak sexual urge. The result is to make her less human, more animal; the laugh is at the expense of the humanity.

In *Tobacco Road*, low-life comedy is made to exist side by side with political and social message. Caldwell ridicules Jeeter Lester and his companions as comic degenerates, and he proclaims their victimization by society. Jeeter wants to plant a crop, but can't because the soil has been exhausted and the merchants won't sell seed and guano on credit. "You rich folks in Augusta is just bleeding us poor folk to death," he complains. "You don't work none, but you get all the money us farmers make." But he will not abandon the land: "We was put here on the land where cotton will grow, and it's my place to make it grow. I wouldn't fool with the mills if I could make as much as fifteen dollars a week in them. I'm staying on the land till my time comes to die."

The political message, the proletarian agricultural motif, is in no important way fused with the low comedy. On the contrary, they work against each other. It is next to impossible to maintain a serious concern for the plight of the Lesters when throughout the novel we are invited to laugh at them for their degeneracy. No doubt it was Caldwell's intention to have us view the degeneracy and squalor as the result of the economic victimization: privileged society has turned the Lesters into swine. But except when making his political pitch Caldwell gleefully expends his rhetoric in making us guffaw at his bestiary. Regard how comically lewd and depraved these Lesters are! he tells us. Watch them fornicate in full view of an audience! Note the way that the woman preacher with the hideous nose quotes Scripture to justify her venery! Ain't it diverting?

We are informed by Robert Cantwell that "as a social document,

Tobacco Road was a highly effective instrument in the various projects of soil conservation and social welfare of the time. . . . Had the characters of *Tobacco Road* been drawn sympathetically, the tragedy they embody would have been at best an echo in prose of the elegy in a country graveyard; as comic characters, they make that poverty unforgettable." There may be some truth to that, but if the New Deal had been forced to make dependence upon the influence of the Caldwell novels in its efforts to marshal public opinion in favor of the Soil Conservation Act, my guess is that the late Henry A. Wallace would have abandoned Washington to return to chicken farming in his native Iowa a number of years earlier than he did.

An altogether more imposing depiction of southern lowlife is James Agee's *Let Us Now Praise Famous Men*. Agee spent his boyhood in Tennessee, he studied at Philips Exeter and Harvard, then went to work for Henry Luce's *Fortune* magazine. During the 1930s Agee found himself increasingly drawn to communism. Though hardly an adherent to the official Party Line, and at all times distrustful of the shallow leftist formulations of his day, Agee declared of the Marxist hypothesis that "an awful lot of things do seem somewhere near and right from that, or essentially that, point of view, as the same things don't from any other." In the summer of 1936 Agee was delighted to receive an assignment from *Fortune* to go south with the photographer Walker Evans and "do a story on: sharecropper family (daily and yearly life): and also a study of Farm Economics in the South (impossible for me): and also on the several efforts to help the situation: *i.e.* Govt. and state work; theories and wishes of Southern liberals; whole story of the 2 Southern unions." It was, he added, the "best break I ever had on *Fortune*."

It was indeed a break; it was pivotal to his literary career. Though the articles he was hired to write proved unacceptable to *Fortune*, they developed into a book that some critics feel is almost a classic. In Geneviève Moreau's summation, *Let Us Now Praise Famous Men* "is an intense spiritual adventure, a search for innocence, and along the way all literature, all culture, is brought into question. It is an experimental, polyphonic work in which all the arts—literature, music, film—fuse. And though Agee repeatedly disavows its artistic purposes, it is as a work of art that *Famous Men* is ultimately valued."

What the assignment to go down to Alabama and write about sharecroppers did for Agee was to get him into the rural South, and into a confrontation with his own origins. For the downtrodden tenant farmers and sharecroppers of Alabama were his father's people. Though the Agees of the Tennessee hill country had not themselves descended from the mountains and into the squalor, deprivation, and hard toil of the Gudgers, Ricketts, and Woods whom Agee encountered in Alabama, James Agee discovered in the houses, lives and ways of these depressed agriculturalists of the rural South a concreteness and significance such as seemed otherwise missing from his adult life in the urban literary and journalistic world of the metropolis. Their lives seemed anchored in actuality. These people were *real*. As he prepared to spend a night in the rickety farmhouse with the Gudgers,

> the feeling increased itself upon me that at the end of a wandering and seeking, so long it had begun before I was born, I had apprehended and now sat at rest in my own home, between two who were my brother and sister, yet less that than something else; these, the wife my age exactly, the husband four years older, seemed not other than my own parents, in whose patience I was so different, so diverged, so strange as I was; and all that surrounded me, that silently strove in through my senses and stretched me full, was familiar and dear to me as nothing else on earth, and as if well known in a deep past and long years lost; so that I could wish that all my chance life was in truth the betrayal, the curable delusion, that it seemed, and that this was my right home, right earth, right blood, to which I would never have true right. For half my blood is just this; and half my right of speech; and by bland chance alone is my life so softened and sophisticated in the years of my defenselessness, and I am robbed of a royalty I can not only never claim, but never properly much desire or regret. And so in this quiet introit, and in all the time we have stayed in this house, and in all we have sought, and in each detail of it, there is so keen, sad, and precious a nostalgia as I can scarcely otherwise know; a knowledge of brief truancy into the sources of life, whereto I have no rightful access, having paid no price beyond love and sorrow.

It is because of this experience, reported retrospectively like the madeleine episode in Proust, that the involvement with the Gudgers in *Let Us Now Praise Famous Men* is artistically important to the author. The "half my blood" and "half my right of speech" are his father's family heritage. Hugh James Agee was killed in an automobile wreck when his son was six years old. James Agee's subsequent life—the years with his mother and her well-educated family of northern antecedents, at Saint Andrews School in Sewanee, Tennessee, at Philips Exeter, Harvard, and in New York City— had constituted a distancing from the social and cultural legacy of his birth and his childhood in Knoxville. Now, in a sharecropper's shack in Alabama, he is made aware of the extent to which that portion of his identity and his heritage had become obscured. But the memory of the past—"so keen, sad, and precious a nostalgia"— can give him renewed access to the circumstance of his own identity in time. *Let Us Now Praise Famous Men*, therefore, comprises the monument and record of James Agee's rediscovery of his southern birthright. The writing of it would ultimately make possible for him the re-creation of remembered experience that is *The Morning Watch* and, most important of all, *A Death in the Family*.

For that very reason, however, the sharecropper book is ineffective as a work of political and social reportage. For despite the extremely detailed portraiture of the sharecropping families, how they looked and talked, where they lived, what they ate, how they worked, how degraded their situation, Agee isn't really imaginatively concerned with them in their own right. It is *his experience there* that fascinates him. The tone painting, the evocations of scenery and circumstance, the continued questioning of his own motives, the expressions of outrage at those who dare to look down upon and pity the humanity of the sharecroppers, the apostrophes to human endurance constitute nothing more, and nothing less, than an exploration of his own sensibility.

Agee isn't interested in the Gudgers, but in how to think, feel, and write about the Gudgers. Under the guise of declining to oversimplify and distort through imposition of any sort of formulaic, stereotyped presentation of sharecropping, Agee is recording his experience in Alabama. As one critic points out, the "lack of order is the order in the text: Agee's straining to communicate reality, and failing, and straining again to give the narrative its form. . . . The form imitates the process of consciousness wherein perception is sudden, inexplicable, quickly lost, and always beginning again. What one feels constantly behind the words on the page is a consciousness laboring toward the world, Nature, the truth." The inability to impose meaningful shape comes because the real meaning was *not* the Alabama experience as such, but his own alienation from what it represented, and how the alienation happened. The place to look for that was not in the details of sharecropper families in Alabama, but in his memories of Knoxville, his childhood, his parents, his divided heritage—"the sources of life, whereto I have no rightful access, having paid no price beyond love and sorrow." Rightful repossession could come only through the resources of memory and understanding: the writing of *The Morning Watch* and *A Death in the Family*, an artistic travail which, pursued intermittently, occupied the remainder of his life.

That Agee declares that the usual ways of writing a book about sharecroppers won't work is quite correct; for he was not writing a book about sharecropping. Agee possessed a deceptive—deceptive to him—ability to engage himself thoroughly and completely in whatever topic came to hand or was assigned to him by an editor or a film maker. As a writer he could get involved in almost anything, and force his energies upon it, without any immediate insight into the relationship of the project at hand to any other aspects of his career or his work. It is the aptitude of the good journalist, the journeyman writer. But Agee was also an artist—an artist who was in search of his true subject, and who had not yet discovered it. In this instance his aptitude misled him, for what Agee was really drawn to wasn't sharecropping and sharecroppers but their symbolic relationship to his own imagination, something that he sensed was tied in with his memories and his origins, but without knowing quite why. So what he tried to do was to invest his portrayal of the sharecroppers with the imaginative dimensions of a significance that really belonged not to the sharecroppers but to the relationship with his past.

Even so, it was not finally wasted. The discovery had been made that led ultimately to *A Death in the Family*. So we can only be grateful for the Alabama book.

The other southern writer of consequence who sought to deal literarily with the Depression of the 1930s, of course, was Thomas Wolfe. Most of what he wrote about the economic and social experience of the Crash is contained in the work entitled *You Can't*

Go Home Again, which was put into shape by Edward Aswell of Harper and Brothers and published in 1940, two years after Wolfe's death, as a "new novel by Thomas Wolfe." We now know that it wasn't any such thing. Aswell pieced it together from a vast heap of published and unpublished writings, some of it dating back to the period of *Look Homeward, Angel*, some of it published in magazines as short novels, some of it written shortly before Wolfe's death. Working from a rough outline left by Wolfe, Aswell cut, spliced, rearranged, rewrote descriptions for consistency, incorporated portions of letters, and wrote transitional passsages himself when he thought they were needed. It is dangerous, therefore, to deal in more than very general terms with Wolfe's actual achievement in reference to *You Can't Go Home Again*. Of all the important American writers of the 1930s Wolfe was by far the worst edited, both at Scribner's and Harper's.

During the years from 1929 until his death in 1938 Wolfe lived for most of the time in New York City, with several extended stays in Europe. The publication of his first novel and the stock market crash both occurred in the fall of 1929. It was not until six years later that his second novel, *Of Time and the River*, was published. All of his work is intensely autobiographical, and since the second novel carried his autobiographical protagonist only up to the late 1920s, he could make no direct commentary there on the ravages of the Great Depression as such. We know that his editor at Scribner's, Maxwell Perkins, was at some pains to insist that Wolfe not allow his Marxist views of the 1930s to become part of Eugene Gant's consciousness during the period covered in *Of Time and the River*, when Thomas Wolfe had held no such views.

Perkins' attitude was that since Wolfe was writing avowedly autobiographical fiction, it was essential that he be faithful to the way his protagonist thought and felt during the time being chronicled. But the difficulty is that Wolfe's fiction is autobiographical not only in the sense that it is about his own life, but also in that he, the writer, is overtly present—*as writer*. Though he does not say "I" (in actuality he did just that in the manuscript entitled *Of Time and the River*, but his editors changed it to the third person for him), he makes his reader quite conscious of his presence as authorial commentator on the events being related, events which earlier had happened to *him*. Thus Perkins' insistence upon chronological authenticity had the result of working against any kind of growing maturity on Wolfe's part as to the meaning of his earlier experience, and as a writer Wolfe needed all the emotional maturity he could muster.

Most of what Wolfe had to say about the Great Depression can be found in two sequences in *You Can't Go Home Again*. One of these is set in New York City a week before the Crash, and describes a lavish party given by George Webber's mistress, Esther Jack, at her Park Avenue apartment. A fire breaks out in the apartment house, the building is evacuated, and the residents and their guests wait outside as the firemen go to work. To extinguish the fire it is necessary to flood the basement, which in turn floods out several levels of railroad trackage underneath. The episode is interpreted by Wolfe as emblematic of the approaching collapse of the wealthy, privileged society of the metropolis in the wake of the stock market debacle and the Depression. When the fire has been put out and tenants return to their apartments, George Webber vows silently to leave the world of Esther Jack and the immense wealth, social inequity, and artistic philistinism that it symbolizes. Wolfe published a shorter version of the sequence, entitled "The Party at Jack's," in novella form. Aswell combined it with additional material, wrote a new ending, and incorporated it in *You Can't Go Home Again*. It is not known whether the additional material was written before or after the version which was published in magazine form. Certainly the novella version is considerably more focussed artistically than that in the book.

A second Depression sequence describes the frenzied business activity of pre-Depression Asheville, which is called Libya Hill, and the calamitous impact of the Crash. Wolfe drew the inspiration for much of this material from his own family's experience. Several sections were originally published as short stories. Aswell combined, spliced, and rewrote to fit it into *You Can't Go Home Again*.

Let it be said at once that there is a great deal of very powerful writing in this later work of Thomas Wolfe's. While I am not convinced that Wolfe ever really found an artistic substitute for the intense lyric self-consciousness of Eugene Gant, his protagonist for the first two novels, he was writing well toward the end, and it may be that as C. Hugh Holman and other good critics have declared, Wolfe was indeed working toward a new and different mastery of his material in a dramatic and social rather than lyrical and personal mode.

It seems to me, even so, that an episode such as "The Party at Jack's" is not altogether convincing as the indictment of the over-refined wealthy that it sets out to be. For George Webber's decision to reject Esther Jack's world seems to come as the result of at least several impulses on the part of George. On the one hand, the society of Esther and her friends is depicted as materialistic, wasteful, callous, effete; ultimately it is based upon the exploitation of the lower levels of society, as personified by the two elevator attendants who die from smoke suffocation in the fire. A second reason for George's distaste for the world of Esther Jack, however, appears to be that it is composed primarily of highly cosmopolitan, successful, supercilious urban folk, many of whom bear such names as Mandell, Heilprinn, Hirsch, Abramson, and who are extremely unappreciative of the merits of earnest young artists from the provinces. The host at the party, Frederick Jack, takes delight in "seeing some yokel, say, fresh from the rural districts, all hands and legs and awkwardness, hooked and wriggling on a cunning word—a woman's, preferably, because women were so swift and deft in matters of this nature." After the party is under way, precisely this is what is done to awkward, ill-at-ease young George Webber. Are all these New Yorkers false, vicious, amoral, predatory because they are wealthy and philistine, or because they are New Yorkers, many of them Jews? One isn't so sure. Still a third reason for George Webber's renunciation is his mistress' age; she is considerably older than he is, and as we see when she pretends that a youthful painting of her was done later than in fact it was painted, she tries to conceal her relative antiquity.

The dramatis personae of "The Party at Jack's" are for the most part a thoroughly unpleasant and unattractive assortment of human beings, and if an earthquake or a stock market crash should come to destroy or cleanse the society they inhabit—preferably a little of both—we might not feel entirely overcome with grief and loss. Still, if what is wrong with them is that they have the misfortune to be New Yorkers—*i.e.*, not Anglo-Americans in origin and ways of speech and appearance—and therefore not to have been born in the South or the Midwest, then isn't the author's attitude a trifle insular and undemocratic? And if what is wrong with George continuing to inhabit the world of Esther Jack is that Esther is considerably older than George and tends to be overly possessive, then is it quite honest to attribute the decision to leave that society principally to the wealth, philistinism, and social callousness?

In other words, mixed in with the social commentary of "The Party at Jack's" is a considerable amount of provincial insularity and personal self-justification. Now we can understand young George Webber, fresh from the provinces and an unpublished author, feeling this way. Indeed, it would be somewhat surprising if he did not. The difficulty is that the older, much more mature author whose autobiographical surrogate young Webber manifestly is, seems also to entertain such emotions. Young George, for example, wasn't present earlier in the episode when Esther Jack's husband looked forward so eagerly to the possibility of a young man from the provinces being humiliated by one of the sophisticates at the party. The author-narrator was there, however, and told us about it with quite the same intensity of feeling that George displayed when later on it happened to him. The author-narrator is quite indignant about the kind of wicked metropolitan society and the kind of nasty urban sensibility that would not only tolerate but actually relish such cruelty to young provincials.

If Wolfe's excoriation of wealth and privilege in the metropolis is compromised by his provincial prejudices, the same is true to at least as great an extent when he turns his attention to the lower levels of metropolitan society. The Irish maids, Swedish doormen, the waitresses and typists, the dwellers in the alleys, tenements, and flats of Depression Brooklyn are so alien to his attitudes and expectations that it is all but impossible for him to write about them other than satirically. Allowing for Wolfe's far more versatile and subtle rhetorical skills, it is almost as if an Erskine Caldwell bereft of his comic instinct had transferred his attentions from Tobacco Road to Skid Row. In the abstract Wolfe can admire the great city and its citizenry, but when he gets down to particulars, what comes out is mostly disgust and despair.

It is true that the magazine version of "The Party at Jack's" does not contain nearly as much of the xenophobia; it is written much more economically and surely. Yet the economy and objectivity are attained in large part at the cost of suppressing the intensity with which George Webber and his autobiographical author-narrator are engaged in the situation. The gain in objectivity is at the expense of vividness; Wolfe's art depends upon the presence of that author-narrator, and without it the fiction tends to be flat and unexciting. So that while the shorter version of "The Party at Jack's" is more focussed and compact, it lacks much of the emotional engagement on the author-narrator's part that makes Wolfe's best work, for all its excess, so compelling.

Let me point out at once that when Wolfe turns to the people back home in Asheville—Libya Hill in the George Webber narratives—and describes the commercial opportunism and real estate mania that brought about the end of the boom there, he is equally as savage in his disapproval. Characters such as Tim Wagner, Rumford Bland, Jarvis Riggs, and Dave Merrit are depicted in terms that are fully as repulsive and denunciatory as those used on the wealthy New Yorkers. Their Anglo-American Protestant credentials do not save them one whit. There is no more withering episode in all of Wolfe's writings than that which portrays the "company man," the two-faced Dave Merrit, all cordiality and good will on the surface, as he savagely browbeats George Webber's friend Randy Shepperson for his failure to meet an ever-increasing sales quota for the Federal Weight, Scales and Computing Company. Libya Hill and its residents are caught in a vicious, inhuman commercial system based on self-delusion and greed:

> They had squandered fabulous sums in meaningless streets and bridges. They had torn down ancient buildings and erected new ones large enough to take care of a city of half a million people. They had levelled hills and bored through mountains, making magnificent tunnels paved with double roadways and glittering with shining tiles—tunnels which leaped out on the other side into Arcadian wilderness. They had flung away the earnings of a lifetime, and mortgaged those of a generation

to come. They had ruined their city, and in so doing had ruined themselves, their children, and their children's children.

It is a searing indictment of American materialism that Wolfe offers us in *You Can't Go Home Again*—and it is the more convincing because in the instance of Asheville Wolfe is able to understand what had caused it. The get-rich-quick mania had come not merely out of avarice, but a thwarted sacramental energy. The people of Libya Hill wanted "some thrilling and impossible fulfillment, some glorious enrichment and release of their pent lives, some ultimate escape from their own tedium." An emptiness in the condition of their lives, a balked need for love and spiritual growth that was not to be reckoned merely in terms of economic indices and material possessions, had led them to grasp so eagerly and fatally at the chance for easy money and extravagant prosperity.

Wolfe and his autobiographical protagonist understand this, because Wolfe is *of* these people; he could see that what the people of his home city did to themselves came out of much the same needs and hopes that had motivated him to pursue a literary career in the shining city beyond the mountains. No such understanding is exhibited when Wolfe writes of the coming of the Depression in the metropolis: the wealthy New Yorkers, the artistic aesthetes of Esther Jack's world, whether bearing Anglo-American or whatever names, are finally alien to Wolfe and to his autobiographical protagonists, and though he tries very hard on occasion to know them, there is a barrier that cannot be overcome. Wolfe's depiction of the city remains that of an outsider, frequently fascinated and as often repelled by what he finds there, but never *of* it. The impact of the Great Depression brought to the fore his political and social outrage, but did not notably increase his understanding. Thus his sympathy is pity rather than compassion, and his anger seems often to be directed as much at the inhabitants of the city for being the kind of people who are to be found in large cities, as it is at the symbols of the wealth, privilege, and injustice that helped to cause the crash.

Yet the final judgment of Wolfe's writings about the Depression years is one of admiration, qualified but real. For Wolfe did his best to understand his experience; he took no cheap ways out, he did not try to avert his gaze from what he saw. He never ceased in his effort to re-create in language his experience of the world, and he sought always to reveal himself nakedly and honestly, without subterfuge or self-deception. As an artist he did not flinch at revealing what manner of man he was, and this self-revelation, which is his basic technique for writing fiction, does not fail to show the worst as well as the best. And he *learned* as he went along. Even the atavistic xenophobia of the early years must be qualified by the episode entitled "I Have a Thing To Tell You," written after a final visit to Germany in 1936, in which he confronts the evil of nazism and the world sickness of the Germans. In C. Hugh Holman's words, "Nothing Wolfe ever wrote has greater narrative drive or more straightforward action than this novella." The Wolfe fiction, finally, *works*: it has its flaws, its failures aplenty, but in its particular kind of vision it is unique. Even *You Can't Go Home Again*, filtered through a clumsy and distorting editorial job, is a work of dignity.

But—to repeat—it is not often very effective social criticism as such, and we must ultimately say of Wolfe what has been noted about Caldwell and Agee: that whatever the considerable achievement of the work they wrote about the Depression, they do not develop and sustain a believable and consistent artistic indictment of social injustice, whether of tenement or tenant shack, which was what they set out to do.

I have sought to show how in each instance the conscious intention of the author seems to have been severely qualified by other aspects of his literary imagination which impelled his artistic attention elsewhere. In Caldwell it was the reliance upon low comedy, in the long-established tradition of southern poor-white humor. For Agee the intention to write about the degradation of sharecropping moved swiftly into an exploration of *his* experience in attempting to do so, an exploration that led him away from Alabama and back into his own past. For Wolfe the intended indictment of Mammon and philistia in the city was seriously compromised by the basic provincial hostility that he brought to bear upon almost all those who inhabit the American metropolis.

Why couldn't these three southern writers deal with the Great Depression in the way they wanted to do?

In Caldwell's instance I read the several assessments of him as an important social critic, and then I go back to the novels, and even so cannot convince myself to take them seriously. Caldwell had a genuine talent for a certain sort of low-life humor, and it comes, as I have suggested earlier, out of a long-standing regional literary tradition. The old southwestern humor involved looking down at the rustic primitives from above, with mingled amusement and astonishment. Caldwell mostly omits the genteel narrator customary to the mode, but nonetheless he is looking down from above at every moment along the way. If we grant Caldwell an underlying seriousness of literary purpose (I find it difficult to do so), then it was betrayed by a vision of caste and class that has been characteristic of southern literature almost from its beginnings.[1] For despite his intention to blame the low estate of the Lester family on the workings of economic determinism, what comes out strongest is a moral contempt for their depravity. Jeeter *says* that the town merchants and the absentee landlords are what prevent him from making a crop; but what Caldwell creates for us is a lazy, unregenerate sinner. Caldwell's view of the inhabitants of Tobacco Road is, in defiance of his intentions, historical and Calvinistic. The depiction of unregenerate mankind is much like Jonathan Edwards': "Thus do all unclean persons, who live in lascivious practices in secret; all malicious persons, all profane persons, that neglect the duties of religion. . . . Thus do tavern-haunters, and frequenters of evil company; and many other kinds that might be mentioned." Unlike Edwards, the Reverend Ira Sylvester Caldwell's son is amused at the uncleanliness and lasciviousness, and he says that the sinfulness is due to the social and economic system. But what he shows is the Mark of the Beast. It is not inappropriate that when the Lesters perish at the end of *Tobacco Road*, they are consumed by fire.

James Agee gives us no such apocalypse. His Gudgers, Ricketts, and Woods are men and women of dignity. But their imaginative significance for him is that they move him backward in time to his origins, to his father's people in the Tennessee mountains: "half my blood is just this; and half my right of speech." The result is "so keen, sad, and precious a nostalgia as I can scarcely otherwise know."* What he saw in Alabama is important because of what hap-

* The fictional name Agee chose for his sharecropper, Gudger, is significantly a North Carolina-Tennessee mountain name. Wolfe also uses it.

pened to him twenty years earlier: the death of his father, the abrupt severance of the link with the east Tennessee hill folk.

The past is also the key to much of Wolfe's performance. In linking the materialism and irresponsibility of the wealthy partygoers to his own presence there as a young provincial, Wolfe ties the episode in with the basic pattern of all his work: the flight from the mountain town in North Carolina to the city and the promise of artistic fulfillment, which is the saga of both Eugene Gant and George Webber. He had sought to put down roots in the city, as exemplified in his compulsive searching out of the details of his mistress' family history and the life of turn-of-the-century New York. But it does not work. The party at Esther Jack's is the occasion of his decision to turn his back on the world of Esther and her friends, a decision he says comes because of the materialism and philistinism of that world, but which is also emotionally bound in with the sense that it is alien to him, foreign to the life that had nurtured and shaped his art. Much of the imaginative significance of "The Party at Jack's" thus lies in his own provincial past.

The imaginative importance of the past in Wolfe's work is even more strongly emphasized in the sequence about the collapse of the boom town economy in Libya Hill. Wolfe and George Webber find the origins of the boom in George Webber's own childhood, in "the barren nighttime streets of the town he had known so well in his boyhood. . . . Yes, it was here, on many a night long past and wearily accomplished, in ten thousand little towns and in ten million little barren streets where all the passion, hope, and hunger of the famished men beat like a great pulse through the fields of darkness—it was there and nowhere else that this madness had been brewed." Their need had been his; in search of fulfillment he had left for the metropolis, while they had remained home and let their frustrated appetite for change and their hunger for meaning overcome their better judgments.

Thus the experience that both Agee and Wolfe looked back to in their effort to understand the Depression was that of the movement away from an older, small-town community with strong rural ties and into the metropolitan society that both of them knew and, as adults, inhabited. And that experience, registered personally, is nothing more or less than the historical experience of the twentieth-century South. In Agee's instance he did not recognize and begin writing about the past at once, but we have seen that it is what the imaginative response to Alabama sharecroppers involved for him. The ultimate result, *A Death in the Family*, was a chronicle of how that separation from the older community occurred and what it meant. In Wolfe's instance the response was more direct.

It has often been noted that the greatest source of strength of southern writing in this century lies in the continuity of its historical imagination. Like Virgie Rainey in Eudora Welty's *The Golden Apples*, the southern writers "saw things in their time." By this is meant not merely the specific history of the South itself (although each of these three authors, including Caldwell, has a very clearly defined notion of southern history). It means a way of looking, an attitude toward the form and meaning of human experience as a process involving a personal, familial identity in historical time.

For the writers we have been examining, this characteristic was not, it seems to me, of notable use in their efforts to write about the social impact of the Great Depression, since it tended to direct their imaginations away from the delineation of the massive phenomenon of the Depression itself and toward a scrutiny of personal and family relationships. But when we turn away from the books we have been considering and think about some of the best southern writing of the twentieth century, we realize that precisely this historical sense is what enables the writers to get at the underlying meaning of the Depression years. For now that the immediate crisis of the Great Depression has long since become history, we can see in what happened during those years an acceleration of the process leading toward urbanism and industrialism, and the final, conclusive shattering of the insularity and self-sufficiency of the old southern system of caste and class. What seemed at the time to be a breakdown in industrialization, a sudden suspension of progress and prosperity, in reality had precisely the opposite result, in that the Depression brought an end to the dominance of subsistence farming and cleared the way for the rapid industrialization and urbanization of the South during and after the Second World War by removing many traditional barriers and hindrances to social and economic change. The Depression forced the South to face up to the need for change; the old ways clearly wouldn't suffice.

Let me briefly suggest how this kind of response to the 1930s manifests itself in a group of four important southern novels, three of them published in the 1930s, the fourth appearing in 1946 but written about events that culminate during the Depression decade. In William Faulkner's *Absalom, Absalom!* young Quentin Compson looks back at his relationship to the life and death of Thomas Sutpen, a vigorous, powerful plebian who had come into Quentin's community many years earlier and in his ruthless, single-minded quest for a dynasty had brought suffering and tragedy to all around him. In Margaret Mitchell's *Gone with the Wind*, a work for which I have a qualified but considerable admiration, a strong-willed young woman cannot share in or understand the community pieties, and will not accept the role of southern lady that her society assigns to her. She learns to cope with war, change, tradition, in ways that appall others but enable her to survive and even flourish. In Allen Tate's *The Fathers* the Buchan family must confront the presence within it of George Posey, who cannot understand the traditional code of manners and behavior. Caught in the impact of war and change, the Buchan family, its northern Virginia home, and the planter civilization it exemplifies are destroyed. The collapse is not only from without, but equally from within, as a survivor, young Lacy Buchan, realizes many years later. Finally, in Robert Penn Warren's *All the King's Men* a young man of patrician family takes up with a strong, charismatic upcountry politician who, free of the blinders and the scruples of upper-class complacency, is able to act meaningfully, though recklessly, in the modern twentieth-century world of economic and political forces and broader human needs. In turning to this man as a substitute for the exertion of individual moral choice, however, the young man and others bring disaster to themselves.

Each of these novels, therefore, involves a powerful central figure who both symbolizes and embodies the force of change. Each deals with the inevitable erosion of a tradition before the onslaught of new times and new needs, and each depicts both the agony and the inescapable necessity of being able to cope with such change. In each instance the meaning of what is taking place is perceived by a young person of tradition and breeding—Quentin Compson, Lacy Buchan, Jack Burden, and in the instance of *Gone with the Wind* the very ambivalent and often unconsciously self-revelatory author herself. In each instance the person doing the perceiving both sympathizes with and is repelled by the iconoclastic central figure.

Thus each of these novels seems in its own way to constitute a response to the necessities of change—a problem that was strikingly characteristic of the years during which the novels were being written. For what is involved is the ability to live and function amid profound social change, and the price that must be paid in order to do so. The older, traditional ways—in three of the novels exemplified by the antebellum South—no longer suffice; yet the new ways are perilous. Is not this the situation of the Depression South, a complex community of human beings come lately to modernity, impelled to accept and often to welcome new ways of thinking and doing, confronting new crises and new economic, social, and political demands, yet very much the inheritor of a powerfully apprehended traditional order that has embodied much that the community would hope to retain as well as much that must be sloughed off?

In these novels, and in the best work of all the modern southern writers (very much including that of Wolfe and Agee), the historical imagination, rather than acting as a hindrance, makes the artistic achievement possible. From the standpoint of almost a half-century's perspective we recognize that it is in works such as these that we can find mirrored the underlying human meaning of the Great Depression of the 1930s.

The American South was never the same after the Great Depression. If you want to find out why, read the literature.

Shelby Foote's Civil War

Publication in November, 1974, of the third and final volume of Shelby Foote's magnificent history of the Civil War makes me think back to the time when he first began it. It was early in 1955, I think, that Random House announced its contract with Foote, who until then had written only fiction. These were the years prior to the centennial of the war, and the book industry was getting ready for it. Since the 1930s, with the publication of Douglas Southall Freeman's four-volume biography, *R. E. Lee*, and then his three-volume sequel, *Lee's Lieutenants*, there had been a rising demand for Civil War military history, and by the early 1950s, with the Centennial less than ten years away, not only publishers but historians both amateur and professional saw a veritable bonanza in sight. The old saw, to the effect that the ideal recipe for a best seller would be one entitled "Lincoln's Doctor's Dog," was being revised; interest in the Great Emancipator was turning into interest in the military events of the war.

The best book titles would be those that could combine the two emphases. T. Harry Williams published a provocative study entitled *Lincoln and His Generals*, which in title and contents was so successful that with the proceeds he built a fine home in Baton Rouge, calling it "Lincolnand." Bruce Catton brought out the first volume of a trilogy, *Mr. Lincoln's Army*; it was a great success, and established Catton thereafter as topmost of a growing crop of professional Civil War chroniclers. Kenneth P. Williams published the first two volumes of what was to be a multivolumed work entitled *Lincoln Finds a General*, in which he began holding inquiry on all the Union military operations, reversing most of the accepted findings and explaining away alleged shortcomings of those generals he admired, in particular U. S. Grant. He even managed to prove, to his own satisfaction at least, that Grant had not after all been taken by surprise by the Confederate attack at Shiloh—this in the face of the famous memorandum that Grant sent to headquarters on the eve of the battle saying that he had scarcely the slightest apprehension of a general attack.

The southerners had long been active, but with Dr. Freeman's leadership, southern historians began writing for a national audience rather than to give comfort to regional loyalties. There was Bell Wiley's *The Life of Johnny Reb*, which detailed the everyday doings of the Confederate soldier in the ranks so successfully that he began a sequel, *The Life of Billy Yank* (which someone suggested ought to be entitled "Lincoln and His Privates"). Stanley Horn had chronicled the campaigns of the Army of Tennessee. Clifford Dowdey contributed *Experiment in Rebellion* and *The Land They Fought For*. Burke Davis began a series of popular biographies of Virginia generals. By the late 1950s there was scarcely a general or a campaign about which someone, somewhere, wasn't writing a book. The rush was on.

There was money to be made in Civil War military history; everyone could sense that. The entrepreneurs began getting into the act. Ralph E. Newman, promoter of the Abraham Lincoln Book Club, changed the name to the Civil War Book Club, and settled in to a career of vending books and nonbooks alike about America's favorite conflict. Carl Haverlin of Broadcast Music, Inc., entered into the spirit of things. T. R. Yoseleff began producing offset editions of such out-of-print compendia as the *Battles and Leaders of the Civil War*. And so on.

In the fall of 1955 the Southern Historical Association met in Memphis, at the Hotel Peabody, and there was a private session held in Ralph Newman's suite to make plans for proper exploitation of the centennial possibilities. I was at the convention to chair a program on history and literature, and a university press friend of mine suggested that I stop by at Newman's suite for the meeting. I rode up on the elevator with two eminent nonmilitary historians of the South, C. Vann Woodward and Francis Butler Simkins; they, too, had been invited and like myself were going along just to see what it was all about. When we got to the suite the parlor was crowded. All the big military boys were there—Catton, Harry Williams, E. B. Long, Bell Wiley, and so on. Newman and Haverlin were doing most of the talking, with the eminent military historians all listening intently. The ice clinked in the drink glasses, the pipe smoke was thick, and the hopes were high.

There was one highly comic moment, for me. Haverlin was discoursing on how the records of the soldiers in both armies ought to be collected for ready reference. Maybe, he suggested, they could persuade Tom Watson—referring familiarly to the chairman of IBM—to put them all on computer tape. I was standing next to Simkins, the biographer of Pitchfork Ben Tillman, for whom the name being cited had very different associations. Francis turned and whispered in puzzlement, "What's *Tom Watson* got to do with all *this*?" Shortly after that Woodward and myself quietly departed from Newman's suite and went down into the relatively pure air of the Peabody lobby.

But the excitement was understandable. It was clear that there was an enormous popular interest in the Civil War, which would surely continue to grow as the Centennial years neared. It was going to be possible at last to write good, soundly researched military history and also make a great deal of money out of doing so. If the scholars didn't take the lead, then the popularizers would surely do it for them. And there was, after all, something of a mandate. A national Centennial commission was in existence, headed by no less a personage than Major General U. S. Grant III, U.S.A. ret. In all the states in which the war had been fought and others besides, Centennial observances were being planned, principally by representatives of the travel industry, who envisioned battlefield reenactments, pageants, sound-and-light spectacles, and mock bombardments attracting tourists by the millions. Should the whole thing be abandoned to the custodianship of such interests? No indeed. Perish forbid, as they say.

So the Civil War Centennial was going to be, in every sense of the word, a golden era, both for scholarship and for selling books. Only it didn't exactly work out that way. For one thing, the book market crested too soon, until by the year 1961, when the actual Centennial observance began, readers (and authors) were already growing weary of more books about the same campaigns and battles, the same generals, the same disputes—based on the same sets of facts and with only minor differences of style and emphasis from book to book. Furthermore, once the publishing industry really got into high gear, there appeared masses of nonbooks, facsimile reprints of out-of-print memoirs, and facile popularizations, which were promoted just as if they were major new historical studies. The usual Gresham's Law operation ensued; the shoddy stuff began to drive out the good, or at any rate to obscure it. Some good historians began quitting the field, though they continued to make occasional forays back in from time to time. Having completed his brilliant biographical study of P. G. T. Beauregard, Harry Williams took up the life and campaigns of another and later Louisiana hero, Huey P. Long. Frank Vandiver, after producing a superb life of Stonewall Jackson and a study of Confederate command problems, moved on to John J. Pershing. And so on. Others, such as Bruce Catton, took to repeating themselves. Nothing of any scope that Catton produced subsequent to the first two volumes of his trilogy on the Army of the Potomac ever quite came up that high standard. As the principal topics were worked over to the point of diminishing return, new studies became smaller and smaller in scope; individual battles, lesser campaigns, minor figures were chronicled in detail. Meanwhile, the picture books, superficial reworkings, and thinned-out reprints continued to appear, dwindling away only as the saturation point was reached even for popular trivia.

More importantly, the Centennial was upstaged by the civil rights movement. At that same meeting of the Southern Historical Association at the Hotel Peabody in Memphis, there was a banquet at which Cecil Sims, William Faulkner, and Benjamin E. Mays spoke on the need for bringing an end to racial segregation. It was attended by almost every historian at the convention. I remember, however, that I left the banquet room a little early and went to the Peabody bar, where I found Francis Simkins and a tiny band of diehards who had refused to attend the civil rights feast assembled to solace their loneliness.

The doings in the banquet hall exemplified what was soon to put a damper on the whole Centennial observance. For it was one thing to commemorate and reenact long-ago battles, provided that one could believe that the animosities and injustices that had caused them to be fought were no longer important, so that one could concentrate on honoring the valor of the opposing armies; it was quite another thing to realize that, despite the blood spilled on the earlier occasion, the issues being fought over were still far from settled. Under such circumstances, one could speedily lose one's taste for battlefield reenactments. What Lee's army had fought for against Grant in the Wilderness was far more justifiable and more admirable than what the T-shirted thugs and club-wielding state troopers represented when they attacked freedom marchers at Selma and Montgomery, but the same battle flag was used to dignify both occasions, and the resemblance seemed somehow too close for comfort.

What happened to the Centennial was symbolized at the very outset of its observance, when committees North and South assembled at Charleston to get the festivities under way. It turned out that several of the delegations from the northeastern states had black members, and the hotels in Charleston refused to put them up for the night, whereupon the other northeastern delegates withdrew in high dudgeon, declaring with good reason that if such things could go on in South Carolina a hundred years after the firing on Fort Sumter, then there wasn't much point in celebrating the Centennial.

Thus, while reenactments and pageants and oratorical observances continued apace throughout the Centennial years, they were not often made into occasions for inquiring into the deeper meaning of the events being commemorated. The thing was determinedly kept on the level of fun and games, and the intellectual leaven was mostly withheld. Back in the 1950s historians had been fond of saying that the forthcoming Centennial represented the chance to teach Americans the meaning of their history. As it turned out, however, the civil rights movement taught some of us the meaning of the Centennial, and we thereupon preferred to look elsewhere for antiquarian adventuring.

Not, however, Shelby Foote. Shelby, too, was present for the meeting of the Southern Historical Association in his home city of Memphis, and at my behest he read a paper on the writing of military history at the session that I chaired. I had come to know him in the early summer of 1955, when in the course of accepting my invitation to take part in the forthcoming session at Memphis he wrote that he wanted to inspect the battlefields around Richmond sometime soon. I was writing a book column for the Richmond *News Leader* at the time and I arranged with the Richmond historian and novelist Clifford Dowdey to take Shelby and myself on the battlefield tour. Clifford had spent a considerable time in close study of the Richmond battlefields, even going over some areas with mine detectors to verify the precise location of certain points of attack during the Seven Days campaign, and he was an ideal guide.

Neither Clifford nor myself was much impressed with Shelby's credentials on that occasion. He was full of opinions, and soon took to lecturing Clifford about the events of the Seven Days battles. On the basis of his experience as a field artillery officer during the Second World War he began experting all over the place, and many of his judgments seemed half-baked. He also endeared himself to Clifford, for whom Robert E. Lee was close to being a demigod, by informing him that the more he studied the events of the war, the less he was coming to respect Lee. "I'm sorry to hear that, Shelby," Clifford replied, though not at all in the tone of someone who was concerned that Civil War historiography would thereby suffer irreparable damage. Shelby also undertook to instruct me about fiction, informing me that no writer had any business associating himself with a university, and that Robert Penn Warren, about whom I had recently published a critical article, was no more than an academic novelist, and that if I couldn't tell the qualitative difference between *All the King's Men* and the fiction of Faulkner, then I too must be an academic. (Since I was then on the faculty of the University of Pennsylvania, this was quite true.)

So when Shelby left, en route I think to New York by way of Antietam and Gettysburg, I was less than completely enthralled over the prospects of reading his projected narrative history of the Civil War. If what I had seen was any evidence, then it was likely to be one of those iconoclastic, experting books, of which there were already too many in existence, in which the judgments of all the better scholars would be flouted and a superficial, amateur expertise substituted in their place.

I began changing my mind, however, that autumn when I went over to have lunch with him in Memphis just before the Southern Historical Association meetings. He was living alone at the time, in an old house on a bluff overlooking the Mississippi River, working on the manuscript of the first volume of his book with only a very large brown boxer dog to keep him company. He showed me a little of what he was doing, and how he was going about it, and I had the sense that however he might like to spout out sweeping generalities in casual conversation, when he put ideas on paper they would be the product of careful consideration and would not be written down until the material had been thoroughly explored and understood. There was nothing haphazard or superficial in Shelby's approach to the task of writing Civil War military history.

The appearance of the first volume of his history, *Fort Sumter to Perryville*, in 1958, not only verified that second impression, but the book itself astounded me by its genuine wisdom. There was absolutely nothing haphazard, nothing shallow about it. It was anything but an arrogant, opinionative work; indeed, what was impressive was the way in which he avoided the customary partisanship. He didn't argue points; he described events. The second volume, *Fredericksburg to Meridian*, appeared in 1963, and its handling of some of the most controversial campaigns of the war bore out all the promise of the first volume. This was truly dispassionate history, free of subjective judgment, yet written with an intensity of language and a narrative art that made the story enthralling to read.

In his second volume, Shelby stated that his intention was that the writing of each book of the trilogy was to take five years. Volume 2 had thus appeared on schedule. But when the next five-year period elapsed, he was still far from being ready with the third and final volume. As a publishing venture, meanwhile, the Civil War had fallen upon dry times by then. The Centennial had passed, and the civil rights movement was turning into something less idealistic and more complex by far, and we were getting ever more deeply embroiled in an undeclared war in Asia, with much unrest and rioting resulting therefrom. How much the state of the nation, the world, and the zeitgeist had to do with Shelby's difficulty over completion of his Civil War narrative I have no way of knowing; but, in any event, it was not until 1974, eleven years after publication of Volume 2 and almost twenty since he first contracted with Random House to undertake the project, that the concluding volume, *Red River to Appomattox*, was completed.

Like its predecessors, the final volume consumes some 400,000 words of print, making a three-volume narrative of almost a million and a third words in all, opening with Jefferson Davis' farewell speech in the Senate of the United States in January, 1861, and closing with the collapse of the Confederate armies and Davis' capture and imprisonment somewhat more than four years later. Primarily it is military history—the story of armies and navies, their commanders, their campaigns and battles, with the Presidents of the Union and the Confederacy depicted principally in their roles as commanders-in-chief of the fighting forces. Such matters as economics, finance, industrial development, politics, and life behind the lines are brought in mostly as they affected the doings of the armies.

Not only that, but it is history in the old style, written in the grand manner. Shelby's models were Tacitus and Gibbon; his research, though profound, is not annotated and attributed, but incorporated into a flowing narrative, and given its authority by the assertion of the stylist-historian rather than by the meticulous citation of sources. In this respect it is comparable to Winston Churchill's history of the Second World War. There are, however, important differences; for one thing, there is no sense of the judgments being imposed by the distinguished author, as opinion. Shelby grounds his evaluations in the details of what happened, and they arise out of the events of the narrative, in order to explain the story. Another difference is that Churchill's history takes its importance and authority by virtue of the fact that it is Churchill who is saying it: a leading participant majestically giving his personal vision of what he and his fellow participants did and thought. Obviously, Shelby could command no such authority, and does not pretend to do so. As historian his role is that of chronicler, and his persona as historian is infused in the facts of the narrative and makes its assertions through the marshaling of the facts. The meaning is determined by the events and controlled by the style.

Unlike Churchill's history, and for that matter unlike Gibbon's, the style of telling is not self-conscious and rhetorical, and seldom calls attention to itself. Here the author's experience as novelist works well for him. As storyteller he places himself inside the narrative, speaking through the language of the telling; but since it is history and not fiction that is being related, the authority and plausibility are achieved principally through the events rather than the way in which they are told. What this means is that he has it both ways; the manner of the storytelling is itself compelling, while at the same time the story being told is decisive by virtue of its clearly having *happened*. The result is that what in the hands of a less diligent and gifted chronicler could have resulted in a slipshod, merely clever narrative emerges instead as the premier military history of the Civil War, the majestic overall account that all knew would one day be written, but that had not appeared thus far.

Shelby has been careful not to call his trilogy a "history," but a "narrative." If there is any basis for this distinction, I have been unable to come upon it; my hypothesis is that he wanted to emphasize that his history was to be a work of art rather than a product of history-as-scientific-research, done in the manner of Gibbon and Prescott, instead of Namier or, say, Frank Owsley. Douglas Southall Freeman, in *Lee's Lieutenants*, was assiduous in documenting every statement of fact that he made, with the footnoted matter often occupying more space than the text itself on the printed page, but I don't think there was any more "science" ultimately involved in Dr. Freeman's operation than in Shelby's. The advantage of Dr. Freeman's method was that someone else could check on the authority for his statements. Shelby did not, I think, need to furnish any such obvious attribution. When Dr. Freeman was writing his histories, so many of the basic facts were obscured or unknown: his *R. E. Lee* and *Lee's Lieutenants* were just about the first accounts of the Confederate campaigns that were not based primarily on what the participants, eyewitnesses, and their contemporaries said had happened, either at the time or afterward in memoirs. Freeman's was the first trained, professional use of the *Official Records* to clarify and rectify the memories and assertions of the participants.

Shelby, however, was composing his history following several decades during which techniques of modern historical research were being brought to bear on almost every important battle and campaign of the Civil War. Where Freeman, for example, had been forced to weigh the three separate versions of the Battle of Gettysburg that General Longstreet wrote during his lifetime against not only the material in *Official Records* but the host of other and frequently passionate contemporary assertions of Longstreet's role during that battle, Shelby could draw on Freeman's documentation, that of Sanger and Hay in their biography, and numerous other important, heavily researched accounts, as well as the *Official Records*. By the time Shelby was writing, just about all the basic facts were known and were available to everyone. There was no real point in his attaching footnoted attribution to his evidence. What he was bringing to the story was a fresh presentation of what the factual evidence, as brought out in the *Official Records* and in numerous accounts based on them, showed. His procedure was to go ahead and describe what happened at Gettysburg, without reference to the controversies, and thus allow his description to constitute his interpretation of where the truth of controversial issues lay.

It is for this reason, among others, I think, that Shelby's history can be characterized as the ultimate achievement to come out of the Centennial. What he has given us is a narrative account of the campaigns of the Civil War based upon a fresh interpretation made possible both by the historical distancing of perspective afforded through the passing of time, and by the several decades or more of history and historiography produced during the upsurge of interest in the war. There comes to my mind something that Shelby said back in 1955. It was no more than a year after the *Brown v. Board of Education* decision, and everyone was talking about what its impact would be. Shelby's response was clear and unequivocal. When

I expressed my reservations (and like many another southerner at the time, I had them) about the practicability of the decision, Shelby replied, "I think they ought to just go ahead and integrate all the way." In 1955 that was pretty sharp language. What I am suggesting is that in a way that I then couldn't, Shelby could separate himself and what he thought was right from the passions and attitudes and beliefs of the southern community, and not be caught between truth and community loyalty. I do not mean by this that in order to write good Civil War military history it was necessary for Shelby or anyone else to believe in racial integration; rather, my point is that Shelby's cast of mind was such that in undertaking to interpret the military events of the Civil War he was not likely to be influenced in his assessment of the campaigns of 1861–1865 by the community's emotional needs during 1961–1965. There was going to be a detachment there that, together with his emotional involvement in the events of the war themselves and therefore of the men who fought in it, was likely to produce an ideal, informed, passionately narrated but dispassionately reasoned historical account. And since that was precisely what was needed as the culmination of the Centennial, so far as the reassessment of the war was concerned, it is fortunate that Shelby's history was begun when it was, and finished when it was, and not earlier.

To illustrate what this means, I want to deal at some length with the way in which the leading historian of the pre-Centennial generation, Douglas Southall Freeman, handled an important contretemps in Confederate military history, and to contrast it with Shelby's treatment of the same problem. I have mentioned the controversy over Longstreet's activities during the Gettysburg campaign, and particularly the second day of the battle. In *R. E. Lee*, published in the early 1930s, Dr. Freeman had come up with a detailed analysis of what happened, in which Longstreet's failure to move his troops up early enough on the morning of July 2, 1863, to occupy the Little Round Top before the Union army had acted to reinforce it in strength was depicted as the most costly of many Confederate failures at Gettysburg. However, by the time that Dr. Freeman got round to writing the third volume of *Lee's Lieutenants*, in the early 1940s, Donald B. Sanger had published an important article in the *Infantry Journal* which demonstrated beyond dispute that no matter what time Longstreet had come up, it would have made little difference. Faced with this evidence, Freeman was forced to concede, in an extended appendix, that all previous criticism of Longstreet's slowness on the morning of July 2 was irrelevant.

But the matter was not so easily put aside as that. For Freeman's earlier censure of Longstreet's apparent failure to move promptly enough was based not merely on what I am sure he thought was the dispassionate scholarly reading of such evidence as was available to him. It was also and at least as importantly an inherited attitude, the product of southern political and social considerations that severely colored Dr. Freeman's capacity for giving an unbiased reading to the evidence. And the mere correction of the facts did not therefore change the larger attitude.

Gettysburg had been the "high-water mark" of the Confederate military achievement; had Lee's army driven the Union forces from the field there, as had been done at Chancellorsville two months before and at Fredericksburg the previous winter, it was believed that Washington, Baltimore, and Philadelphia would have fallen, whereupon England and France would have given the Confederacy *de jure* recognition as an independent government, and southern independence would have been achieved. (My own belief is that nothing of the sort would have happened, but that is another matter.) Thus the Confederate defeat at Gettysburg meant in effect the loss of the war, and the men, or man, who were responsible for the defeat were the cause of the loss of the war. After the battle, Lee had said without hesitation that *he* was the one responsible for the defeat. But few loyal ex-Confederates ever really believed that, and Lee himself is quoted as having remarked, several years after the surrender of his army, that if only Stonewall Jackson had been alive and present there, he would have won the battle and the South would have secured its independence.

The logical deduction to be made from Lee's postwar remark is that in his own view it was the failure of Generals Ewell and Early, and in particular Ewell, to drive the Union forces from the field and occupy Culp's Hill and Cemetery Ridge on the first day, when the Union right was still weakly defended, that was responsible. And Ewell himself later remarked that it took a good many blunders to cause the Confederates to lose the battle of Gettysburg, and he had committed more than his share of them.

But Ewell was a Virginian, like Lee, and did not make a satisfactory villain. His failure at Gettysburg was duly reported, but that was not enough. After the surrender, however, General Longstreet, who was not a Virginian, had gone down to New Orleans. In prewar years, he had been a friend of General Grant's. Taking the results of the war literally (and Longstreet, unlike his uncle Augustus Baldwin, who had written the *Georgia Scenes*, was a very literal-minded man), he had accepted the fact that there was now only one nation and one government, and had proceeded to cooperate all too fully with it. Indeed, he had even gone so far as to turn Republican, had commanded the metropolitan police against white mobs during a bloody riot in Reconstruction New Orleans, and later had accepted an appointive office under Grant. In addition, he had published a newspaper article about Gettysburg in which he had said that he had strongly urged Lee not to fight it.

There ensued a controversy, begun by Colonel William Allan and carried on stridently thereafter by various participants, including General Early, in which it was contended that Longstreet, by moving so tardily on the morning of July 2, had cost the Confederate army the chance to occupy Little Round Top—bringing about the loss of the battle, the war, and southern independence. Longstreet was thus made into the villain—the South, and Virginia in particular, had found the scapegoat it needed. Furthermore, Longstreet did not help matters by attempting on several occasions to reply to the charges, each time embroidering the facts and enlarging the discussion in which he had sought to dissuade General Lee first from fighting the battle at all, and then from ordering him to send Pickett's troops charging against Cemetery Ridge on the third day. He was not a very articulate controversialist, his memory was failing him as he grew older, and his bewilderment and frustration at becoming the scapegoat for the Confederate defeat betrayed him into making absurd claims in his own defense. To read the dialogue be-

tween Longstreet and Lee as reported in Longstreet's long and pon-
derous memoir, *From Manassas to Appomattox,* one might think
that it was Edmund Burke or Daniel Webster, not James Longstreet,
who had been counseling General Lee during the campaign. (Dr.
Freeman reported that the book was ghostwritten by an ex-lieuten-
ant of Negro troops.)

Now Douglas Southall Freeman was a Virginian. The son of a captain in the Army of Northern Virginia, he had grown up among Confederate veterans. He had attended Johns Hopkins and there mastered the techniques of scholarly research, written his doctoral
dissertation, and turned to journalism as a career. Dr. Freeman was
a passionate man, and his biography of Lee, which was decades in
the writing before it began appearing in the early 1930s, was a labor
of intense love and admiration for the general and his cause. It is
well known that to the end of his life, on his way downtown each
day, as he drove past the statue of Lee on Monument Avenue in
Richmond, he saluted his commander.

When Dr. Freeman got around to Longstreet and his role in the
Confederate defeat he was not exactly disposed to be admiring. I
knew him slightly, and he once showed me his Civil War library. I
took down his copy of *From Manassas to Appomattox,* and just as
I had heard, written upon the title page were these words: "To count
the number of lies, count the number of lines." His treatment of
Longstreet throughout *R. E. Lee* and *Lee's Lieutenants* was, at crucial junctures, quite unfavorable. Unlike the early controversialists
and later amateurs such as Hamilton Eckenrode, he was careful to
provide citations for all of his factual assertions, and I have no doubt
that he thought he was being quite historically objective. He portrayed Longstreet at Second Manassas as so tardy in unleashing his
devastating assault against Pope that the safety of Jackson's corps
was in some jeopardy for a while. Now Longstreet did take his time
in preparing his attack, but nothing in the wartime documents in-
dicates that General Lee, who was with Longstreet, thought that
the attack was overly delayed. What Dr. Freeman was doing, again
I think without realizing the extent to which his passions were gov-
erning his research, was setting the stage for Longstreet's tardiness
on the second day at Gettysburg. He made much of a remark to the

effect that Longstreet was a savage fighter but "so slow" to get moving, which Lee was quoted as having made to another Confederate officer; Lee may well have said it, but the Confederate who quoted it did so after Lee's death, during the postwar years when Longstreet was being transformed into the culprit at Gettysburg, and I have always wondered to what extent remarks reported on such circumstances can be credited.

Again, in the spring of 1863 Longstreet's corps was on independent assignment in southeastern Virginia and North Carolina, with the primary objective of gathering food and supplies for the forthcoming campaigns. When General Hooker threw his army across the Rappahannock, Lee was left to face him with a greatly reduced force. There was no way that Longstreet could have rejoined Lee in time for the battle, and Lee in no way suggested that he should have been there. But Dr. Freeman interpreted Longstreet's Southside campaign as an effort on Longstreet's part to prove his genius for independent command after the manner of Jackson, portrayed it as a failure, and suggested that Longstreet was reluctant to pull out from Suffolk and rejoin Lee because he did not want to give up his independent operation, with the implication that it was this recalcitrance on Longstreet's part that imperiled the vastly outnumbered remainder of the army before Chancellorsville. There was really no wartime evidence at all to indicate that Longstreet was getting delusions of grandeur about his capacity for independent operations, but that was how Dr. Freeman read the evidence—as a foreshadowing of Longstreet's disastrous behavior at Gettysburg.

With Gettysburg itself, we have seen how in *R. E. Lee* Dr. Freeman accepted the commonly held notion that Longstreet failed to move on the Little Round Top in time, and then had to recant in *Lee's Lieutenants* in the face of incontrovertible evidence that the Federal army was already in position there. But this did not really change Dr. Freeman's verdict on Longstreet's performance at Gettysburg. He portrayed him as going far beyond his role as subordinate in his insistence that the battle not be fought, and then when he was overruled, sulking, moving slowly and reluctantly, refusing to cooperate, and even trying to shift the burden of responsibility for ordering Pickett to move against Cemetery Ridge on the third day onto the shoulders of a young lieutenant colonel of artillery.

Now it is quite clear that Longstreet did not want to fight the battle; that he kept trying to get Lee to move around the Round Tops toward Washington and force the Army of the Potomac to give up its strong position along Cemetery Hill; that he was so opposed to making an attack on the second day that when ordered to do so he became savagely insistent that his division commanders execute Lee's battle plan literally even though some modifications were in order; and that he was very unhappy indeed about having to send Pickett up Cemetery Hill on the final day. But the real point all along is that at almost every juncture Longstreet was right, and Lee was wrong, and Longstreet's counsel against attacking Meade's army at Gettysburg was based on a quite accurate appraisal of the situation. His obvious reluctance, his continued attempts to get Lee to change his plans, his surliness about making the attack on the second day, and his intense disapproval of the charge up Cemetery Hill have a much simpler and more charitable explanation than Dr. Freeman's suggestions that as a corps commander he was getting too big for his britches and so when Lee asserted his authority Longstreet became petulant and behaved like a spoiled child. Longstreet didn't want the battle to be lost, and knew that if fought under such circumstances it would surely be lost, and he was upset and sick at heart over the setback he saw was in the offing and the cost that was about to be paid in Confederate casualties. This wasn't insubordination, delusions of grandeur, overweening egotism; it was the behavior of a man who must stand helplessly by while the chief he has so admired and trusted is making a terrible mistake that will surely jeopardize the cause for which both have fought so hard.

This is the conclusion really warranted by a dispassionate reading of the wartime evidence. But Dr. Freeman apparently never even considered it; his view of Lee, Longstreet, and Gettysburg was still so much the product of the loyalties, pieties, and frustrations of the postwar controversy, the South's need for a scapegoat, and the resentment against Longstreet's turning Republican after the war, that all his great skill at scholarly research notwithstanding, he came up with essentially the same version of what went wrong at Gettysburg that the earlier, largely unresearched accounts had given.

Nor did it end there. When after the Battle of Chickamauga in the fall of 1863, Longstreet's corps, which had been transferred to the West for the campaign, was sent on an expedition against Knoxville and Longstreet was unable to do very much there, Dr. Freeman portrayed the campaign as proof of Longstreet's failure at independent command without Lee to direct his movements, and suggested that it was only thus that Longstreet finally got the itch for independent operations out of his system. Again, nothing in the wartime records supports this view of what Longstreet had in mind; if anything, the evidence would seem to be that Longstreet was opposed to Braxton Bragg's directing him to move his corps northeastward, believing that he would be able to do little and that Bragg's army would be severely weakened in the face of strong Union forces being concentrated at Chattanooga (in which instance he was all too correct, as the battle of Missionary Ridge proved). The East Tennessee operation was a failure, but not because of any lack of capability on Longstreet's part, and it was protracted not because of Longstreet's yen for independent command but in spite of Longstreet's desire to remain either with Bragg's army or else to get back to Virginia.

The point of this long digression is to show how, writing his books when he did, so skilled and devoted a military historian as Douglas Freeman, preparing the first really professionally researched account of the Army of Northern Virginia's campaigns, could be guided in his approaches and his conclusions by attitudes and emotions based on the heated passions and resentments of wartime and postwar reactions to the loss of the war, and thus come up with a highly biased account of what happened. Yet had it not been for that passionate involvement in his subject, the desire to chronicle for all time the heroic exploits of his father's army and his father's great chieftain, Dr. Freeman would never have written his magnificent volumes at all, and the historiography of the Civil War would be very much the poorer today.

Shelby Foote, however, coming along several decades after Dr. Freeman's labors, and with a very different and less partisan emotional involvement in his subject, could draw on the research of Freeman, Sanger, and others, yet not be swayed from examining the facts independently of received opinion as to their meaning. The result is that Shelby's picture of Longstreet's performance during

the war is very different from Freeman's; he does not portray Longstreet as either obstinate, overly ambitious for independent command, or insubordinate. The only part of the conventional indictment that he tends to accept in any way is the slowness to get into
action, and even this he sees as an almost inevitable by-product of
Longstreet's ability to hit hard and to employ his forces to maxi-
mum effectiveness. Shelby does not argue the matter; his verdict on
Longstreet comes out entirely through the way in which he describes the campaigns that Longstreet fought.

Shelby could write about Longstreet without personal bias controlling his reading of the evidence because Shelby was not himself
involved in fighting the war over. One would be hard put, I think,
to determine, from a casual reading of any of the campaigns described, whether the author was a southerner or a northerner. I don't
mean by this that Shelby doesn't have his loyalties, and that they
don't come out here and there. But he is able to view and to describe
the planning and the execution of a campaign alternately from each
side's point of view and make the reader look at the events from
that perspective. What I found myself doing again and again, for
example, was identifying with the objectives of the Federal commanders as they plotted their campaigns. and then with those of the
Confederates as they plotted their defenses. That is precisely what
Shelby wanted his reader to do, and what, if his narrative was to
succeed in telling the military history of the war, the reader must
be led to do. Dr. Freeman's great works were, by contrast, written
entirely from the Confederate point of view, which was quite fitting
and proper and was part of the impulse that caused them to get
written. But Shelby's book is the product of a later generation of
southerners; Shelby was able to write as he did *because* Dr. Freeman and his generation had written and felt as they did.

I have gone into the Longstreet controversy because it illustrates
the distance that has been traveled by the best historian of the Centennial generation from the inherited partisanship present in the
work of even the best historian of the previous generation. It ought
also to be pointed out that in Shelby's treatment of the civilian
leader of the Confederacy, Jefferson Davis, he shows an even greater

emancipation from earlier prejudices—not so much Dr. Freeman's as those of other and lesser historians. The South had lost the war despite some very effective fighting by its armies. Under such circumstances it was not very likely that the conquered southern people would attribute their defeat to the generals who had led their armies. Instead, the civil government, through its failure to support the armies, made a much better target. Since Jefferson Davis was President of the Confederate States, it might be expected that he would come in for much of the blame. But at the same time, few southerners claimed that Davis had ever lost heart, or failed to give his best at all times, and it was clear that after the war was over, he had paid the highest price in imprisonment, confinement, and humiliation that any of the major figures had had to pay. Thus, for a hundred years the general picture of Jefferson Davis that has been given in works of southern history is of a man who was loyal and determined, but also intolerant of others' opinions, sensitive and vain, aloof and inflexible, unable to do the compromising that was necessary to keep the various southern governors and editors united, and so forth—in short, an honorable, high-principled man, but the wrong man for the job. Some have blamed him for his high principles and rigid idealism at a time when a flexible approach was needed; others have asserted just as passionately that he lacked the courage of his convictions and would not exercise the decisive leadership needed in desperate times. Given the declining fortunes of the Confederacy, there was no way that Davis could have pleased many people for very long, and given the outcome of the war, it was inevitable that his mistakes would be magnified. Had the North lost the war, Lincoln would have been remembered in the same fashion; when things were going badly for the Union in 1862 and again in late 1863, he was being blamed for the same kinds of things for which Davis was criticized.

Shelby, however, was able to see through much of the wartime and postwar cloud that surrounded Davis' reputation, realize the extent to which the customary criticism of Davis' performance as Confederate president was based on the South's need for a target to direct its frustrations against, and he came up with a depiction of Davis' behavior as President that, though it does not brush over his shortcomings, is very sympathetic. He does not accept, for example, the conventional argument that Davis' insistence upon keeping Braxton Bragg in command of the Army of Tennessee, over the objections of all his corps commanders, was simply due to his pridefulness, his unwillingness to listen to criticism, and his obstinacy in holding to his decisions, even though the war in the West was all but lost thereby. He explores the advice Davis got, the alternatives before him, and the way he went about making his decision, and concludes that under the circumstances there was little else Davis could do. One is hard put to see, after reading Shelby's account of the four years of war, how Jefferson Davis could have done very much better than he did for his country.

Shelby's account of the Union leadership is somewhat more conventional, for the reason that, no doubt because the North won the war, there is considerably less historical dispute as to what happened and why. The chief subject of argumentation about northern generalship has been the military capabilities of General Grant. Was he merely a butcher who won his campaigns by relentless hammering, heedless of his casualties, or was he a great commander, a skillful tactician who took over in the East where others had failed and bested the Confederacy's most resourceful general? As might be expected, southern commentators have tended toward the former view, since it results in the ascription of the loss of the war by the South to factors of superior manpower, industrial resources, and much greater availability of supplies, rather than to any shortcomings on the part of Confederate fighting talent. In reaction, some northern partisans have insisted upon Grant's genius as a battlefield tactician, and have sought to number him among the great captains of history. Shelby is obviously no great admirer of Grant as humanitarian, but neither does he portray him as a military butcher. Grant had the strength, and he knew how to use it. His greatest talent was in his ability to move his troops skillfully and effectively. In the forty days campaign in the spring and summer of 1864, from the Rapidan to the Cold Harbor, he was consistently outguessed and outmaneuvered on the battlefield, but at no time was he kept from continuing to apply force against Lee's army. He moved his troops efficiently, and he prevented the wily Lee from maneuvering him out of position. It is true that this was possible because he had the strength to do it, but a less skillful commander could not have kept that strength so relentlessly applied against the enemy.

Lincoln, of course, looms large in Shelby's account of the Union conduct of the war. At this date there is probably very little that Shelby or anyone else could add to our understanding of Lincoln's performance as war president—it would be difficult to improve on T. Harry Williams' analysis, for example. What impresses me about Shelby's handling of Lincoln is the extent to which he brings out not only Lincoln's humanity and magnanimity but his extremely skillful role as wartime political strategist. Lincoln's greatness of spirit is joined with Lincoln's executive ability. At no time is Shelby given to the use of Rich, Beautiful Prose and the Purple Patch, but there is one moment when he feels impelled to point out the masterfulness of Lincoln's performance, and he does it by including in his narrative, as the culmination of a description of Lincoln's handling of the command problem of the Army of the Potomac in the spring of 1863, the text of the famous letter to General Hooker. The wisdom and adroitness of the Union president's actions, detailed in the account of the way in which Lincoln settled on Hooker to replace Burnside as commanding general, are given the final seal of admiration and approval by the presentation of Lincoln's words themselves. I found Shelby's overall account of Lincoln's magnificent performance as commander in chief of the fighting armies more convincing and more satisfactory than any other I have read, including Bruce Catton's.

Three volumes of Civil War military history, each of more than 400,000 words, is a great deal of Civil War military history. Yet is is difficult to see how Shelby could have done the job more economically. His narrative, despite its broad scope, is no popularization— by which I mean that complex matters are not made simple for the reader who cannot or does not wish to involve himself in the complexity. On the other hand, I think that this involved story is told so well that its enjoyment will not be restricted primarily to the Civil War buff. As a novelist, Shelby is very much a psychologist, and characterization is a good novelist's necessity; writing his military history he has made much of the human beings who are the principal figures. Not only Lee and Grant, Davis and Lincoln, but Sherman, McClellan, Buell, Farragut, Porter, Meade, Thomas, Longstreet, Jackson, Forrest, Bragg, Joe and Albert Sidney Johnston, Sheridan, and Stuart all emerge strongly. And without going in for the kind of mystical transcendence business that Bruce Catton likes to do, Shelby has a strong feeling for the soldiers who made up the armies that the generals directed.

The books are full of good anecdotes and moments of fine humor. But the Civil War was a grim business, and if there are military historians who tend to get so involved in the excitement of a campaign or battle that they forget the savagery and agony, Shelby is not one of them. I think his obvious distaste for Grant the man comes primarily from that general's disregard for his own men's suffering. One of the most gruesome scenes in the history is that describing the aftermath of Pemberton's repulse of Grant's assault on the Vicksburg fortifications in May of 1863.

> For three days—six, in the case of those who had fallen in the first assault—Grant's dead and injured lay in the fields and ditches at the base of the Confederate ridge, exposed to the fierce heat of the early Mississippi summer. The stench of the dead, whose bodies were swollen grotesquely, and the cries of the wounded, who suffered the added torment of thirst, were intolerable to the men who had shot them down; yet Grant would not ask for a truce for burial or treatment of these unfortunates, evidently thinking that such a request would be an admission of weakness on his part.

Finally, Pemberton could no longer stand the sight and petitioned Grant "in the name of humanity" to accept a brief cessation of hostilities in order to remove his dead and dying men. Grant accepted, and in Shelby's words, "at 6 P.M. all firing was suspended while the Federals came forward to bury the dead where they lay and bring comfort to such few men as had survived the three-day torture. This done, they returned through the darkness to their lines and the firing was resumed with as much fury as before." This sort of thing often gets left out of Civil War military history; not, however, out of this one.

For these reasons, therefore, and many others besides, I feel that Shelby Foote's three-volume history of the Civil War is the best military account of the four years of conflict that has thus far been written. And it is so well written! The style holds it all under control, develops the story beautifully and suspensefully, elucidates the problems, makes complex matters clear, captures the humanity of the participants. This study is a model of historical narration. Unless I miss my guess, it will be the classic full-length presentation of the American Civil War, worthy to stand alongside the great works of narrative history. It seems unlikely to me that it will ever be superseded.

The Boll Weevil, the Iron Horse, and the
End of the Line: Thoughts on the South

I. *The Boll Weevil*

On hot afternoons in the summertime—this was in the middle-
to-late 1930s—I sat in the bleachers at College Park in Charleston
and when the baseball game was not too interesting I watched for
the Boll Weevil at the Seaboard Air Line railway station. It was
called the Boll Weevil because when the little gas-electric locomo-
tive-coach was placed in service in the early 1920s the black folk of
the South Carolina sea islands through which the little train passed
fancied its resemblance to the bug that had moved northward and
then eastward from Mexico to devastate the cotton crops.

The little Seaboard gas-electric coach, of course, devastated no
cotton crops. As a railroad train the Boll Weevil wasn't much. There
were two of them in actuality, a northbound and a southbound
train, operating each day between Savannah, Georgia, and Hamlet,
North Carolina, the latter being a railroad junction point a few
miles beyond the border between the two Carolinas. The trackage
they traversed was not the Seaboard's main line, which was the
New York-Florida route that crossed through South Carolina well
to the interior. Rather, the railroad's low-country branch constituted a large bow in the line, a two-hundred-mile-long loop that
dropped southward from the main line junction at Hamlet down
toward the seacoast, then southwestward to Charleston and to Sa-

vannah not quite a hundred miles farther, where it rejoined the main line. It served the truck farming and—until the coming of the little black bug—the cotton industry along the coast, and transported passengers, mostly black, who wished to travel between the little way stations, towns, and flag stops and Charleston or Savannah, the only two communities of any size along the route.

The northbound Boll Weevil came through Charleston from Savannah shortly before midday. Its southbound counterpart from Hamlet customarily arrived about three o'clock in the afternoon. It was the latter that I watched for. At some point during the weekend doubleheader Municipal League baseball games it would make its appearance, clattering across Rutledge Avenue and rolling to a halt at the little stucco railroad station at Grove Street just beyond the left-field limits. No ceremony attended its advent. Perhaps there would be a taxicab or two, but usually only a railroad baggageman and a handful of outward-bound passengers were there to greet it.

The Boll Weevil's route lay closer to the coast than the Coast Line's. Until the 1900s the only way to travel between Charleston and the numerous coastal islands had been by slow boat; shallow-draft launches with steam and later make-and-break gasoline engines had traversed the creeks, estuaries, bays, and rivers with passengers and cargoes from the islands, made their way to the city, and tied up at Adger's Wharf. But now most of the sea islands were linked to the mainland by bridges, and the remoteness of the low country, which had lasted from colonial times, was coming to an end.

The Boll Weevil, however unprepossessing in appearance, thus represented a phase in the process whereby the several centuries of comparative isolation that had characterized the life of the Carolina seacoast were giving way to the mobility of modern industrial America. No longer were goods dependent upon water transport, or upon horse and mule drayage along rutted, sandy roads, to get into the hinterlands. And if there was no job for a black farmhand in the low country—no need, for example, to pick cotton any more, thanks to the little black bug from Mexico—the train was there to take him to the city.

So the sleepy little Boll Weevil gas-electric train that waited around for such an interminably long time at the stucco station up at College Park, just beyond left field, and which I would watch on summer afternoons during the 1930s, was in its own way emblematic of something perhaps every bit as disruptive, as devastating, as the insect that had moved up from Mexico in the 1910s to eradicate the cotton crop. What it represented and embodied was *change*.

Throughout the South there were many trains like the little Boll Weevil. In Eudora Welty's beautiful novel *Delta Wedding*, a little train named the Yellow Dog—in actuality the Yazoo and Delta—brings cousin Laura McRaven from the city of Jackson to the cotton lands of the Mississippi Delta—a mixed train, "four cars, freight, white, colored, and caboose, its smoke like a poodle tail curled overhead." Into the flat plantation country of the Delta it transported travelers from Jackson and from the world beyond, and though it seemed so diminutive and harmless, with its friendly engineer Mr. Dolittle who occasionally halted the train en route so that the conductor could gather goldenrod, it was not harmless but instead powerful and inexorable, as Miss Welty suggested, and what it brought and signified was ultimately irresistible; time and change, the world outside the confines of the plantation.

Nowadays there is no more Yellow Dog, and no more Boll Weevil. Even when I sat in the bleachers at the baseball games in the 1930s and watched the little train arrive at the Seaboard station, it was already outmoded, for the trains had been an earlier phase of the change. By the 1930s automobiles, buses, and trucks were the principal means of conveyance between the city and the islands. The dirt roads were being widened and paved. There were highway bridges connecting most of the sea islands with the mainland. Few places in the low country were really remote any more. All over the South this was taking place—had, indeed, already taken place by the middle 1930s.

The old isolation was ended, and the towns and cities were expanding into the open countryside. When I had first begun attending the games at College Park I had walked home through fields, leaving the built-up area along Grove Street to cut through a mile of open land, crossed a marsh creek over a little wooden bridge, then walked through a grove of trees to our house on a bluff overlooking the

Ashley River. But by the late 1930s the entire area was rapidly being built up, and where for two hundred years there had been planted fields and marshland were now frame houses and multiple-occupancy dwellings. For there was a growing need for new housing in Charleston, occasioned by the influx of new people into the city to work at the Navy Yard, the steel mill, and other industrial installations to the north of the city limits. True, those city limits were still where they had been located at the time of the Civil War, along Mount Pleasant Street, a block north of our house. But now there was a sprawling and largely unlovely industrial community stretching out for ten miles and more to the northward.

One day I was waiting for a bus—the trolley cars were gone by then—at the corner of King and Wentworth streets downtown. When it pulled up to the curb there were already so many riders aboard that there was no room for anyone else. It was the going-home hour and another bus would be along shortly, I knew, so I prepared to wait. A woman who was standing near me was not willing to wait, however. She went up to the closed doors of the bus and began rapping on the glass panels in a vain attempt to gain admittance. "I want in!" she called. "I want in!"

She could not be a native Charlestonian, I knew, because she would never have said it that way if she were. She would have called, "I want to come in!" or "I want to get in!" No doubt she and her family had come from Ohio or somewhere else in the Midwest to work at the Navy Yard. Many people were moving to Charleston, from the Upstate, the other southern states, and the Midwest and North as well, for there were imminent signs of another war, and a tremendous defense industry was getting into high gear. There were many more buses in service, but also more waiting, because the area north of the city was becoming so thickly populated that the South Carolina Power Company simply could not purchase new buses rapidly enough to accommodate the demand.

Meanwhile the Boll Weevil kept to its rounds. I would catch sight of it from time to time while riding downtown or coming home on the bus. Sometimes I wished I might go for a trip aboard the little train. I wanted to board it at the station on Grove Street and make the journey with it up the coast and then inland, all the way to its northern terminus at Hamlet, North Carolina. I could then transfer to a main line Seaboard train such as the streamliner, the Silver Meteor, and continue on to Richmond, where my aunts, uncles, and cousins lived. But of course that was not the way to travel from Charleston to Richmond. To go there one drove up to North Charleston and boarded one of the Atlantic Coast Line trains.

By then the Second World War had come. My family moved from Charleston to Richmond, where my mother had come from, and soon after that I was in the Army. I was stationed first in Alabama and then in Connecticut, and most of my fellow soldiers were from the North and Midwest. Some were quick to point out to me, when I attempted to describe what I so liked about life back home, that many of the more pleasant qualities of that life were possible because of the availability of a disadvantaged labor force to do the unpleasant work and thus permit the famous "gracious living" enjoyed by the white folks. But if that were true—and I began to see that in certain crucial respects it was all too true—I could not feel that it was a sufficient explanation for what I felt about life in my part of the country.

Later I was sent to Fort Benning, and for almost two years I lived near the city of Columbus, Georgia. Here was a community of less than 50,000 which almost overnight was the civilian adjunct of an army camp of 120,000 troops! Housing, transportation, business, entertainment, recreation facilities were inconceivably overcrowded and inadequate. From my occasional visits to Columbus I could understand why it was that when sometimes I encountered a fellow soldier who had been stationed at or near Charleston, his attitude toward my own home city as a place to visit was usually so very hostile. Of course the city he had found so unpleasant and inhospitable was not the real Charleston, as I always hastened to explain, but a place that within a matter of several years had suddenly been forced to accommodate itself to the presence of three times its own population, ringed as it was with military installations. The chances were that on his visits to the city he had encountered very few actual Charlestonians; most of those storekeepers, taxi drivers,

USO workers, shop girls and other civilians he had met were recent arrivals.

I doubt that the question ever occurred to me whether, when the war was done, my native city could or would go back to being what it had been just a few years ago. Yet had it not been changing even when I was living there? "I want in!" the woman at the bus stop had declared in her midwestern accent and idiom. Was the city I remembered, with the fishing boats and the White Stack tugboats tied up at Adger's Wharf, the little train waiting at the station just past the ball park, the barber shop which like my father I always patronized (with its familiar clientele and its barbers who conducted themselves so professionally and yet so accommodatingly), Broad Street with its lawyers, bankers, realtors, insurance men, the local "establishment" as it were, where my aunt was a secretary and where there were so many persons I knew and who knew me and my family—was this place, which I knew so well and liked so much, both for its virtues and its vices (and both were numerous), not the real, unchanging Charleston? And after the war was won would I not go back there to live, as I was sure I wanted to do?

Several times when I visited my relatives in Charleston during the war while on leave from Fort Benning, I had seen the little Boll Weevil in its familiar setting up by the station at College Park. But there was one occasion when I caught sight of the little train in a very different context. It was when I was on furlough to Richmond, where my parents were living. The train to Richmond, which I boarded at Atlanta, stopped at Hamlet, North Carolina, sometime after midnight to change crews and engines, and I made my way out of the crowded coach, which was filled with sleeping travelers, and stepped down onto the platform to look around. It was cold. The station was a large, old-fashioned wooden affair, with tracks on both sides. I walked back along the platform, past the station and toward the rear of the train, and gazed out into the winter night at the town's main thoroughfare. Except for the lights in the lobby of a railroad hotel, all was dark. After a minute I strolled back toward the station, and on the way I happened to glance down a section of track along a side street that crossed the main line, whereupon I spied a familiar silhouette. It was the Boll Weevil, waiting overnight

tion at College Park I got off and walked over to Rutledge Avenue to take the bus downtown. I thought to myself that even if the Boll Weevil was gone, at least I had finally made the trip.

It was none too soon, for within a few years all passenger service on the Hamlet-Charleston-Savannah branch was discontinued. And in the 1960s when the Seaboard and Atlantic Coast Line railroads were merged, even freight traffic along the tracks that led by the ball park and over the trestle at the foot of Grove Street was ended. The old wooden bridge across the Ashley River was torn down. No longer would young Charlestonians lie in bed at night as I had once done and hear the night freight train from the south whistling far off in the darkness, and then gradually draw near the bridge, until as the wheels rolled onto the timbered structure the iron flanges set up a deep, singing reverberation on the rails, which grew hoarser as the train crossed over the river and entered the city.

No, the train was gone for good, as indeed were steam locomotives, the Boll Weevil, Adger's Wharf down on the waterfront with the shrimp boats and tugboats and little cargo launches with their make-and-break engines, and many another artifact of youth and young manhood. And each separate visit, over the years, seemed to broaden the loss. The barber shop down on King Street, where once there had been eight barbers, all of whom I knew by name and who knew me, was now down to one elderly man, tending shop by himself. The comfortable old Fort Sumter Hotel on the Battery was converted into condominium apartments. The hulk of the ferryboat *Sappho*, moored throughout my youth in the tidal flats just beyond Gadsden Street, had long since disappeared under a landfill. The old Southern Railway roundhouse on Columbus Street, where on Sunday mornings my father used to take us to see the trains, was gone, and a supermarket occupied its former place. East Bay Street, where the wholesale houses had been located in antebellum buildings, had lost its hegemony to more accessible places in the built-up northern area; there was little but empty store fronts and a few conversions into apartments. Missing in particular was a red wagon wheel which had always hung suspended from a bracket above the entrance to one hardware dealer. My father had installed it in 1913, when he had been a youth working there.

Gone, too, along with the places and the emblems were those Charlestonians of my father's generation who had once lived among these things and made them substantial and significant. For almost all of those men and women, my elders, the adult citizens of the city when I was a child, and whose lives and positions and concerns and opinions had seemed so important and so formidable, were dead now, while the few who still survived and whom I sometimes encountered here and there were frail and old, human relics as it seemed, more like tourists such as myself than inhabitants, now that their onetime peers and companions, the social context in which they had fitted, were gone. They appeared oddly diminished and shrunken in stature, caricatures of their former selves. So that on each successive visit to what had once been my home, I found that what had constituted its substance and accidence both had dwindled. To the extent that the places, objects, people, and associations of my childhood—a southern childhood, in and of a southern city—had constituted whatever there was of reality and permanence to my younger experience, then that reality was becoming more and more a matter of absence, loss, and alienation. I was, that is, steadily being dispossessed.

2. *Will Barrett's Iron Horse*

The experience recounted thus far, however intensely felt by myself, is in no sense unique. It differs from similar experience for others only in the particular details in which it has been presented. Insofar as it is appropriate to most persons who, like myself, have grown away from a community that has been very much caught up in social transition and widespread change, it is valid for numerous modern southerners. Moreover, though its meaning lies, I think, at the center of the southern literary experience of our time, in the form that I have reported it so far it is inert, useless: merely a species of nostalgia. As presented, it presupposes a kind of absolute cultural, social, and historical order, designed and believed to exist permanently, and then interprets all subsequent changes within that order, all alteration in the complex substance of its embodiment, as a diminution of reality, an erosion of what should by rights have been immutable: in short, as disorder, loss, chaos.

But while such a way of viewing one's experience is perhaps unavoidable as a starting point, it is also partial, superficial, and really a distortion of reality rather than an evocation of it. And if that were all there was to the southern literary imagination as it views the past, there would be little point in paying much heed to it. For the truth is that, as I have suggested earlier on, just as there was at no time an absolute, unchanging, permanent form to the life of the Carolina low country, but instead at all times change and alteration, so my own memories of places, people, institutions, and artifacts of my own childhood and young manhood are composed not of fixity and diuturnity but of elements that were very much caught up in change, however they may have once seemed immutable to me.

I had thought of the little Boll Weevil train as fixed and determined in its arrivals and departures at the Seaboard station. But the railroad crew that operated it reported that it had constantly broken down and been behind schedule, and what it meant for the agricultural life of the low country had been mobility, change, the coming of the city to the sea islands and the movement of the black folk to the city. When during the war I had caught sight of the Boll Weevil late one winter night in North Carolina, and had felt so powerfully that it belonged not there on the unfamiliar siding but to summer afternoons at the stucco station in Charleston, I had been facile. It was not the little train, but myself, who was in what seemed to be the wrong place and wrong season. And what made the present time and place seem unsatisfactory was that I was attributing a greater emotional importance, a more self-sufficient identity and a freedom from contingency, to the earlier experience. Whereas the truth was that only *because* of the later experience—because I *saw* the little train in Hamlet that night—was the earlier experience made to seem so important, so intense, to seem, in short, so very *real*. In actuality the authenticity of the experience, and its importance for me, lay neither in the isolated memory of the little train at College Park as such, which was an act of mere nostalgia, nor in my reencounter with the train at Hamlet, which because of its seeming inappropriateness was so pathetic. Rather, the authenticity and importance resided in the relation of the one to the other—in the profound vividness of the experience of time and change, a vividness that I myself, through my participation, was able to bring to it. And it has been just such vividness, but magnified and enriched many times through artistic genius, that has constituted the achievement of the best of the modern southern writers.

There comes immediately to mind a scene from a brilliant novel by Walker Percy, *The Last Gentleman*, in which precisely this kind of perception is delineated, and which I now propose to discuss at some length. The novel, which like much of Percy's fiction contains strong autobiographical elements, involves the hegira of one Williston Bibb Barrett from Mississippi to New York City and then back southward and later westward in search of a way to unite action and conviction, and much of the motivation for Barrett's journey is ascribable to the collapse and futility, as he sees it, of the old southern stoic attitude of aristocratic fortitude he had been taught to believe in, a collapse exemplified by his own father's suicide.

Like more than one young man in southern literature, Will Barrett has the expectation of a proper and assured role for himself, but cannot identify the possibility of any such role existing in his own changed circumstance, even while he remains unwilling and unable to accept the kind of moral and social wasteland in which no such assurance is available. Like the speaker in Allen Tate's beautiful "Ode to the Confederate Dead," he stands at the cemetery gate, as it were, grieves at the inescapability of the fact that he cannot believe in the validity of the communal pieties, yet also cannot settle for an existence in which no such pieties are possible. "What shall we say who have knowledge / Carried to the heart?" Tate's protagonist asks. "Shall we take the act / To the grave?" In Will Barrett's instance he manages to stop, en route westward, outside his old home in Mississippi one night and look on from the darkness of the oak trees while his aunts sit out on the porch in traditional southern style—watching a give-away quiz show on television!

He remembers the night when his father, a lawyer (and much resembling Percy's cousin, William Alexander Percy), had walked up and down the street beneath the oak trees as usual, awaiting the outcome of a public battle he has led against a lower-class faction that seems to resemble the Ku Klux Klan of the 1920s. His son sat on the steps, tending the old-fashioned 78-rpm drop-record phonograph, on which a Brahms symphony was being played in the darkness. By and by the police come to tell the father that his fight has been won, the riffraff have broken up their meeting and left town. Instead of rejoicing in his victory, however, the father tells his son that its price has been the destruction of any pretense to superior moral and ethical standards on the part of his own class of onetime ladies and gentlemen. The illusion of aristocratic virtue and rectitude having been shattered, the father has only his private isolated sensibility to fall back upon. "In the last analysis, you are alone," he tells his son, and walks off again. "*Don't leave,*" his son begs. But the father goes into the house, climbs the stairs up to the attic, places the muzzle end of a shotgun against his breast, and pulls the trigger.

Now an older Will Barrett stands among the oaks remembering the sound of the shot, and meanwhile hearing the television commercial that his aunts are watching. He reaches out in the darkness and his hand encounters an iron hitching post, molded in the form of a horse's head, about the base of which an oak tree has grown until now it entirely surrounds it. He touches the tree bark:

> *Wait.* While his fingers explored the juncture of iron and bark, his eyes narrowed as if he caught a glimmer of light on the cold iron skull. *Wait.* I think he was wrong and that he was looking in the wrong place. No, not he but the times. The times were wrong and one looked in the wrong place. It wasn't even his fault because that was the way he was and the way the times were, and there was no other place a man could look. It was the worst of times, a time of fake beauty and fake victory. *Wait.* He had missed it! It was not in the Brahms that one looked and not in solitariness and not in the old sad poetry but—he wrung out his ear—but here, under your nose, here in the very curiousness and drollness and extraness of the iron and the bark that— he shook his head—that—

This is a marvelous passage. What Will Barrett wishes he could tell his dead father is that those public values and truths upon which his life and conduct had been predicated, and which had finally seemed to have so eroded that he had killed himself, were false, or at best only partial and ancillary. *Wait,* he keeps telling his father in his imaginary expostulation, in repetition of that traumatic moment in the past when he had vainly begged his father not to leave. The triumph over the riffraff, the great horn theme of

Brahms, he insists, were false victory and false loveliness because the ideals they were being made to embody were illusory, a species of ideality removed from the world, as it were. His father had felt that his struggle with the red-necks (corresponding, one should note, to Walker Percy's grandfather's victory over the Klan in the 1920s, as described by Will Percy in *Lanterns On the Levee*) was the assertion of absolute integrity in a graceless modern world. In being achieved it had revealed to his father his own isolation, since it had forced him to see that those who were on his side in the dispute, and who supposedly represented the lofty morality that he believed in, were in no way absolutely superior in ethics and morality to those they had defeated. He tells his son that the lower orders had once been "the fornicators and the bribers and the takers of bribes and we were not and that was why they hated us. Now we are like them."

But what Will Barrett knows, out of his own subsequent experience and observation, is that there never was any such generation of earlier heroes who were exempt from human stain and contingency, so that his father's ideal of aristocratic virtue, however nobly motivated, was actually a romantic escape from the compromised actuality of human life in time. Such a view necessarily presupposed a former time in which men were better and wiser, more disinterested and virtuous than humans could ever be, as well as a society that had been more nearly free from all temptations to covetousness, avarice, lust, and cruelty than had ever existed on earth.

Thus any change in circumstances and conduct would have to constitute a falling away from perfection, and to the extent that the change continued in time, the arrival of crass days, a moral and social wasteland, the death of the gods. So his father's belief that a mere political victory would reaffirm the antique virtues and insure their permanence was doomed to disappointment once his father realized that the golden age had not thereby been re-created. What his father had done was to attempt to insulate himself from time, change, and mortality by retreating into a private code of aristocratic virtue and honor, truth and beauty that gave him the illusion of human perfectibility, and when this was shattered by being tested in the actual world, there seemed nothing left for him but to be destroyed with it.

In the same way, the notion that the great horn theme of Brahms, to which the father had been listening on the night of his suicide, enunciated an ideal of absolute and timeless beauty was also ultimately self-contradictory. For as Will Barrett sensed, "The mellowness of Brahms had gone overripe, the victorious serenity of the Great Horn Theme was false, oh fake fake." Percy is alluding, I think, to a characteristic of Brahms's symphonic music that I have also noticed. Brahms builds up to huge, slow-moving thematic statements that seem to assert a kind of hard-won triumph of spirit, and which in their massive harmonics pronounce an ultimate resolution superior to merely human difficulties and leaving no further occasion for striving or disruption. Thus when the last notes of the symphony die out, one has a sense not of triumph but of sadness, for since so supernal a resolution cannot be continued indefinitely but must come to an end, one feels, as it were, alone and abandoned in a jaded world. The quality that Will Barrett identifies and deplores in Brahms seems to be a sort of victorious exhaustion, an elimination of all further possibility of growth or extension, that corresponds mightily to the *fin de siècle* romanticism of Swinburne, Dowson, the *Rubaiyat*, "The City of Dreadful Night," and, be it noted, of the poetry of William Alexander Percy himself. Thus, in having Will Barrett declare that his father had looked for beauty in the wrong place, what Walker Percy means, I think, is that music that asserts as an ideal a quality of perfection that seems to rule out all further human involvement can only become hollow and intolerable.

The place to look for beauty and for truth, rather, is "here, right under your nose, here in the very curiousness and drollness and extraness of the iron and the bark." For the iron horse's head of the hitching post, though ornamental, was cast for use by men, while the oak that has grown around it has drawn it into time and change rather than abstracted it from all future contingency, and in the union of the two is the miracle of growth and fusion, producing a quality of excess and uniqueness that goes beyond the merely usable or fortuitously natural, even while deriving its strength and beauty from time and change.

Such an achievement cannot ever involve a static perfection. The iron hitching post was given its form by men, to serve a purpose and yet to be ornamental as well, and though that purpose is outmoded, the very element that has outmoded it—change—has given it its marvelous new possibility: of being as one with the oak tree.

All this, it seems to me, is implicit in that remarkable passage from *The Last Gentleman. Wait!* Will Barrett begs his father. *Don't leave!* For the boy needed his father, but the father's way of seeing himself and his duty did not, finally, encompass any obligation to or need for a future so fallen from perfection as to seem meaningless. The father could not see that the presence of the boy there with him in the dark, tending the phonograph as he walked back and forth beneath the trees, was itself a refutation of his premise that *"in the last analysis,* you are alone" (italics mine)—for human virtue and meaning were not to be found solely within oneself, as measured against an autonomous, static ideal of timeless perfection, but instead were human qualities growing out of continuing existence in time, never perfect, never complete and self-sufficient in themselves, but always in vital relationship with ongoing experience.

The great horn theme seemed to separate itself from all regeneration, assert an ideal of pure, abstract beauty that mocked mere human striving. Similarly, the worship of the past as an age of superhuman heroes made the present into a time of certain decline and fall, and the future into something meaningless. Instead of the past being allowed to illuminate and strengthen the authenticity of the present, it is made to destroy it. For the presence of the boy there on the steps, overseeing the drop-record phonograph and watching his father, is what the past has created; and the boy's need of his father—*don't leave!*—validates the genuineness of the past, because it provides a means for the best qualities of that past to continue to have meaning in time. And it is *that* kind of continuity, and not the blind preservation of what had once been human existence in time as static, changeless icon, untouched by the hurly-burly of continued experience, that keeps the past meaningful and makes its exemplars truly heroic. Otherwise that past, which Will Barrett's father saw as the sole repository of virtue, is rendered empty and abstract—as futile as the world-weary, life-denying "victory" of the great horn theme, a beauty so removed and isolated from human need and desire as to produce emptiness and despair.

Looking out from under the shadow of the oaks, Will Barrett does not blame his father for having left him. On the contrary, he is filled with love and pity for his father, for he knows that his father, like himself, was caught in a situation not of his own making, and was unable to extricate himself from it. Indeed, it might even be said that it was *because* his father had taken his life, in despair over what he considered the impossibility of being able to stay with him, that he was now able to recognize the murderous falseness and inadequacy of the ideal of the solitary man. The sound of that shotgun blast in the night, the hopelessness that had caused his father to pull the trigger of the twelve-gauge Greener, was what had sent him on his own search, which however prolonged and agonizing represented the only way that he might ever learn to break through the walls of solitude that might otherwise have imprisoned him as well.

What he learns, finally, is that solitary integrity is not enough for a man, that one cannot live merely in private measurement against a personal ideal. There can be no *I* without a *Thou*. The plea, "Wait. Don't leave!" is the recognition of human need, and the heeding of the plea is the acknowledgment not only that one is needed by another, but that acceptance of another's need is *in itself an assertion of need*. It is there, in ongoing involvement with what is outside of one's own otherwise solitary self, that one's identity in time can be affirmed: not through a strong-willed transcending of life but *in* and *through* life, immanently: the iron horse encircled by the living cortex of the great oak, the two elements become extraordinary in their marvelous need-in-separateness: unique and mysterious in their configuration—the handiwork of God.

The difference, as I see it, between my experience with the Boll Weevil and that given by Walker Percy to Williston Bibb Barrett in *The Last Gentleman* is that in effect the novel commences where I was willing to leave off. What I had done was to see the past—the little Seaboard gas-electric coach in its place at the station in Charleston—as something absolute and completely self-contained, in and of itself. And God said, Let there be Light, one might say; and He created the Boll Weevil. Because the train was there for me to see, it became part of my experience, and it belonged there at the ball park. But since, being human, I existed in time, I grew away from the experience it symbolized, and because its vivid, emblematic quality was important to me, I could only interpret any change in my relationship to it, any distancing of its image in time, as a falling away from perfection. Each subsequent stage in my relationship to it—seeing it at night on the siding, far from its familiar context; finding the diesel locomotive in its place when I went to board it at Hamlet; and finally, seeing the tracks along which it ran and the trestle over which it crossed the river torn up and removed—constituted a diminution of its reality to me. For I had associated the little train, to repeat, with a time and place that had seemed very real and permanent to me. The memory of the train was nostalgic, in that it revived the memory of the time and place, as a kind of golden age before the Fall; but since it was no more than that, I had to confront the fact that it was gone forever, with nothing in my present experience seemingly able to replace it in its vividness and solidity.

In the same way, Will Barrett's father in *The Last Gentleman*, confronting the fact that the old times, the old standards of aristocratic probity, were gone, and not even the temporary victory over the rabble can restore them, saw no further hope, no standard of moral conduct that could adequately replace what had been lost.

But not so his son, who out of his grief and loss at his father's death is made to see the limitations of such a way of viewing oneself and one's place in time in the inevitable hopelessness of his father's plight. Through an act of the resolute will his father had managed for a period of time to convince himself that the old times were not gone; but the evidence of his eyes and senses finally shattered the illusion. Will Barrett will make no such attempt, because he cannot; his father's suicide made it impossible for him to be satisfied with any repetition of his father's way. What he comes to see, therefore, after a long and painful search, is that no man may impose his heart's-desire view of reality upon the world without isolating himself from that world. Human reality in time, and his relationship to it, must be found in one's continuing engagement with the world, an engagement that because it takes place in human time must accept and incorporate change as well as continuity. Ac-

relationship involves an acceptance of one's need for what is outside oneself, and the obligation to seek to be oneself *in* that exterior world. A difficult task, truly, requiring as it does neither abject surrender nor prideful disdain, but ongoing engagement.

3. *End of the Line*

And what has that to do with the present and future South, whether Walker Percy's or mine or anyone else's? Simply (yet with what complication!) that we live in a region upon which history has enforced so pervasive a heritage of order and form and community, so powerful a set of loyalties and expectations, that we cannot sidestep the extraordinary strength of our identification with it. So decisive is that sense of identification, even today, that to an important degree it determines our personality. When I say, "I am a southerner," or "I am from Charleston," I am, no matter how I may disguise it, uttering an expression of pride in identity. It matters not that Walker Percy's experience of the South and his role within it may be in certain respects very different from mine or someone else's (his grandfather owned plantations in the Delta and served in the Senate of the United States, while mine owned a little grocery store down by the railroad tracks in Florence, South Carolina, and spoke in a German Jewish accent); the similarities are far more important than the differences, and that fact of itself might help to explain *why* the region could and still can exert so strong an influence upon its inhabitants and command so much of their loyalties. For genuine human communities, as contrasted with mere economic and social combinations, are hard to come by in this world, and that is what the South has been.

But the temptations and dangers involved in such an identification are perilous, too. It is too easy, and too tempting, to surrender one's own individual personality to it, to construct an absolute moral and ethical entity out of a relationship which, because it is human and in time, cannot ever afford absolute certainty to one. That way lies idolatry. This is what Allen Tate meant when he wrote to his friend Donald Davidson in 1942 that "you have always seemed to me to hold to a kind of mystical secularism, which has made you impatient and angry at the lack of results. We live in a bad age in which we cannot give our best; but no age is good." Donald Davidson, like Will Barrett's father, sought valiantly to fuse his own identity with the community he loved in its time and place, and when, as was inevitable, that community, being made up of humans, changed, he saw the change as a fall from perfection, and thus as a betrayal, and he spent his energies in a vain attempt to arrest the change and deny its manifestations. Increasingly the South that he loved became a heart's-desire land which bore less and less relationship to the actual Tennessee community he lived in, until his life became almost totally a rear guard action against any accommodation with change, and in which each engagement was fought as if it were Armageddon, or perhaps Gettysburg. Entered into with the noblest of motives, waged with unremitting courage and high personal honor, Donald Davidson's battle ultimately deprived him of all contact with the real world that poetry must inhabit if it is to take its images and meanings from life.

It is temptingly easy to forget what Stark Young warned his fellow Nashville Agrarians about when he declared in his contribution to the Agrarian symposium *I'll Take My Stand* that "we must remember that we are concerned first with a quality itself, not as our own but as found anywhere; and that we defend certain qualities not because they belong to the South, but because the South belongs to them." But it is also rather too easy to pursue the opposite course: to give in utterly and uncritically to change, to attempt to abdicate any responsibility for determining one's own moral and ethical relationship to it. For one's identity lies not in the change as such, but in what is undergoing change, and though we cannot arrest change, neither can we yield ourselves over to it entirely and still hope to retain any worthwhile integrity or identity in time. We are, in human terms at least, the product of our past, and our task is always therefore to adapt what we are to the inevitability of change, so as to secure and strengthen what we are and can be: to seek to control and shape change so as to help it become part of *us*. In that transaction lies human identity in time, and it would be foolish indeed for us not to attempt to preserve such hard-won virtues and accomplishments as we possess. For we have no way of knowing that adequate and acceptable replacements will be available if we give them up uncritically in exchange for the unknown.

The South has been with us for some time now, and there seems to be little reason not to assume that it will continue to be the South for many years to come. It has changed a great deal—it is always changing, and in recent decades the change has been especially dramatic. But there is little conclusive evidence that it is changing into something that is less markedly southern than in the past. After all, why should it? Does anyone, for example, seriously believe that the liberation of an entire segment of its population, its black folk, into full participation in the region's political and economic life will make the region *less* distinctively southern in its ways? Is not the reverse more likely? Does it seem plausible that, merely because they now live and work in towns and cities rather than in rural areas, the bulk of the southern population both white and black will abruptly cease to hold and to share most of the values, attitudes, concerns, and opinions that have hitherto characterized their lives?

Is the South becoming the "no-South"? Does the southern community cease to exist once it becomes urban and industrial? Not if we are to place any stock in what the sociological and political indices report, or what Walker Percy and other novelists and poets tell us. To think of change simply as destruction of the South's distinctiveness is misleading. Instead of concentrating our attention solely upon what industrialization, urbanization, racial integration, and so forth are going to do to the South, we might consider what so powerful and complex a community as our South is going to do to and with them. For the South has long had a habit of incorporating seemingly disruptive change within itself, and continuing to be the South. The historian George Tindall wryly records the long chronology of supposed demises of the "Old South." Each juncture in the region's history—the Civil War, the end of slavery, Reconstruction, the New South movement of the 1880s and 1890s, the Populist revolt, the impact of the First World War, the boosterism and business expansion of the 1920s, the Great Depression, the New Deal, the downfall of King Cotton and the rise of a more diversified agriculture, the break-up of the one-party system and the Solid South, *Brown* v. *Board of Education* and the end of legal segregation, the sweeping industrialization and urbanization of the 1960s and 1970s, the newfound prosperity of the so-called Sun Belt, the election of Jimmy Carter as President with strong backing from black southerners—has been proclaimed as signalizing the end of the line, so far as the preservation of regional identity and distinctiveness are concerned. Yet an identifiable and visible South remains, and its inhabitants continue to face the same underlying human problems as before, however much the particular issues may change.

At the conclusion of *The Last Gentleman*, Will Barrett, having lived in New York and journeyed to Sante Fe, will presumably go back to Birmingham, Alabama. He will not return to Things As They Were; but then, things are never as they once were. Those who proclaim Walker Percy's fiction as existential, thereby symbolizing the passing of the South and the conclusion of the twentieth-century southern literary mode as such, miss the point, it seems to me. The details of the southern heritage are deeply embodied in Percy's imagination, and in taking on the continuing human problems of self-definition, belief, good and evil, man's place in society from the perspective of a changed set of social and historical circumstances, Percy is doing what every major southern author before him has done. For at no time was there ever a static, changeless society known as the South, inhabited by fully realized, timeless human exemplars known as southerners, for whom there was no problem of self-definition in changing times. The evidence of southern literature, it seems to me—of which Percy is the latest practitioner— is that in every time and place men have faced the task of reconciling individual and private virtue with an inescapable need for fulfillment within a community of men and women, and there is always the requirement to redefine the ethical and moral assumptions of one's rearing and one's present social circumstance amid change. In *The Last Gentleman* Will Barrett has no doubt, really, that he wants to live a "normal" life; his consuming problem is the discovery of a way whereby he can believe in the virtue and value of such a life, rather than merely viewing his role in it as a kind of game plan, a calculated, abstract exercise of the will in which he imposes a private meaning upon what is outside and around him entirely in terms of its usefulness for himself. What he realizes, finally, is his absolute need for what goes on and is involved in that life—for what is ultimately outside of and unknown to him. Only with this acknowledgment of absolute dependence can he go back to his girl and his job and his life in Birmingham.

Now it seems to me that far from representing an end to the so-called traditional southern literary mode, *The Last Gentleman* is a redefinition of it, one that is necessary if it is to continue to have any significance. It represents, on its author's part, a reassessment of certain fundamental human truths, involving community, order, mutability, and belief, in a changed social circumstance. Without such a reassessment, whereby ethical and moral assumptions are translated into a usable idiom, the assumptions would soon become empty and meaningless. And as Will Barrett well recognizes, any such redefinition can be only partial and inexact, for the human beings who hold to the assumptions and seek to act upon them are finite men and women.

Once more, and for the last time, the Boll Weevil: for its demise, the merger of the Seaboard and Coast Line railroads, the discontinuance of all railroading along the trackage that led by the baseball field in Charleston, the removal of the old wooden trestle across the Ashley River, were not after all the end of my imaginative involvement with the little gas-electric coach that plays so inordinately emblematic a role in my memory of the past. There was a summer day, only several years ago, when I was driving from Charleston back to my home in North Carolina. The route led through the town of Hamlet, and since it was getting on toward midday when I neared there, I decided that I would leave the marked route, drive over to where the railway passenger station had been located, have a look around, and then find a place to eat lunch.

It has been twenty-five years since the day I had ridden down from Richmond, spent the night at the railroad hotel, and then gone to board the Boll Weevil, only to find it replaced by a diesel locomotive and air-conditioned coaches. Now I found the station itself, looking much as it had in the past, except that save for one small area reserved for Amtrak passengers, it was all boarded up. I went over to look at the train announcement board. There were only two passenger trains a day each way listed upon it. Not only had the branch line service to Charleston been long since discontinued, along with other such branches, but with the takeover of all passenger service by Amtrak, the onetime Seaboard service to Atlanta and Birmingham had been eliminated. Now the only passenger trains were New York-to-Florida runs.

The station platform was empty. I remembered it as it had been during the war, when the station had been filled with travelers, the lunch room crowded, porters busy with baggage carts along the ramps, railroad workers checking the condition of the wheels and braking equipment on the strings of coaches, switch engines shunting coaches, pullmans, baggage and mail cars back and forth to make up consists for the northbound, southbound, westbound, and eastbound runs. The life of the town of Hamlet, I thought, had once centered upon the activities at this station. Now it was deserted, boarded up.

I found the place where one night during the war I had spied the little Boll Weevil waiting alone in the darkness, far away from where in my mind's eye I felt it ought to be. Now there was only an empty stretch of siding next to an old brick warehouse, with the weeds grown high about the crossties and the rails rusty from long disuse.

I wondered whether the old wooden railroad hotel was still functioning. I walked a block southward. It was still there and, surprisingly, still doing business. No doubt its clientele of trainmen still found it useful for overnight stays between freight runs.

The restaurant was open, so I went in and sat down at a booth to order lunch. The room was crowded, and as I waited for my meal to be served, I looked around at my fellow customers. To judge from their age and appearance, most were not railroad workers but employees in the stores and offices along the main street nearby. What caught my eye, however, were four young women installed in a booth diagonally across from where I sat, eating lunch together while several youths stood nearby bantering with them. Three of the girls were white. One was black.

Twenty-five years ago, if I had been here at lunch time, such a sight would have been inconceivable. As they talked away, eating, chattering, making jokes, laughing, giggling, I thought of how much political rhetoric, how much scheming and planning and denouncing and defying and editorializing and drawing up of legal briefs and passing laws and the like had been expended in my part of the country in the vain effort to prevent those four girls from eating lunch together in that restaurant. How many dire predictions of social catastrophe, how many lamentations over the imminent destruction of the Southern Way of Life, the violation of all that was sacred and noble, had come thundering forth on all sides!

Yet here they were now, eating lunch together, and here was this restaurant in a southeastern North Carolina town on a summer day, with the clientele laughing and talking and eating, and the waitresses serving up the hamburgers and salads and cokes and coffee and iced tea and pie, and the floor fans droning away, and except for the presence of the black girl there and several other black customers at other tables, whom I now saw, nothing seemed importantly different from what I might have seen there had I stopped in for lunch on that day when I rode the successor to the Boll Weevil down to Charleston, or for that matter, from what I would have seen if a decade before that I had been able to board the train at the station near the ball park as I had dreamed of doing, and made the trip all the way up to Hamlet.

How remarkable it was, to have been part of all that had happened since then! For indeed I had been part of it; nor was it yet concluded. Here was I, at the place where a third of a century earlier I had known that the train was bound for, and had wanted to go there with it. Only now there was no more train. Those same years that had contained the stress and struggle and strife which had ultimately made it possible for those four girls, three white and one black, to go out for lunch together after three centuries of law and tradition to the contrary, had also witnessed the decline and the demise of the little passenger train that I had once so admired and loved. Yet could I honestly say, if in effect the end of a place for the

Boll Weevil in the scheme of things had been, symbolically, the price that had to be paid in order for me to see those four girls eating lunch together in this restaurant, that the cost had been too high?

So that I could not and must not think of the memory of the little train as something unique and unqualified, frozen in time and inviolate, and of which all subsequent encounters and experiences were a species of decline and fall. For both I and the train had been part of a complex fabric of social experience, having moral and ethical validity, whose form had been the shape of time. It had been *real*, it had *existed*, and for me the little train was process: identity *in* time, not outside it. Its diminution did not represent merely loss, but change, of which I was a part, and which, because it had happened to me in my time, was mine to cherish. And it was not ghostly and subjective, with no further existence except as I could remember it, but substantial and in the world, authentic *because* it was part of time and change, emblematic of my own involvement in that world, and proof that I had been and still was alive. It was *in* time that it was able to be what it was for me, *in* its contingency: droll in its extraordinary extraness—the oak tree growing around the iron horse's head. And if I wanted to understand who I was, what my country was and why, it was there that I must learn to look.

Notes

William Faulkner: The Discovery of a Man's Vocation

1. "A Word to Young Writers," in William Faulkner, *Essays, Speeches and Public Letters*, ed. James B. Meriwether (New York: Random House, 1965), 162–65.

2. Faulkner, *Absalom, Absalom!* (New York: Random House, 1936), 9–10.

3. *Ibid.*, 174.

4. Joseph Blotner, *Faulkner: A Biography* (New York: Random House, 1974), I, 428.

5. Faulkner, *Absalom, Absalom!*, 89.

6. William Faulkner, *Flags in the Dust*, ed. Douglas Day (New York: Random House, 1973), 147.

7. John Faulkner, *My Brother Bill: An Affectionate Reminiscence* (New York: Trident Press, 1963), 139.

8. Faulkner, *Flags in the Dust*, 163.

9. In viewing Faulkner's characters as divided into a pattern of man of action versus man of sensibility, I am drawing liberally upon the insights of a former student of mine, Daniel V. Gribbin, who in an excellent dissertation, "Men of Thought, Men of Action in Faulkner's Novels" (Ph.D. dissertation, University of North Carolina at Chapel Hill, 1973), has demonstrated how this approach to characterization is central to most of the fiction of the late 1920s and the 1930s.

10. C. Hugh Holman, "The Unity of *Light in August*," *The Roots of Southern Writing: Essays on the Literature of the American South* (Athens: University of Georgia Press, 1972), 155.

11. Appendix, in William Faulkner, *The Sound and the Fury & As I Lay Dying* (New York: Modern Library, 1946), 10.

12. Cleanth Brooks, *William Faulkner: The Yoknapatawpha Country* (New Haven, Conn.: Yale University Press, 1966), 109.

13. Jackson J. Benson, "Quentin Compson: Self-Portrait of a Young Artist's Emotions," *Twentieth Century Literature*, XVII (July, 1971), 143–59.

14. Faulkner, *The Sound and the Fury & As I Lay Dying*, 170.

15. Faulkner, *Absalom, Absalom!*, 185.

16. *Ibid.*

17. Blotner, *Faulkner: A Biography*, I, 187.

18. Faulkner to Malcolm Cowley, November, 1944, in Cowley, *The Faulkner-Cowley File: Letters and Memories, 1944–1962* (New York: Viking Press, 1966), 15.

19. Blotner, *Faulkner: A Biography*, I, 493–94.
20. Cowley, *Faulkner-Cowley File*, 15.
21. Floyd C. Watkins, "Faulkner, Faulkner, Faulkner," *Sewanee Review*, LXXXII (Summer, 1974), 520.
22. *Ibid.*
23. Faulkner, *The Sound and the Fury & As I Lay Dying*, 181.
24. "Books and Things," in William Faulkner, *Early Prose and Poetry*, ed. Carvel Collins (Boston: Atlantic-Little, Brown, 1962), 71.
25. Faulkner, "Verse Old and Nascent: A Pilgrimage," *Early Prose and Poetry*, 115.
26. Faulkner, "Books and Things: American Drama: Inhibitions," *Ibid.*, 96–97.
27. *Ibid.*, 96.
28. Faulkner, "A Note on Sherwood Anderson," *Essays, Speeches and Public Letters*, 6.
29. *Ibid.*, 10.
30. Faulkner, "Verse Old and Nascent: A Pilgrimage," *Early Prose and Poetry*, 117.
31. Quoted in Blotner, *Faulkner: A Biography*, I, 811.
32. Faulkner, "To the Youth of Japan," *Essays, Speeches and Public Letters*, 83.

Scarlett O'Hara and the Two Quentin Compsons

1. Quoted in Frank Luther Mott, *Golden Multitudes: The Story of Best Sellers in the United States* (New York: Macmillan, 1947), 256.
2. Clifton P. Fadiman, "Faulkner, Extra-Special, Double-Distilled," *New Yorker*, Oct. 31, 1936, in Robert Penn Warren (ed.), *Faulkner: A Collection of Critical Essays* (Englewood Cliffs, N.J.: Prentice-Hall, 1966), 290.
3. Joseph Blotner, *Faulkner: A Biography* (New York: Random House, 1974), II, 977, 927.
4. William Faulkner, *Absalom, Absalom!* (New York: Random House, 1936). 16–17.
5. *Ibid.*, 315.
6. Margaret Mitchell, *Gone with the Wind* (New York: Macmillan, 1936), 31, 32, 35.
7. Faulkner, *Absalom, Absalom!*, 358.
8. *Ibid.*, 356.
9. Mitchell, *Gone with the Wind*, 705.
10. *Ibid.*, 64–65, 293.
11. *Ibid.*, 419.
12. *Ibid.*, 640.
13. Faulkner, *Absalom, Absalom!*, 11, 260.
14. Cleanth Brooks, *William Faulkner: The Yoknapatawpha Country* (New Haven, Conn.: Yale University Press, 1963), 298.
15. Floyd C. Watkins, "*Gone with the Wind* as Vulgar Literature," *Southern Literary Journal*, II (Spring, 1970), 97.
16. E. Merton Coulter, *The South During Reconstruction, 1865–1877* (Baton Rouge: Louisiana State University Press, 1947), 153.
17. Mitchell, *Gone with the Wind*, 418–19.
18. Thomas Nelson Page, "Marse Chan," *In Old Virginia, or, Marse Chan and Other Stories* (New York: Charles Scribner's Sons, 1887), 1.
19. Mitchell, *Gone with the Wind*, 701.
20. Faulkner, *Absalom, Absalom!*, 9.
21. Malcolm Cowley, *The Faulkner-Cowley File: Letters and Memories, 1944–1962* (New York: Viking Press, 1966), 13–14.
22. Mitchell, *Gone with the Wind*, 718.

Art and Artistry in Morgana, Mississippi

1. Eudora Welty, *The Golden Apples* (New York: Harcourt, Brace, 1949), 53. All citations are to this edition and will hereafter be given parenthetically.
2. Eudora Welty, "Some Notes on Time in Fiction," *The Eye of the Story: Selected Essays and Reviews* (New York: Random House, 1978), 172, 173.
3. "The Song of Wandering Aengus," *The Collected Poems of W. B. Yeats* (New York: Macmillan, 1951), 57–58.
4. Marcel Proust, *Remembrance of Things Past*, trans. K. R. Scott-Moncrieff (New York: Random House, 1932), II, 1001.
5. Welty, "Katherine Anne Porter: The Eye of the Story," *The Eye of the Story*, 40.

In Search of the Country of Art: Thomas Wolfe's *Of Time and the River*

1. Thomas Wolfe, *Of Time and the River* (New York: Charles Scribner's Sons, 1935), 14. Citations throughout are to this edition and are given parenthetically.
2. Andrew Turnbull, *Thomas Wolfe: A Biography* (New York: Charles Scribner's Sons, 1967), 34.
3. Thomas Wolfe, *Look Homeward, Angel* (New York: Charles Scribner's Sons, 1929), 155.
4. Robert Penn Warren, "A Note on the Hamlet of Thomas Wolfe," *Selected Essays* (New York: Random House, 1958), 184.
5. John Peale Bishop, "The Sorrows of Thomas Wolfe," in *Thomas Wolfe: A Collection of Critical Essays*, ed. Louis D. Rubin, Jr. (Englewood Cliffs, N.J.: Prentice-Hall, 1973), 70.
6. Warren, "A Note on the Hamlet," 183.
7. In this essay I have sought to deal with Eugene Gant, not Thomas Wolfe, and with the published text of *Of Time and the River*. Wolfe scholars, notably Richard S. Kennedy, *The Window of Memory: The Literary Career of Thomas Wolfe* (Chapel Hill: University of North Carolina Press, 1962), have demonstrated that the published version was in important respects not the book that Wolfe himself intended, that it contains segments of unpublished books, including several short novels originally shaped for magazine publication, and that much of it was originally written as first-person narrative and was changed to the third person when it was edited at Charles Scribner's Sons. I agree emphatically with C. Hugh Holman's conclusion, in his study of the problem of the point of view in the novel, that the shift away from the first person was decidedly for the worse. *The Loneliness at the Core: Studies in Thomas Wolfe* (Baton Rouge: Louisiana State University Press, 1975), pp. 76–85. That it was Wolfe's responsibility, and that a writer with more confidence in his own art would not have yielded to the judgment of his editor, Maxwell Perkins, in the matter does not excuse the fact that of the important American writers, Wolfe was probably the worst served by his editors. Just what the shift to the third person meant to the coherence of Wolfe's fiction can be vividly seen by comparing the episodes involving Bascom Pentland and the visit to England in *Of Time and the River* with "A Portrait of Bascom Hawke" and "No Door," in *The Short Novels of Thomas Wolfe*, ed. C. Hugh Holman (New York: Charles Scribner's Sons, 1961).
8. Wright Morris, "The Function of Appetite," in *Thomas Wolfe: A Collection of Critical Essays*, ed. Louis D. Rubin, Jr., 96.

Index